Swimmer
in a
Dark Sea

Pierce Timberlake

2019

Arjuna's **A**rrow
PUBLISHING

Swimmer in a Dark Sea

Portions of this book have been previously published and copyrighted by the author as Kindle ebooks:

Fear of the Dark © 2013, 2016

Sex, Not-Sex, and Love © 2013, 2014

The Art of Living Forever © 2013, 2014

Ideology and the Real World (originally published as *Style as Ideology / Ideology as Style*) © 2013, 2014

Bullies, Victims, and Heroes © 2013, 2017

Critical Numbers © 2013, 2017

Living the Dream, Dreaming the Life © 2013, 2017

Chaos Theory in a Tokyo Bar © 2013, 2016

Living the Dream, Dreaming the Life & *Critical Numbers* & *Bullies, Victims, and Heroes* were all originally published as *Triad three inquiries* © 2017

Cover photo by JOHN TOWNER on Unsplash

Address inquiries to pwtlake@hotmail.com or markcharalambous@gmail.com.
Available at Amazon.com and other online outlets.
www.arjunasarrow.com

First Edition

ISBN-13: 978-0-578-49783-9

For Nancy

Contents

Part 1

Fear of the Dark

When Thomas was four years old, he experienced the first foreshadowing of an adult consciousness. While this did not occur at any single moment, Thomas later associated its beginning with his family's move from Florida to South Carolina.

Thomas' father had been one semester short of graduating from college when he'd gone off to World War II; finishing that last term and getting a degree had long been at the back of his mind. So, in late summer of 1951, Thomas Sr. took a leave of absence from the Air Force, packed wife and son into their black 1950 Mercury, and set out for his old school. They drove out of Eglin Air Force Base, across Florida, up through Georgia, and into South Carolina, eventually arriving in Clinton. Their first stop there was Thomas Sr.'s old college, where he visited the college president in his office—Thomas Sr. had been one of the school's star athletes before the war, and he was royally received. Then the family went on to their rental house.

Thomas' family spent the next few weeks settling in their new home. Fall semester hadn't started yet, and Thomas' parents used the time to unpack, arrange furniture, and visit Thomas Sr.'s old friends (mostly coaches and sports directors; classmates had graduated and moved on). Thomas' parents even located neighbors with children around Thomas' age; Thomas found he had been assigned new friends.

It was around this point that Thomas began to think a little differently. He had previously existed in the dream-like world of a small child, only marginally self-aware. At about age four and a half, however, his mind seemed to form a structure on which memories could be hung.

Many new thoughts entered his mind; many questions occurred to him.

Thomas' qualitative leap in awareness might have been triggered by his new surroundings, or maybe he had coincidentally reached a culminating moment in neural development. For whatever reason, during those months in Clinton, Thomas' life began to have a chronology. Reality became more coherent.

(Much later, adult Thomas still had a few memories of his life before moving to South Carolina, but they were hazy and indeterminate, unclear as to place and time. In one almost hallucinatory vision, he was wading in the ocean—it would have been the Gulf of Mexico—on a very hot day, the dazzling blue sea reflecting a blazing sky above, everything so bright that his eyes hurt. He had not yet learned to swim, and was seeing how far out he could wade before the water was over his head. This seemed to be his earliest memory; he might have been three years old.)

Thomas' shift in consciousness was marked by four new ideas during the semester in South Carolina:

First, he was made to understand that he could die. And a little later, that he inevitably *would* die. This came in a conversation with his mother, Patricia, after he had done something she considered dangerous. (In his mother's view, "dangerous" described at least half of everything Thomas did.)

Initially Thomas wouldn't believe her. "I'll just go to sleep," he said, "and then I'll wake up."

His mother shook her head. "When you die you don't wake up. Ever."

4

"Yes I will."

"No." Firmly. "You *won't*."

Thomas pondered this for a long time.

The second idea had to do with religion, and was more of a cluster of ideas. His father's college had a religious affiliation, in fact was named after a Protestant denomination, and the Christian faith was taken seriously there. It was explained to Thomas that there was a God, a Someone who had total power over him, and who was always watching. Always? In the bathtub? On the toilet? Modesty was a relatively new feeling for Thomas, one not yet tempered by experience, and any infringement made him distinctly uncomfortable. And he was further informed that this same Someone could even read his thoughts. Thomas found this even more worrisome: He had little control over his thoughts, he felt that he might at any moment think something bad, even blasphemous (he didn't know the word, but he vaguely intuited the concept). Somehow adding to his uneasiness were the severe tone of the high, narrow steeples and stained glass windows of the college chapel, the solemn preaching by the minister behind his pulpit, the histrionically earnest hymns performed by the choir that Thomas Sr. sang in on Sundays. Occasionally Thomas and his mother would shop in town, and in the stores Thomas would see small plaster figures of Jesus. The scaled down saviors seemed to stare sightlessly into nothing, or into an eternity that made Thomas feel lost and minute. He found the whole idea of religion unsettling and eerie.

His mother explained to him that God was on their side, that He had made each of them, and everything, and all of the world.

Thomas asked the obvious question: "Who made God?"

His mother had no real answer to this—no one else ever has, either—so she said, "Well, He just *is*." Then she praised Thomas, saying the question showed he was intelligent, and changed the subject.

Thomas also pondered this uncaused God business for a long time. Between implacable death and an uncaused Creator, Thomas experienced an existential anxiety of exactly the sort religion can often protect us from, but it didn't work that way in Thomas' case. His fear may have resulted from a miscommunication of religious concepts, or a frightful presentation of its iconography, but for Thomas, religion was a considerable problem.

The third new idea was sexuality. For the first time in his life, Thomas was consciously aware of sexual feelings. Not that he had any idea of sexual function, but he would sometimes experience an odd giddiness when he looked at the young coeds on campus, and wondered about the swelling under their sweaters, the roundness of their hips under the plaid skirts, their smooth legs above the saddle oxfords. Around this same time he inadvertently encountered his mother coming out of the bath and realized that it wasn't just breasts and hip shape: Females had a different arrangement in other respects as well. (When Thomas later asked his father why his mother lacked a certain appendage, Thomas Sr. jocularly told him that Fez, the family's cocker spaniel, had bitten it off.) Thomas had no idea what these gender differences signified, but it was all exciting ... though he felt uncomfortable that his mother was in any way involved, and he worried again about God knowing his thoughts. This nascent sexuality, however, seemed to be the one thing that could take his mind off of his fear of death and infinity and Uncaused Causes. And his fear of skeletons ...

Living skeletons, ghosts, and related phenomena comprised the fourth new idea. Goblins, witches, and most of all skeletons, had become real and terrifying. The faces of horror were provided by the upcoming Halloween's imagery, and by the covers of pre-code comic books. Thomas was never allowed to actually read these, but they were ubiquitous in stores, and their cover illustrations told the story. They routinely depicted a horrified individual, usually a woman, alone in a cemetery at night, standing over a grave; skeletal or semi-decomposed arms were reaching up from the ground, grasping her wrists, and drawing her down. Thomas developed an intense fear of the dark. At night he became afraid to enter unlit rooms in their rental home; he didn't know what creatures might be in there; he wished someone else would go in first and turn on the light. He had to force himself to walk through the door, then feel desperately for a light switch.

Thomas' parents weren't much help with these new ideas. His mother was kind enough, but didn't really know what to say when Thomas tried to formulate questions. The situation was even worse with Thomas' father.

Thomas Sr. became aware of his son's obsessive fear, and found it ridiculous. His great and often repeated joke was to wait in an unlit room until Thomas walked in, then step abruptly out of the darkness with uplifted arms and make a low, weird sound. This never failed to terrify Thomas.

Thomas Sr. was half amused, half exasperated. "For Christ's sake!" he'd say to Thomas, "you know it's me!"

The frustrating aspect was that Thomas always did know, in some part of his mind, that it was his father. He even sort of understood that ghosts, living skeletons, goblins and so on didn't actually exist. But he was still panicked. Because how could he be *sure* they didn't exist? What if, just this once, it *wasn't* his father in the darkness?

* * *

Thomas' father had originally attended college on a full athletic scholarship. He ran the quarter- and half-miles—440 and 880 yards, respectively—though the 440 was his specialty. (By the time Thomas was an adult, track athletes were running 400 and 800 meters, comparable but slightly shorter metric races.) At a time when runners were stereotyped as slim and lanky, Thomas' father was built like a football player, square and mesomorphic. Still, he usually managed to muscle his way around the track faster than anyone else in the race. He won state championships in the quarter-mile in both high school and college.

In order to get full value for their investment, the sports faculty at Thomas Sr.'s college coerced him into other sports when track wasn't in season. He boxed ("Just keep your guard up," he told Thomas), put the shot ("It's all in the legs,"), and tried basketball. He didn't offer Thomas any one-line advisories for basketball, which apparently he couldn't get the hang of. In fact, he found the sport frustrating:

"It was idiotic," he told Thomas. "First, we'd all run in one direction. Then, just as I'm getting up to speed, everyone would turn around and run the other way! And then we'd turn around again! One time, I ran right into the damned wall."

Becoming aggravated with this, Thomas' father went to the college's athletic director. "Look," he told him, "my job is to bring home the state championship in the quarter mile. Your job is to provide me with an education. I've given you the 440 championship every year; I shouldn't have to do this other stuff." The athletic director agreed, and Thomas Sr. stopped worrying about basketball. He did grumble that they had him mopping the gym floor in the off season. Years later, when Thomas read how "full ride" college athletes are treated in a more modern era, he got the sense that things had changed.

Looking back as an adult, Thomas thought about his father trying to get up to maximum quarter-mile speed in the confines of a basketball court, and running into the wall. Thomas thought it seemed emblematic of Thomas Sr.'s approach to life: all heart—in the athletic sense—and zero nuance.

* * *

Thomas was never told why his father hadn't finished college on the first try. He knew he'd gone into the army but he also knew he hadn't been drafted; as an officer candidate in the ROTC he wouldn't have been, and anyway Thomas Sr. was vehement about not having been a draftee. He came from an old military family with a long, proud history—his father had been a Brigadier General in the Army—and being drafted, rather than volunteering, would have been dishonorable. Years later Thomas put together what must have happened: In his senior year in college, Thomas' father had been "spiked" in a pre-season indoor track meet. (Spiked: the runner behind him drove the spikes of his track shoe into the back of his father's leg—accidentally or otherwise—

grievously tearing the calf muscle and Achilles tendon). Thomas' father had spent several weeks in a hospital bed. He had always talked about this as an imposition on his athletic career, but it also must have been a serious obstacle to attending classes. At the end of his interrupted semester, Thomas Sr. had decided to go ahead and enlist. The Second World War wasn't going to wait.

* * *

Thomas Sr. finished his make-up semester in early 1952, was duly awarded his Bachelor of Arts Degree, and the family returned to Eglin. Nothing overly frightening happened to Thomas in the next few years, with two exceptions:

The first exceptional event occurred when Thomas was five. Thomas and friends Dennis, also aged five, and Davy, aged three, started a forest fire in a large heavily wooded area within the confines of the air base. They didn't mean any harm. They had become very impressed with scouting—Dennis' older brother was a Boy Scout, and his mother was a Cub Scout den mother—and Thomas and his friends thought they could experience the scouting mystique by setting their own campfire. It didn't occur to them to isolate their little flame by clearing away the surrounding underbrush, and soon a small campfire spread into a very large campfire. Firefighters and military police quickly became involved, and eventually Thomas found himself being threatened by his parents in the most dire terms: He would be taken away by the Air Police, locked up indefinitely, separated from his family, subjected to unspeakable torments ...

Thomas took these threats very seriously and was very seriously frightened by them. So much so, in fact, that when his parents went out for a social visit later that evening, leaving Thomas alone in the house, he locked all the doors and windows, and hid under his bed (presumably a place where the Air Police would never think to look.) When his parents eventually came home, they were unable to get in, and Thomas, under his bed, took a long time to hear them pounding on the walls and doors ... Thomas was soon in even more trouble.

As frightened as he was of all this, however, Thomas was still far more frightened of religion and skeletons.

The second event occurred after Thomas had started school. He began with first grade, since kindergarten the previous year had been overcrowded and difficult to get a child into, a consequence of the first wave of boomer babies hitting the schools. Young kindergarten candidates were put on a waiting list and their parents had to advocate for them. Thomas' parents didn't think it was worth the trouble and didn't bother; Thomas started with First Grade.

First grade was a strange new world for Thomas, as it must be for most children, but generally things seemed to go well enough. Many of his classmates appeared to be significantly ahead of him at reading and arithmetic (maybe because they'd gone to kindergarten), but nothing about the overall situation was frightening. It just seemed to Thomas that he had no idea what was going on, a feeling he was used to.

Then Halloween came. Thomas' parents were engaged in some secretive business which didn't involve him, and it was made clear that if he hung around he would be in the way. So, on Halloween night Thomas was put in his costume and given over to the care of Dennis' mother. She took Dennis, Thomas, and a couple of other boys to their grade school, where a campus-wide Halloween festival was in progress. The students, and even most of the teachers, wore costumes, and the classrooms and cafeteria were made up in orange and black construction paper, and generally in mock frightening decor. Even though this was the school Thomas had attended every weekday for almost two months, nothing looked familiar to him—he couldn't find his way around his own school, and he didn't recognize any of his classmates through their costumes. (Although several recognized him, especially the little girls—six-year-old girls may be smarter than six-year-old boys. At least smarter than Thomas was.)

In a short time Dennis' mother had separated herself from the little group of boys, telling them to stay together and stay in the area while she chatted with other moms. The boys went off on their own, mingling with the crowd and getting as far as possible from parents. Thomas was mesmerized by what seemed a strange and exotic environment, and after a while found that he'd become separated not only from Dennis' mother, but from the other boys as well. He was lost in his own school.

Thomas walked aimlessly through the buildings and playgrounds for a while, hoping that he would run into someone he knew. But no luck; the school seemed to have grown in some surreal way, become strangely large, not to mention packed with masked strangers. After a half hour or so of forlorn wandering, Thomas gave up. His only hope, he decided, was to walk the mile or so back to his home.

The first several blocks after Thomas left the school were in an area of residential quarters, reasonably well-lit and occupied, and walking through them didn't cause him too much anxiety. Eventually, however, he came to the part of the trip he had been trying not to think about.

While both the school and Thomas' home on Hatchee Road were surrounded by dependent family (Wherry) housing, they were separated from each other by a large wooded area, a different reach of the same forest in which Thomas, Dennis and Davy had started their fire the year before. This forested area had no infrastructure at all; it was basically an untouched wilderness within the airbase, small as forests go, but big enough for a child to get lost in. Before starting school, Thomas and his friends had been drawn to it irresistibly (when the sun was up), though hardly a day passed without his mother warning against it. It was, she told him, a place of snakes, and maybe even alligators. (This *was* Florida.) So, other than walking through the woods themselves, a psychological impossibility for Thomas this night, and probably a bad idea anyway, there was only one way for him to get from the area of the base where the school was to the area where his home was: a dark, lonely road, a two-lane blacktop that curved steeply down through the woods.

Down, as the school was on substantially higher ground than Thomas' home. From the top of the hill Thomas saw no sign of the bottom. No lights, no buildings; the road curved sharply and vanished into the forest. The grade was steep enough that a car in third gear, with no foot on the gas pedal, would coast downhill at a speed greater than 40 miles per hour. (Or at least that's what Thomas Sr. had told the air policeman that had stopped him for speeding on this same curve, a few months before.)

Thomas' problem was to pass down this road and survive. He wasn't worried about snakes or even alligators; the real issue was that the woods hid an army of ghosts, witches, hobgoblins, and skeletons. Turning around and walking back to the school might have been more logical, but Thomas didn't feel that he had any real choice: He was somehow compelled to go forward. Like a threatened animal, he wanted his lair.

Thomas remembered his journey down that road for the rest of his life, his most intense experience as a child, though no doubt its very intensity distorted the accuracy of his recall. Still, looking back as an adult, he thought it had gone like this:

running ...

Thomas considers his strategy. He will run the entire distance to his home, and he will keep as far as possible from either side of the road, avoiding the tree branches that reach out for him with skeletal fingers. He will stay in the very center of the road, keeping his feet on the painted divider stripes. Since this puts him at risk of being run down by a car (perhaps moving faster than 40 miles per hour), his fear of the supernatural will place him at real physical risk. Somewhere in his mind he realizes this, but it doesn't dent his resolve. He tells himself he will listen for cars, and swerve quickly to the curb if he hears one coming.

Standing on the last fringe of the residential area and pondering the descending road before him, Thomas remembers that he is still wearing his costume, a single piece coverall of very thin, garishly tinted synthetic material over his street clothes, and a light, stiff mask secured by an elastic string. The little child's costume feels out of place away from the school, and somehow pathetic.

Thomas catches sight of a remote something on the far shoulder of the road. It is quiet and unmoving, but seems to be a figure: someone silently watching him. Thomas stares back at it. It can't be a person, he thinks; it keeps too still. And yet the shape of it could be read ... as a tall, powerfully built male figure in a dark overcoat. And above the coat, framed by the turned-up collar, Thomas sees ... a skull. The blind, insane visage grins back at him.

Thomas' mind goes totally blank; he stands frozen. Finally he dares to move slightly to one side. Perspective shifts just enough that the shape becomes disproportionate, no longer readable as a human figure. Just a trick of faint light and shadows. But Thomas is afraid to look away from it. He doesn't trust it. It might change back.

Eventually Thomas decides he can't stand here staring at it forever. He looks down the road one more long moment, takes a deep breath—and starts running.

Not too fast the first few strides, but then he breaks into a wild, headlong sprint. Down the hill—arms pumping, legs flying, an uncontrolled run that should be dangerous on a slope, but he doesn't sense any possibility of falling. He is shorter than an adult, and he runs all the time. Thomas Sr. was state champion in the 440 (as he never tires of telling Thomas), and Thomas has inherited his athleticism to a slight degree—he has discovered that, in first grade, he can already outrun all the second graders. Now, he'll outrun the darkness, the demons, the overcoated skull-man. The road flies by beneath his feet. Adrenalized energy is the answer Thomas has come up with; physical vitality is his counter to the darkness ...

* * *

Many years later ...

...Thomas, now an undergraduate majoring in Philosophy, found himself remembering that Halloween night and reflecting on his youthful panic. What, he wondered, had he been so afraid of?

Thomas was sitting alone on a late afternoon in his college's student union coffee shop. He tried to focus on a book he was reading, but he was also worrying about an imminent exam, and another part of his attention kept being drawn to Rachel, an attractive coed who worked part-time in the coffee shop and was bussing tables nearby. Seemingly out of nowhere, memory of that Halloween came to Thomas, with no obvious antecedent chain of thought. By now Thomas was accustomed to the elliptical nature of his own mind—apparently un-triggered memories were a commonplace for him—and he didn't try to retrace his thinking. Instead, he forgot his surroundings and allowed himself to re-experience the run, this time applying an analytical mindset.

Thomas thought that his intense mental state that night was a culmination of feelings and attitudes that had started in South Carolina. It had something to do with Thomas Sr. frightening him in dark rooms, and the fact that we all someday die, and the strange excitement provoked by the coeds, and the unexplained and apparently unexplainable origin of the universe ... it all tied together in some mysterious way that Thomas felt, but couldn't articulate.

Thomas reflected that Freud, whom he had recently been reading, would have had no trouble dissecting this complex of emotions and fears: According to psycho-analytic theory, at age four Thomas should have been in the midst of his Oedipal Complex. Freud would have said that the cause of Thomas' anguish was guilt produced by a desire to kill and replace his father, and have sex with his mother—all of this so he could return to that place of peace and security he unconsciously remembered, the womb. This desire to return would also entail a castration anxiety, since if Thomas were sexually maimed (by his father), he couldn't use intercourse to get back inside.

Thomas thought that returning to the womb through sexual intercourse sounded sort of intuitively plausible as a psychological mechanism, until you remember that our species has two genders. How would it work for a woman? She can't symbolically return to her lover's womb; he doesn't have one. Is she trying to return to her own womb? And anyway, would a child have even the faintest idea of coitus, or of a maiming that would remove his ability to engage in sex? Even if he subliminally remembered the uterus, would he really think of his genitals as the means of getting back into it?

Sometimes, in the nightmarish dreams Thomas had had during his childhood, he was pursued by a hulking monster he could never outrun, a monster that turned out to be his father. This fit very obviously with Oedipal theory, the idea of his father as castrator. It seemed to Thomas, though, that this monster-as-father association had more to do with Thomas Sr.'s habit of ambushing him in dark rooms: the large creature in the darkness really was Thomas' father—no symbolism required.

While Thomas thought all of this Freudian paraphernalia had a certain plausibility (maybe), he decided it didn't ring true in his case. He had another explanation:

Thomas had clearly been frightened by the prospect of termination, of his own non-existence—the skull or skeleton is the universal symbol of death—but he thought he was bothered even more by something else. He thought skeletons and the rest formed the unreasoning mask of a deeper issue: Thomas was profoundly disturbed by the fact that there was no explanation for the existence of the world.

Before the brief conversation with his mother, Thomas didn't remember thinking about the concept of initial cause. If it had crossed his mind at all, he had unconsciously assumed that there was some explanation, and no doubt the adults were on top of it. Then, at age four, Thomas realized he had no idea of how anything existed, and neither did the adults.

The more Thomas thought about it, the more it seemed that not only did he not have an answer to the question of where everything came from, but there couldn't be an answer. No matter what original Cause you come up with to explain everything, that Cause itself would always need a preceding cause, initiating an infinite regression of causes that never finally explained anything.

Plus, this tied in to other questions that had arisen for Thomas as a young child: Does space really extend forever, as his father had told him? Thomas couldn't get his mind around such an idea, but if he tried to imagine a boundary, that didn't work either—something always had to be beyond a boundary. And the same paradox applied to time. What happened before God made the world? How could time go on forever? How could it not?

This hadn't been an intellectual issue for young Thomas; it was deeply emotional. He felt unsupported, as though reality, suddenly exposed as having no foundation, was a fraud that might collapse at any moment. We had been walking on clouds all along, and telling ourselves it was solid ground. Now Thomas knew the chilling truth. He felt at the mercy of an as yet undefined solipsism, an ultimate loneliness.

Undergrad Symposium

College-age Thomas' musings were interrupted by the arrival of four friends, the usual group, which, along with himself, he thought of somewhat ironically as "The Symposium."

After laconic initial greetings and brief exchanges of news, the five of them moved quickly into their serial debate. Thomas thought his friends could easily represent the conflicting metaphysical impulses in his own mind. On one side of the issue were the atheists: The clever and sometimes mocking Richard, a Biology major, and the calm and quiet Stephen, majoring in Physics. On the other side were the believers: History major Theo was a vehement if somewhat surly advocate of Christianity, while the milder and more reasonable Timothy studied at a nearby seminary. Thomas, as a

Philosophy major who had decided he was an agnostic—
"Doubting Thomas"—saw himself as the natural
mediator. Though more often than not, he was attacked
by both sides.

Richard was in yet another debate with Theo.

"If you don't believe in God," Theo asked, "what basis do
you have for morality? How do you explain altruism?"

"This again?" Richard said with a hint of exasperation.
"We've covered it before. Morality, and altruism, can be
explained by Darwinian mechanisms."

"Not really," Theo said. "Explanations like that
ultimately depend on humans being rational—they
aren't."

"Why is it then that atheists are often more ethical than
theists?"

"That sometimes happens," Theo conceded, "but it
doesn't prove that atheists have any basis for morality.
The fact that their 'morality' always resembles that of
their surrounding religious culture shows that they are
just ripping off the local faith—'moral' atheists have
been plagiarizing the Ten Commandments forever. Their
moral code is parasitic. Why do secular moral codes
always conform to religious moral systems? Because
they're stolen from them." Theo thought it over. "A
believer may not be perfect, but at least you know where
he's coming from. How do we know what to expect from
an atheist, no matter what he says? The fact is that
people are naturally bad. We have to be coerced into
moral behavior. That requires a divine master."

So, Thomas thought, we're a flawed species that religion
attempts to correct. But it seemed to him that the

believers who made the attempt were flawed themselves, so it always went awry.

Richard and Theo had had this discussion before; nothing was ever resolved. Richard decided on a different tack. He turned to Thomas.

"What does Philosophy have to say, Thomas? Do we have to have God to behave?"

"I'm not sure of the agnostic explanation for the basis of morality," Thomas replied, feeling for what tack to take. "I'm not sure that any morality can be derived completely through rational argument. Though I've tried to do that myself a few times, in some papers I've turned in. But I don't feel I can take a stance on it right now."

"Afraid to commit again," Richard said. "Agnostics! It takes more balls to be a believer or an atheist than an agnostic. Come on, Thomas. Take a position. Stand for something."

"It's not a question of machismo," Thomas said, annoyed. "My ideas are either valid or not. Their bravado quotient has nothing to do with it. Anyway, if I'm being rigorously logical, I have to be an agnostic: God cannot be logically proven nor disproven. And neither religion nor science can explain the ultimate beginning of things."

"Ultimate Cause can be understood," Richard said, "through science. In fact, I expect to see a scientific explanation within a few years." Richard thought for a moment, then drove on. "When you say you're an agnostic, Thomas, you're saying that the odds of God existing are 50-50. I can acknowledge a faint possibility of God myself, but 50-50? Nowhere near that."

"Thomas' position follows from science, and demonstrates its weakness," Theo said. "An agnostic, after all, is someone who says, 'I have no scientific proof that God exists, therefore I don't believe in Him.'"

"You're both wrong," Thomas said. "I'm not giving odds here. I'm saying I simply don't know if there is a God. No percentage is implied. Admitting you don't know something, rather than trying to sell some phony decisiveness, is the only honest position when you really don't know. And the truth is that none of us know; we just like to tell ourselves we do. And Theo's definition of an agnostic is no good either. A person who chooses to disbelieve because he lacks proof is an atheist who is an atheist for a particular reason, not an agnostic. An agnostic makes no claim either way. An agnostic reserves judgment."

Thomas paused, not satisfied with his thoughts. Richard, he knew, would say—had said—that a morality inspired by fear of divine punishment wasn't really moral. That seemed valid, but what, exactly, would an atheistic set of morals be based upon? Would Darwinian survival or sheer reason really arrive at a code of behavior that was applicable in all circumstances?

"So Theo ..." Thomas said, trying to ferret out a thought, "morality has to be based on fear?"

Timothy the seminarian decided to enter the conversation:

"Christian theology concedes the flawed character of real Christians. Our moral efforts are too weak and basely motivated to redeem us. Salvation can only be found through the grace of God. Character development is a gradual and ongoing process that occurs after we accept Christ."

"Which brings us back to belief," Thomas said. "If we honestly can't believe in a divinity, then we can't have a moral life?"

"Belief is the center," Timothy said. "Behavior follows. But you *can* find belief. There may be no airtight proof of God, but there are powerful clues. Look, everything we know of is contingent upon something else. That must include the universe. What could the universe be caused by except something *outside* of the universe?" Something supernatural?"

Timothy smiled. "And you know what else? The truth is that, deep down, you *know* that God exists!"

This stopped Thomas in his tracks. "I do?" he asked. Do I? he wondered. Thomas found that, despite his first impulse, he couldn't arbitrarily dismiss this contention (as he knew Richard would).

"Maybe God exists," Thomas said slowly, "but why is there all this other? Like, why did He sacrifice his son? Why that business with Abraham and Isaac? Why did he torment Job? The whole paraphernalia ... Why?"

"Why did Jesus have to die on the cross?" Timothy said. "Because humans carried a debt of sin, and a debt must be paid. Someone must always pay the cost! Jesus paid our debt for us."

Richard shook his head. He noticed Rachel, who had paused from bussing tables and seemed to be quietly listening to them. Perhaps hoping to derail Timothy's momentum, Richard called out to her.

"Rachel—what about it? Is there a God?"

Rachel lifted eyebrows. "Sorry," she said. "I can't do that magic man in the sky thing."

Timothy kept his composure, but Thomas thought he looked faintly sad. Thomas was a little surprised himself. He didn't know Rachel well, but he thought a fair number of people were still believers, and she seemed pretty normal. Admittedly she had blue hair, a small tattoo, and a nose ring, but still ...

Timothy's voice interrupted his thoughts.

"You really don't feel any need for him?" Timothy asked Rachel.

Rachel shrugged. "Do you guys need him?"

No one answered for a moment, then Stephen, the Physics major, spoke for the first time.

"I don't need God," he said. "We don't need God. Science doesn't need him for an explanation. The origin and structure of the universe is understandable. It can all be attributed to gravity. God is unnecessary."

For Stephen, Thomas wryly reflected, science had already discovered the Uncaused Cause; Richard's "few years" weren't needed.

Stephen smiled his beatific smile. "And I'm not afraid of the dark."

But I was, Thomas thought. Afraid of the dark. Maybe, a little, I still am ...

* * *

Thomas reflects, post symposium

Later that evening, stretched out on the couch in his living room, Thomas pondered the afternoon's conversation:

God, Thomas thought, is as He may be. That is, He exists or He doesn't, but if He does, He exists independent of human beliefs or institutions. (Thomas was not interested in a relativistic God.) Religion, on the other hand, is a human invention, with its own structures and purposes. Believers of almost any stripe seemed to make the tacit assumption that their version of religion was identical to God himself. For example, if school-sanctioned prayer was ruled to be illegal in the US, fundamentalists would cry that God is being kept out of our schools. Clearly then, their religion and God are one and the same.

(Thomas reflected that if God is omnipresent, as usually described by these same religionists, He should be impossible to keep out of anywhere. And of course, anyone who wants to is always free to pray within their own mind. The fundamentalists' real complaint is that they are not being allowed to present their religious practices in a way that suggests they are supported by the entire society.)

Humans, Thomas thought, are human, whatever beliefs they espouse. Character varies, and specific religions reflect the character of the humans who created them, in combination with the later evolution of the religion. Religions can have many purposes, some noble, some less so. One of the purposes, not so noble perhaps, was the coercion and control of humans by other humans. Whatever the original goal of such coercion, even if it was meant for our own good, it could easily turn darker over time. And the question of who gets to determine our own good is always there. An assumption of the equivalence of God and religion hides the human-tainted character of theistic beliefs.

What did Thomas believe, really? He had proclaimed to his friends that he was agnostic, because he felt logical rigor demanded it. It was impossible to prove God existed, and equally impossible to prove that He didn't. (Maybe even more impossible to prove that He didn't, if impossibility could be qualified.) Since Thomas didn't see any way to logically or empirically resolve the point, his formal position had to be agnosticism. What about his informal position, his intuitive feeling? Agnosticism also, but with vague theistic (and maybe Deistic) leanings. It just *felt* like there was something more to it all than what could be directly observed. Sometimes he thought he could almost make out some pattern in it all—too many coincidences, too many events that almost made sense. Thomas had read analyses that explained these perceptions as merely the result of the over-developed pattern recognition ability of the human brain. Maybe ... but Doubting Thomas didn't doubt just the claims of religion. He doubted everything. He followed the logic of how randomness could appear as pattern, but he thought another explanation was possible. A superior force of some type could be behind it, or could co-exist with randomness, asserting an occasional influence.

Perhaps this was why Timothy had rocked him when he said we knew God existed. In some part of his mind, Thomas still did think God existed. He knew that this sentiment might be the residue of being raised in a sort-of Christian household, and of being subjected all of his life to religious references, from casual cursing, to panel cartoons in popular magazines, to common turns of phrase. At any rate he felt there was a distinct possibility that some mysterious element beyond the tangible world existed. We could call that mystery God.

Thomas understood also that his theistic intuition might be mere wishful thinking. Western religion was generally associated with an afterlife, and Thomas would like a post-mortal reunion with people he'd known in this world. And he also had a hard time accepting the idea of his own non-existence. But he realized that an afterlife was not a necessary adjunct to theism—some religions didn't even promise it—and it even might be possible to have an afterlife without a God, depending on the structure of the universe. In any case, Thomas wasn't counting on anything. The afterlife would happen or it wouldn't, but he was convinced that this world, the earthly plane, existed for its own sake, to be fully engaged in, and not as some test, or prelude to another reality. An afterlife might exist, but while we were here we should focus on being *here*. (Hence Thomas' reach toward Deism. Deists believed, among other things, that God made the world, but did not intervene in its further development.)

Whether agnostic or semi-believer, though, Thomas was not inclined to follow any conventional religion. When he read the Bible or any other holy book, he found it too easy to interpret the ideas presented as the guesswork of the ancients, long dead individuals whose speculations had, over time, become codified into doctrine and eventually rigidified into dogma. These ancients, mostly men maybe, or maybe not, had sometimes been very intelligent, and they had stretched their imaginations heroically in their attempts to understand a complex and often hostile universe. They were of another time and culture, however, and did not know much of what has since been learned. Contradictions in their ideas were easy to find, questions could be raised at every point.

In debates with believers, Thomas would point these inconsistencies out. The believers would try to give answers, but Thomas could usually shoot those down as well. Eventually a theist would say something like, "God moves in mysterious ways. We can't expect Him to conform to our understanding." (Or, if the theist was Islamic, "You don't know the mind of God!")

"Then why," Thomas would ask, "have you been sitting here for the last half hour describing to me the mind of God? Describing His ways? You seem to think you know the mind of God well enough, until I call you on the contradictions, and then we fall back on God's 'mysterious ways'. Tell me from the start that no human can understand a divine being, or explain Him to me logically all the way through, but don't try to have it both ways. (And didn't Paul say—Romans 1:20—that the invisible must be understood by the visible?) Besides, isn't God supposed to be a better deal than an accidental world? From a human standpoint, what is the difference between a totally enigmatic God and a random, senseless universe? In both cases, we don't really know what to expect. In both cases the world is unfathomable and we have no hope of control."

Sometimes a Christian would complain that Thomas was focusing on the Old Testament God, the harsh and vengeful Yahweh. Christ, the Christian would say, offers a different picture. He does in fact, Thomas agreed, but Yahweh was still fair game in a debate with a Christian: Christians named the Jewish Bible as their "Old

Testament"; when Thomas had been coerced into attending Sunday school as a child, the lessons taught by his Presbyterian teacher had certainly included stories from the Old Testament. Whatever incongruent picture Yahweh presented, the Christians had never disavowed Him.

Still ... was there a God? Thomas mentally shrugged. Yet again, Thomas considered the standard issues, the usual biblical paradoxes skeptics liked to point out. And questions like, could God create a rock He couldn't lift? None of this amounted to much, in Thomas' opinion. Most of these objections could be gotten rid of pretty easily. Paradoxes like the lifting of an un-liftable rock were like the irresistible force/immovable object conundrum: mere verbal constructs that made no sense in the real world. (It also occurred to Thomas that a common atheistic debate tactic was to point out illogicalities in a specific religion, then think they had shown religion in general to be absurd. Not a valid progression.)

Thomas thought that commonly raised issues, such as the problem of evil in the world, had been pretty thoroughly resolved. God gave Man free will, which meant Man was able to choose evil as well as good, and some men and women always would choose evil. Why give Man free will in the first place? Theists tended to answer this in ways that centered around humans, but Thomas had a different idea. God gave humans free will because otherwise God is trapped in a universe where everything He sees is just another reflection of Himself. Man has free will for God's benefit, not Man's. Only if Man had free will could humans present something of real interest to God. This would be important to an ultimate being, because He faced the possibility of ultimate boredom. Believers never considered what seemed to Thomas a basic question, whether God could grow bored. Perhaps Believers didn't want to consider it because it made God seem too human, in some ways a frightening idea. But perhaps God was more human than we thought; the Bible after all said God had made Man in his own image, and a psychological resemblance would be most significant. The jealous, angry, Old Testament God seemed human enough.

Or perhaps believers felt a capacity for boredom made God seem weak, and they didn't want to impute any negative qualities to an all-powerful being they constantly heaped praise upon. A human who possessed omnipotence would certainly need to worry about boredom; why not God? He was in the position of being the ultimate solipsist ... all powerful in a sad universe of boredom and loneliness. ("Ultimate" solipsist because, unlike a run-of-the-mill human solipsist, God would know for certain that He lived in a world that was also His own mind.) So God invents humans to surprise Himself ... in ways both good and bad. God invents evolution, so animals can transform in unexpected ways, and surprise Him. God would find more interest, surprise, and wonder in the universe if He didn't micro-manage everything.

All of this was presenting God in a much different light than most believers seemed to prefer, but it occurred to Thomas now that many of the paradoxes of the Bible would be resolved simply by letting God be more human. If God had to be perfect in every respect—and believers were afraid to say otherwise; God might get angry—then inconsistencies were inevitably created, and these inconsistencies fed the arguments of the atheists. The idea that a Creator must be absolute in every way was not required by any actual logic. The notion was far more suggestive of a psychological need on the part of believers than any realistic assessment of what God might be like. Thomas thought that allowing an imperfect God countered various atheistic lines of argument.

It was important to let God change and evolve over time; that would certainly erase inconsistencies. Thomas suddenly realized that God, as presented in the Christian Bible, *had* to have changed over time. When Abrahamic religion was Jewish only, God could be seen as being in one state. With the advent of Christianity, however, God made a transition to a more universal plane. Why would a messiah appear at a certain moment in human history, unless God had re-thought something? Unless God had changed, in response to the activities of His creation?

Whatever had caused it, at a point in historical time God had changed, or at least reconsidered, and this had led to the manifestation of Christ in the human world. If God had changed, He could not have been perfect and complete before. At the very least, it implied that God existed within time, and would respond to events that occurred within time.

Thomas closed his tired eyes, rubbed them with finger tips. For atheists, he thought, the problem was more general. Partly, maybe atheists were just people more inclined to doubt, but Thomas thought that, to at least some degree, they were reacting to the sometimes oppressive certainty of believers.

For many people, what seems to be most crucial in a belief system is that it tells them what they want to hear, what they wish to be true. For example, that they

31

will live forever, or be reunited after death with friends and family, or will always be loved. If the doctrine presented is sufficiently appealing, these people will find ways to believe it. This is understandable: Of what use is an utterly bleak ultimate truth? If the news isn't good, wouldn't we be better off not knowing? Maybe ignorance is bliss. We'll just assume that what we want to be true is true, suppress any doubts, and get on with it.

For others, though, belief can't be mediated by wishes. Pascal's wager—that by believing, we have something to gain and nothing to lose, so we might as well believe—requires too much detachment. Even if we want to put faith in a doctrine, some of us can't escape the need to be convinced that it's true. Maybe this evolved from an instinct for survival: If we know everything with absolute accuracy, we can expect that nothing will catch us off-guard. But however that may be, the fact is that no matter how appealing an idea is, if some people aren't deep-down convinced of it, they will always be haunted by an underlying uneasiness.

And there were more basic problems with scripture. It wasn't merely that we can find logical discrepancies in the Bible, or that we are put off by Jehovah's treatment of Abraham or Job, or that we aren't all Jewish, or that some believers paint themselves into corners with their obsessions and semantic paradoxes. The real problem is that the Bible presents a picture of the world that is inconsistent with both our everyday experience and scientific evidence.

Life, on the one hand, permeates the surface of our planet with a fantastic diversity of forms and sizes, shaping itself in ways that humans find sometimes beautiful, sometimes grotesque, but that allow survival in a vast range of environments. The picture of life on Earth suggests infinite flexibility on the part of any Creator. Some major religions, on the other hand, want to yoke us with the most petty rules and protocols, the most narrow, human-centric (while theoretically God-given) dogmatism.

Would a being capable of creating this vast and complex universe care how many times we said *Our Father* or *Hail Mary?* Would He worry about how many times a day we knelt facing Mecca? Would he have a stern attitude toward sex, the means, supposedly invented by Him, by which all higher life forms continue their species? Would He really need our constant flattery, our continuous reassurances that He is, indeed, superior to us? Would the God of this amazing cosmos really be an insecure pedant?

The more Thomas thought about the God presented by the religiously intolerant, the more he thought their God's personality resembled their own. The fundamentalists had grafted their own character traits—self-righteousness, judgmentalism, anger, rigidity, obsessive-compulsive disorder—on to God. They found that God corroborated their every bias. Thomas profoundly doubted that God would be an insecure pedant, but he saw how God could easily be imagined that way by insecure, pedantic humans. As the old chestnut went, God created Man in His own image, and Man returned the favor.

Thomas applied this common charge to fundamentalists, but he himself was also guilty. When he wondered what a judgmental God might think of him, he realized he could be in trouble. This was not a big concern most of the time, but to the extent that

Thomas worried about it at all, he countered by assuring himself that any real God of this vast and diverse world could not be petty, small-minded, or mean-spirited. In fact, Thomas would be very surprised if God didn't casually forgive Thomas his every trespass. Thomas expected any supreme being to be sanguine, tolerant, reasonable, objective ... in short, a fellow much like Thomas himself. Or at least as Thomas liked to imagine himself. Thus Thomas also cast God in his own image.

And if none of this saved him, Thomas thought, perhaps God had a sense of humor. It sure looked that way at times.

* * *

Somewhat wryly, Thomas reminded himself that he was not a theologian. Take it back to a more basic level, he thought. Don't try to know more than you actually know. So what did he know?

Matter versus Intent

Thomas saw that there were two possible explanations for all of reality: Matter and Intent.

What was Matter? No more than what it sounded like: dust, random atoms, inert substance and, most significantly, the various fields, energies, and tendencies by which this stuff interacts with itself. If we believe in matter and nothing else, we are allowing that chaos can randomly evolve into orderly systems. Theists have an issue with this, and it is intuitively problematic. Which, however, doesn't make it necessarily false.

What was Intent? It may appear to be simply an indirect way of referring to God, but there is a difference. If we remove the concept of God from its mooring in established traditions, it can become very ambiguous. When we make God sufficiently abstract, the term could mean any principle that originates phenomena or brings order to the universe—including a blind force with no self-awareness. Stephen's cosmos-initiating gravity could then be described as God. In which case God is barely different from matter.

The term *Intent* does not allow this, since it implies conscious purpose. Gravity, or electro-magnetically propagated radiation, or the law of averages, or the tendency of individual units to self-organize in aggregate, isn't Intent.

To compare the two explanations, Thomas came up with a somewhat editorialized description of each:

Matter

Matter (which somehow exists) interacts with itself and with more abstract forces, such as gravity and electromagnetism (which somehow exist) to spontaneously bring chaos into order. Order out of chaos is not so intuitive, but the idea is that in a sufficient amount of time, in a state of unbounded random physical process, everything will eventually come into being. Including Order. (Thomas had recently been reading Nietzsche also, and this reminded him of Nietzsche's concept of "eternal recurrence": In endless time and space, not only will everything happen, but it will happen over and over again.) Perhaps this form of the order out of chaos idea is difficult because we can't get our minds around an endless period of time.

Intent

Intent (which somehow exists), having somehow formed will and purpose in a void, without the benefit of interactive experience, brought the world into being: matter manifested, swirled in Intent's wake, coalesced according to Intent's design, became all that we know ...

Seen in this very simplified way, devoid of Original Sin, or Abraham and Isaac, or the Resurrection, or the Prophet, or Vishnu, is there anything more inherently plausible—*or more scientific*—about either scenario? Thomas remembered the idea Richard had rejected, that the odds of God's existence were 50-50. But viewed as Matter versus Intent, Thomas thought that 50-50 odds seemed reasonable.

In the end, of course, neither Matter nor Intent provided an adequate explanation. Neither answered the question of an Uncaused Cause.

A third scenario was possible: Matter and Intent co-evolved, each reacting to the other. Intent became increasingly aware as it learned from observing Matter, influenced Matter in turn, but did not totally dominate it. Matter eventually became more orderly and Intent continued to evolve, at some point developing true mind and will. The early state of Intent could have been extremely inhuman, alien to our sensibility, perhaps explaining why the universe appears so vast and indifferent to us. But ... Intent would continue to evolve.

This third, combined, concept seemed the most persuasive, to Thomas at least, since it permitted a way for Intent to develop by interacting with something outside of itself, while it still accounted for the universe's significant degree of randomness. Thomas couldn't pretend, however, that it answered the basic question of where anything had originally come from.

Thomas saw yet again that the question had no answer. God required an origin; gravity required an origin; electromagnetism required an origin, and so on. Given the structure and dynamic of human intelligence, it didn't seem there could possibly be an explanation for any of these. Maybe our brains would someday evolve to a higher level, and we would be capable of a perception that would explain it all. In our current state, however, the cosmos' apparent need for an uncaused Cause is something we are incapable of dealing with. Richard's suggestion that science would make it all clear by and by, and Stephen's notion that it already had been explained by gravity, were not credible.

So: at the center of everything was an enigma neither religion nor science could explain. In a way it was liberating, Thomas thought. You were left free to be religious, or secular, whatever suited you. It was your choice. Still ...

From the standpoint of pure logic, Thomas felt forced to conclude that the world didn't exist, it was all impossible, and we ourselves don't exist.

Except that we do. Putting aside solipsism (which doesn't explain it either), we had to accept the reality of each other and the cosmos. The enigma is always there, but so is the world. And usually we can get along by concentrating on what is immediately before us, not worrying about the rest. We simply ignore the fact that we spend our lives running down a poorly lit road, with darkness on either side.

A question of right and wrong

So, maybe none of it mattered anyway. However we got here, we're here. Deal with life as you find it. The big questions have no pragmatic use.

Except ... Thomas remembered Theo's question: What is an atheist's basis for morality? Moral behavior certainly intersected with everyday life. Did morality require religious belief? And Theo had also said that humans were innately bad.

Are we evil?

Thomas recalled a novel he had been forced to read in high school, William Golding's *Lord of the Flies*. In this book, a group of British schoolboys is cast ashore on a desert island. Lacking any adult supervision, the boys at first try to maintain a civilized order, electing a leader, assigning tasks, and seeking to be rescued. (In the movie adaptation of the book, they initially, and somewhat endearingly, follow the protocols of their schools, even wearing school uniforms and chanting while marching in order.) Soon, however, civilization erodes away. By the end of the book, the boys are semi-naked savages, obsessed with their wild, brutal hunting culture, and practicing human sacrifice.

Lord of the Flies was generally interpreted as presenting the conflict between what is savage and chaotic in people, and what is humane and orderly. The primitive hunting life is identified with evil (no noble savages here); order and civilization are identified with good. Golding seemed to believe that our ferocious side is more basic than our tendency toward good: Humans, he's telling us, are innately evil.

Thomas thought that Golding's novel, with its allegorical force and narrative clarity, strongly represented a certain dark view of humanity. Golding's perspective was far from unique, however. A negative assessment of humankind has come from many other sources, some claiming scientific support, some purely philosophical. Christianity, the predominant religion of western civilization, teaches that we are born into sin.

Lord of the Flies was first published in 1954, in the immediate aftermath of World War II and the Holocaust, so Thomas could see where Golding might have gained such a bleak view. But was Golding right? Is a violent and bloody hunter a fair representative of who we really are? Are we in fact evil?

Maybe we're bad to the bone ...

But Thomas thought not. He felt that logic ruled out the possibility. His reasoning went like this:

First, the empirical evidence offered by both history and prehistory is that the human trajectory is from lesser to greater organization, from competing tribes to larger functional groups. The scenario depicted in *Lord of the Flies*, deterioration into savagery, is exactly the opposite of what historically happened. We began as savages but over time moved increasingly toward order. There have been many setbacks, but our overall direction appears to be toward cooperation, away from conflict.

Second, the good/evil duality may be meaningful to us in various spiritual ways, but it also has pragmatic value. *Good* generally moves, by some route or other, toward what is perceived as helping our species to survive and thrive—on all levels, both physical and spiritual. (Note that this thriving is of the group, not necessarily of the individual.) *Evil*, conversely, is that which does not serve us. In this view, Are we evil? isn't a meaningful question. The Good/Evil duality is a tool; it doesn't define us.

Third, if we had qualities that made us essentially evil, we would be blind to them. We would take such qualities for granted; in fact we probably wouldn't be aware of them at all. We certainly wouldn't regard them as evil. Their wrongness would be recognizable only to an occasional outsider, a visionary or a madman or an extraterrestrial.

Or maybe to a deity.

In short, it would be paradoxical for us to define evil in such a way that it defines us. It would be like a pride of lions voting against meat.

So, while individuals may be evil—due to a sociopathic nature brought on by stunted brain development, traumatizing experience, or defects of the soul—people in general can't be evil. Religious and philosophical advisories to the contrary must be seen as attempts to coerce and direct. Logic says that as a group we are not inherently bad.

These arguments felt sound to Thomas at first, but then he wondered if they weren't a little too easy. Was there evidence to support an opposing view? Maybe so ... because now Thomas remembered something else.

Thomas' summer vacation in Europe

When Thomas was thirteen, the Air Force had sent his father to Ramstein, a NATO base in West Germany (as it was then known). Thomas and his mother and brothers had joined Thomas Sr. a few months later and the family had lived in Germany for the next three years. During their stay at Ramstein, Thomas Sr. had spent much of his time off taking the family on car trips to various parts of Europe. In the summer between Thomas' freshman and sophomore years in high school, Thomas Sr. decided the family would visit the Adriatic Sea.

They drove down through southern Germany, stopping at a freshwater lake named Chiemsee, where they enjoyed the sunshine, the Bavarian landscape, and water sports, swimming and kayaking. (Not *Lake* Chiemsee, Thomas learned; the *see* in Chiemsee meant *lake*, presumably cognate with the English word sea.) After a few days at Chiemsee, they continued on through Austria, Switzerland, and into Italy. They settled into a beach house in Lignano, a popular vacation spot on the north-eastern coast of the Italian peninsula.

Thomas' memories of Italy were vivid: The Adriatic Sea was gentle and very shallow near land; Thomas could wade out until people on the shore were mere dots and still have his shoulders above water. The weather was sunny, warm without being oppressive, and the people seemed emotional, expressive, vivacious, and usually friendly.

On the beach, Thomas remembered being mesmerized by a gaggle of sun-browned, bikini-clad young Italian women. They always stayed together, never seemed to go into the water, and frolicked on the sand brandishing bodies that were nubile, beautiful, and perfect—or at least so it seemed to Thomas at age fifteen. Probably none of them were more than five years older than he

41

was, but the gulf between them and Thomas felt cosmic. They were as bright and untouchable as the sun.

Dress code on the beach was relaxed. In addition to the bikinis worn by gals, some young males wore bathing suits that were hardly more than jockstraps—though this wasn't common; most men wore more conventional swimwear. There were unspoken rules, however. An elderly German couple was observed to change clothes on the beach under a large beach towel, something that was commonly done on German beaches. The Italian crowd didn't like it. When they noticed what was happening, they fell silent en masse and stared at the German couple, watching them grimly until they had finished.

This clothes-changing process seemed modest enough, since the towel covered everything except heads and necks. The bikinis and conventional bathing suits commonly worn on the same beach, not to mention the almost pornographic jockstrap swimsuits, were far more revealing. However, it was clear there were some lines that shouldn't be crossed.

The German couple studiously ignored the watching Italians. Thomas thought their attitude might have been, *We're old so we'll do what we want—we no longer have the energy to deal with other people's issues.*

After a week or so on the beach, Thomas' family visited Venice, not too far from Lignano. They spent the day on water busses (no gondolas), took in architecture that seemed baroque if not medieval, observed glass-blowers creating colorful, curving shapes, and tried to absorb the highly textured ambience of the city.

A trip to Rome was also suggested, but it was farther away and Thomas' father was uncharacteristically short on enthusiasm; Thomas wondered if his reluctance had something to do with Rome's association with Catholicism, and his father's known bias against Catholics. Whatever his reasons, Thomas Sr. said something about heavy traffic and they didn't go. After another week on the beach, the family got into the station wagon and headed back to Germany.

Their return route took them near the remains of the concentration camp at Dachau. Thomas Sr. decided that it would edify them to stop and make a tour ... a somber final note to their sunny, Italian vacation.

* * *

Thomas didn't know what to expect at Dachau. Seventeen years had passed since it had been liberated in 1945, seventeen years since the execution of at least some of the guards by American soldiers and liberated inmates, though this part of the story wasn't generally known in 1962. The place seemed too mundane—the rows of one story buildings were bland, certainly not aesthetic but not exactly ugly, just kind of dull and meaningless. And the place seemed too small to contain the events that had occurred there.

Groups of people of various nationalities were also walking around the camp, but not a great many; the site didn't feel overcrowded with tourists. The other visitors were as quiet and slow moving as Thomas' family. Eventually Thomas encountered in one of the buildings a sort of shrine that looked to be erected out of found objects. They were told by a placard that it was a memorial made by camp survivors.

Thomas didn't quite know how to think about Dachau. Was he expecting demons in the walls? Satanic clouds overhanging? The buildings were bland, the day not bright but mild and clear. When Thomas had read about what had happened there, no emotional or philosophical response seemed sufficient. In person, the place felt inert. There was a sort of pervasive lack of aliveness.

Thomas and his family left in silence.

* * *

Thomas saw that Dachau and the other camps, and what they represented, forcibly informed his vision of human nature.

Thomas couldn't think of Dachau as some freak aberration. He had read enough history to know that the genocidal impulse manifests across the range of global cultures. Defining exactly what constitutes genocide can be controversial, but if we avoid being distracted by arguments about boundary cases, the general picture is clear enough.

You don't, for example, have to build camps and ovens. If you turn soldiers loose on cities and villages of unarmed civilians, with orders to evacuate and/or kill the population, this clearly qualifies. It would also seem to qualify as genocide when powerful leaders knowingly make decisions that will result in the death of huge numbers of their own citizens—as Stalin did in the 1930s, for example, or Mao Ze-Dong did in Tibet in the late forties, and did again in China in the 1950s and 1960s. Pol Pot, in Cambodia in the 1970s, combined brutal policies with outright murder.

In the twentieth century alone, the list of genocides was staggering, running from Armenians killed by Turks in 1915 to 1920, to North Korean leader Kim Il Sung's purges and camps in the late forties, to Menghistu in Ethiopia in the 1970s, to Rwanda in the 1990s, to give just a cursory accounting. If we use intent as a criteria, rather than effectiveness, Thomas suspected that the list of genocidal factions would begin to seem endless. Genocide was never a uniquely German custom.

The point for Thomas was that the repugnant foregoing history looked like a series of group efforts, not just the work of a few sick individuals. So ... how are we as a species not evil? If recurrent genocide isn't evil, what is?

Evil

Thomas decided that before it was possible to assess whether we were evil, he needed to clarify the concept. What do we really mean when we say *evil*? It has been defined many ways: as a negation—not a something, but an absence of something; as disharmony within divinity, or within the balance of nature; as dross, an inertness that intrinsically resists the life force. It has been divided into "natural" evil, earthquakes, tornadoes, etc., versus "moral" evil—the behavior of humans. It has also been described as part of an equivalence: Evil and good form a sort of yin/yang balance, where one doesn't exist without the other.

While any or all of these views may have validity and provide insight, when we ask if humans are evil, we are not referring to an abstract tendency in the universe. We are talking about a category of human behavior, a class of actions over which we have some control— actions we could choose not to take.

This raises the issue of free will. The problem with free will is that it is always possible to trace our behavior, at least hypothetically, to some arbitrary influence. No matter what we do, our behavior must be influenced by something, whether it's experience, genetics, or the quality of our souls. If one or more of these is ultimately the decisive factor, it is possible to define free will in such a way that the whole concept becomes self-contradictory. Our will is never free because it is always caused by something beyond our control. Free will becomes oxymoronic, logically impossible. But if we don't have free will, how can anything we do be called evil?

A problem also exists with cultural relativism. Different cultures define evil differently. Shouldn't we be tolerant of other belief systems? Who's to say that the idea of evil held by our group, whichever group "ours" might be, is more valid than that held by any other group?

Thomas' response to the first question: We may or may not have free will, depending on how you define the term, but it gains us nothing to assume we don't. Lacking free will, the discussion becomes pointless; we're talking about something we can't do anything about.

In response to the second question: The idea that all truths are equally valid adds up to no truth being valid—there is no truth. We can accept this concept but, again, it isn't useful. If everything is equally true, it doesn't matter what we do. Action is generally goal-oriented, and if all truths are equal, how do you set a goal?

The ideas that we have no free will and that nothing is finally true may in fact be accurate. The point that these are philosophical and behavioral non sequiturs by no means disproves them. Maybe all our actions are beyond our control, and maybe there are no absolute truths. However, for reasons both pragmatic and intuitive, Thomas chose to assume that some things are more true than others, and that we have some way of making choices that comes from within our unique, individual selves. He would call this free will.

And as for relativism, Thomas thought he could establish some common ground between cultures as regards evil. Virtually any culture defines evil as human misery in some form, and those behaviors and attitudes that tend to increase human misery. What is thought to increase misery may vary from culture to culture, of course. Lack of political freedom may vex members of one culture, another may loath economic insecurity, while another may be tormented by desecration of their sacred icons. Most groups abhor sickness, physical pain, the inability to thrive. Ultimately, these can all be seen as contributing to human misery.

The above consideration implies that the idea of evil has an exclusively human basis. It could also be possible that the concept of evil comes from sources beyond us; maybe God has defined evil. Another possibility is that evil is defined by the intrinsic nature of reality, an idea sometimes associated with "Natural Law."

The first of these two extra-human sources is self-explanatory: a divine being. The second is the idea that morality—the distinction between good and evil—is based on principles that are inherent in the order of the universe. These principles can be figured out by human reason. Good and evil would exist in the same way mathematical truths exist: self-evident, independent of human or divine will. Two plus two equal four, with or without divinity. Good is good and evil is evil, with or without God.

Thomas thought about Timothy's notion of a debt owed by humans. We carried a debt (of sin), Timothy had said, and a debt must be paid. (A theistic version of the physicist's "no free lunch", perhaps.) Thus, Christ died on the cross to resolve an obligation, to pay off our sins. Aside from the obvious question—how does *Jesus'* sacrifice get *us* off the hook?—Timothy's wording suggested other puzzles: To whom exactly would such a debt be owed? Or was debt simply an intrinsic, non-sentient principle, like natural law? If even God was subject to debt requirements that He could not cancel, there must be something higher, or beyond, God. Moral principles that superseded a divine being.

a basic question ...

Thomas thought of a way to get at the natural law concept. In his mind he asked Timothy and all believers to consider the following question: Suppose God tells you, in a direct and unequivocal way, to do something normally considered evil, such as murdering random strangers. He doesn't give you a reason, no claim of doing it for a greater good. He tells you to do it, and that is the only reason you should need. If you obey without qualm or reluctance, then there is no distinction for you between divine word and what is intrinsically good and right. If you hesitate for even a moment, however, you are admitting that you are moved by some morality beyond what God tells you. This is true even if you think natural law comes originally from God. Even if it does, the law against murder still has force, in defiance of

God's subsequent will. The law has become established in its own right.

Thomas saw that this might be another issue that swayed an individual toward either belief or atheism. For an atheist, God could be taken as a loose cannon, requiring His adherents to do things like flying airplanes into buildings full of innocents. (Of course, a true atheist would think that God never asked you to do anything; you merely interpreted your concept of Him as asking you to be a murderer.)

A believer, on the other hand, thinks any message from God will always be facilitative, something that benefits humanity as a whole. God will always ask us to do only what is best for us. The depiction of Yahweh's behavior in the Old Testament is sometimes hard to reconcile with this.

Thomas remembered Theo's contention that, with a believer, you at least knew where their morality was coming from. This didn't really provide much reassurance, Thomas thought, given the human genius for re-interpreting virtually anything—any scripture or moral code—to suit our needs of the moment. It doesn't matter where the morality you started with came from, if you can always rationalize your way around it.

Evolved Morality

The other question was whether morality could be arrived at purely through Darwinian survival mechanisms, as Richard said. But while some evolutionists claimed that it could, theists predictably denied the possibility. Thomas decided to think about how such a morality could come into existence.

Thomas had once spoken with a foreign student, an Australian, who was a fellow Philosophy major. Thomas' colleague had been adamant that Darwinism could not explain what he called an "altruism instinct." This philosopher's basic goal seemed to be to discredit Darwin; his method was to contend that if Darwinism was correct, any species with an altruism instinct would long since have become extinct. Since humans had such an instinct and hadn't become extinct, clearly (to him) Darwin was wrong. Because, he said, any group unhampered by a tendency toward altruism "should and would" overrun groups that were hobbled by gentler instincts.

Thomas had found the logic very dubious. To start with, the Australian philosopher seemed to be confusing group and individual dynamics. Machiavellian individuals might succeed by deceiving or double-crossing moral individuals, at least until those with morality learned to watch out for their tricks, but an immoral or non-altruistic group, a group composed of completely self-oriented individuals, would lack all cohesion. A group can't function without internal unity; unity would not exist if all members of the group were only out for themselves and behaved ruthlessly toward each other. A certain degree of deference to, and concern for, other group members was vital if the group as a whole was to compete successfully. There should be no need to point out the survival advantage of a group whose members could defer personal desires in order to act in unity. (And actually, Thomas was not so sure the "should and would" theory of immoral success would even apply to individuals. At least some of the time a moral individual could deal successfully with an immoral one, otherwise, one on one, the bad guy would always win. But he doesn't.)

Of course, Thomas reflected, his fellow philosopher had put it a little differently. He had referred to an "altruism instinct", not just the ability to put aside immediate personal gain for the sake of group success. Thomas saw that how you labeled this apparent human tendency made a difference in how you might explain it. If you called it an altruism instinct, you might explain Mother Teresa. If you called it an instinct toward group cooperation, you merely were explaining the social behavior of most people, an easier and more necessary task.

Instincts, Thomas thought, manifest to different degrees in different individuals. In some people, for example, a lustful instinct was nearly overwhelming, while for others it was just one motive in a constellation of drives and forces. The term "altruism instinct" could cover a range of behavior. It could signify anything from simple generosity on one hand, all the way to a willingness to die for a stranger on the other. And some people would barely experience it at all (or not at all). On one side you had Albert Schweitzer, on the other Al Capone. A normal person, with a mixture of selfish and unselfish motives, could be seen as having a mild version of the same altruism instinct that would be more fully expressed in an extremely self-sacrificing individual. Or, conversely, a person who makes the ultimate sacrifice might be showing an extreme, even distorted, example of a usually milder group cooperation instinct. You did not, Thomas thought, have to explain all of the outliers when you were defending the concept of a given instinct. If your theory explained the behavior of the vast majority of people, a normal degree of aberrancy could account for the rest.

Beyond this was the evolutionary idea that the survival of genetic material, not of individuals, was the real thrust of evolution. Thus, a person who gave herself up to protect family members was acting for the survival of her gene pool (probably not consciously). This could be a valid idea, though it had to be stretched quite a bit to explain cases where the sacrifice was made for non-group members and even total strangers. Maybe these were also aberrant outliers? Thomas didn't find the defense of genetic material concept to be completely dismissible, but thought that an instinct toward group cooperation, carried to an instinctual extreme in some individuals, was more explanatory.

Thomas remembered Theo's contention that people were naturally bad, that morality based on non-religious principles was merely plagiarism of divine law. Why, Theo had asked, do secular moralities always seem to be consistent with their cultures' religiously derived moralities? Because, Theo had answered himself, they were plagiarized from them.

With a faint inward smile when he imagined Theo's reaction to it, Thomas came up with another explanation: Maybe it was the other way around, maybe religious law was stolen from tribal folk law. For example, how had the ancient Jews behaved before Moses brought the commandments down from the mountain? Had their lives been a constant chaos of betrayal, adultery, theft, false witnessing? Very unlikely; they would never have survived as a group. They probably already had a rough version of moral law, explicitly specified or not, that paralleled the Ten Commandments. Maybe Theo's plagiarism, if you wanted to call it that, went in the opposite direction. The Commandments were most likely a codification—

and perhaps clearer articulation—of pre-existing tribal law.

* * *

Thomas considered: If altruism, or something like it, was actually just a survival mechanism that facilitated group cohesion, group members would not necessarily apply it to outsiders. So, did history provide examples of groups whose members treated each other morally, but treated non-group members immorally? Or was altruism applied evenly to all? The answer was depressingly obvious: History was filled with cases of people who were perfectly kind to others in their tribe or culture, while treating outsiders abominably. (In fact, it appears that the Ten Commandments themselves were only intended as tribal law, not applicable to outsiders. The Old Testament depicts the Israelites invading areas occupied by other tribes and killing those already there, people who had not harmed the Israelites but whose land the Israelites wanted.) And yet ...

And yet brutal treatment of outsiders wasn't always the way it went. Even early on, there were a few exceptions, and more as history progressed. Sometimes outsiders were treated well, even nurtured. Why?

Thomas tried to imaginatively reconstruct early human history: At first the inconsistency between treating fellow tribespeople one way and outsiders another way probably caused little emotional conflict. Survival was challenging, and the well-being of the *other*, the non-member of your group, was irrelevant. Life had to be dealt with on a very basic level. As groups grew to include factions that had once been competitors, however, it must have become apparent that humans from other tribes are not so dissimilar from us—we are more alike than we are different. (To be a racist, or any sort of bigot, you must focus on minuscule differences between people, while ignoring vast similarities.) Many early historical people must have had enough imagination to extrapolate: If the peoples we once thought of as alien turned out to be so much like us, then perhaps our current enemies, the members of groups not yet assimilated, are also like us.

So we continued to make war on our rivals, did our best to exterminate them, but somewhere in our consciousness lurked the realization that we were killing individuals much like ourselves. It is at least possible that this double vision, this ability to see an enemy as akin to us even as we see him as an enemy, led to the original formation, or at least an extension, of the sense of guilt. Only a nagging feeling at first, perhaps, but it continued to develop.

The original concept of evil would have just been that which hurts or thwarts us. Eventually, this new realization on our part gave evil a deeper and more subtle shade: Now, we could be evil.

* * *

Still, what would be the process by which an inchoate, pre-verbal instinct modified into a set of vague moral precepts, and then modified from that into formal laws? What original instinct would ultimately be a pathway to morality? Thomas thought about it. He eventually decided that the best candidate was empathy.

Empathy

Working in the intensive care unit of a hospital, many years further on, Thomas had further occasion to consider the nature of empathy. Hospital work had brought him face to face with the dying and the dead, and it was a sobering but enlightening experience. Of the many events that had lingered with him from this period of his life, one in particular seemed to bear on empathy now. Thomas had come on the floor one afternoon to find out from RN Jodi that the patient in room 242, Mr. Jones, has abruptly, but not unexpectedly, passed.

Mr. Jones had previously agreed to make usable portions of his anatomy available to Donor Services, an outside group contracted to obtain body parts from patients who still breathed, but whose brain function had ceased. The harvested organs, tissue, and so on, were stored in cooled containers to be subsequently re-used by patients in particular need of them. It turned out, however, that because of Mr. Jones' advanced state of age and illness, the only usable parts of his physical remains were the corneas of his eyes. Harvesting corneas was relatively simple, and did not require that the patient be kept alive (or at least breathing) while it was done. Mr. Jones had therefore been allowed to pass, and Donor Services had been canceled. Harvesting of his corneas would be handled within the hospital.

Cornea excision and storage was something of a specialty skill, so Jodi notified James in ED, who had the requisite training. When James had a break in his Emergency Department duties, he came upstairs to the Intensive Care Unit with a small container, and a tool like a scaled-down, oddly-shaped spoon.

James was a handsome male RN in late youth. Though he spent most of his time in the ED, his secondary function as a gatherer of corneas kept him moving about among the various floors, and he was generally known throughout the facility. He had long, dark hair tied back in a ponytail, and he was personable, well spoken, and serious. He currently had a live-in lover relationship with a female MD.

Jodi, a tall, dark-haired woman who had gone from pretty and slim to pretty and mildly buxom under the stress of hospital work, asked Thomas if he would like to watch the harvesting. James, on good terms with Thomas also, seconded the invitation.

"Sure," Thomas said, not quite knowing what to expect, and James, Jodi and he went into Mr. Smith's partially darkened room.

Mr. Jones was still in his bed. A recently deceased caucasian, he looked much as he had while alive, except all pink was gone from his skin, leaving him with a vaguely yellowish cast. He was, of course, unmoving. Without fanfare, James approached the bed with his spoon-knife and container. Jodi stood close by Mr. Jones, who had been her patient, patting his forearm and making reassuring comments to him, calling him "honey." Since he was no longer alive, this seemed odd to Thomas, and he wondered if Jodi believed the dead could hear.

James deftly scooped, twice, with his tool; in a moment the pupils of both eyes were gone into the container. Thomas blinked; he had expected the whole process to be more elaborate, and that only the corneas would be taken, rather than the entire pupils. But why not do it the simplest way possible? Only the cornea had any further use; damage to the rest of the eye was meaningless. Take more than you had to, and you could be more certain the corneas themselves would be intact.

It was quicker and simpler not attempting to separate cornea and pupil at this stage. The portion of Mr. Jones' eyes still in his head now looked like very small, half-eaten hard-boiled eggs. Thomas could see that the insides were filled with dark fluid.

"James," Thomas asked, "how did you get into this line of work?" Referring to cornea-harvesting, not nursing. At this time of his life Thomas was curious as to how people found themselves in uncommon jobs, such as hand-modeling, deodorant-testing, changing bulbs in aircraft warning lights on high towers, designing credit scoring systems, harvesting corneas, and so forth.

James told them how he had first observed cornea-harvesting being done and found himself responding strongly. "I knew right then this was what something I wanted to do," he said. "It felt right for me."

James left with the corneas and Thomas pondered his words. He understood that the corneas would be useful to living people, and that a valuable service was being provided by harvesting them. Feeling good about helping people was one of the major rewards of healthcare work. Still, Thomas had thought that the actual task of harvesting corneas would be odious or uncomfortable. The harvester would persevere in the face of this, sustained by the austere satisfaction of a good deed performed in conflict with the natural instinct not to dig someone's eyes out. But James' enthusiasm seemed to spring from something less lofty, more personal. He seemed to derive a visceral satisfaction from his task.

Thomas thought about it, but finally couldn't fully understand James' attitude, any more than he could grasp why Jodi reassured a corpse. Maybe James had so internalized the value of harvesting that the act was satisfying in itself. Perhaps Jodi's sympathy for her patient couldn't immediately turn itself off, even though the patient had died. Maybe if they had more time to explain, their mindsets would come to seem more normal. But what did Thomas think was normal, and why? Later that evening he reflected on this, and certain realizations came to him ...

As long as it is happening to someone else, why should we be bothered by eye-scooping? *Our* eyes aren't affected. Except, in our unconscious minds, they are—it *is* happening to us. If we are normal people, not numbed by experience or an aberrant mindset, we vicariously experience everything we see happening to others. This is why we wince when we see someone sliced with a razor, wrinkle our noses in disgust when we watch someone eating something foul, or jerk back in shock when we see a pedestrian slammed into by a high-speed vehicle (even if only in a movie). We react as if we are experiencing these events ourselves. This is *empathy*.

It is the reason we get anything out of using fiction, and it is why we may watch in fascination when two beautiful people feign love-making on a movie screen— empathy works for pleasure as well as pain.

Since the behaviors we most commonly see in others are innocuous, the impact of empathy may not always be noticed. We can react with powerful emotion though, when we see people engaging in activities that are both intensely personal and foreign to us, such as sex in a different mode. We may be outraged and want to ban their behavior. *We* wouldn't act like that, and we don't want to be forced to experience it vicariously because someone else is doing it.

As a Philosophy major in college, Thomas had written papers speculating about the basis of morality. He had conjectured that it came from our accumulated wisdom, presented as a kind of situational shorthand, with the aim of creating an environment that ultimately benefits everyone. In a pre-literate and pre-intellectual era, however, he thought that empathy must have been the first glimmering of, the first instinctual and emotional reach toward, morality. Empathy could lead to a principle common to most major religions and many secular philosophies: Treat others as you would be treated. Because somewhere in your mind, you are being treated as you are treating them.

What exactly is empathy? It is a faculty for vicariously sharing someone else's experience. We sense another individual's inner state through a semi-conscious perception of expressions and body language, and a re-creation in our own minds of their experience, based on how we would react to the same stimuli.

What empathy is *not* is sympathy, though people frequently speak as though both were the same. Sympathy is a sentiment, an emotion of pity and concern toward another person. Empathy, on the other hand, is a felt understanding of someone else's emotional or physical state; it doesn't necessarily inspire kindness. For example, we may understand exactly what emotions led a murderer to act, without forgiving him in the least. We know we might have felt those same emotions ourselves in his situation, but we believe that we would not have given in to them, we would not have committed murder—and he shouldn't have either. In such a case, empathy may actually lead to stronger condemnation, less mercy. While empathy can lead to sympathy, there is no necessary link. This is another way empathy facilitates morality, as morality also is not always kind.

Empathy is the basic ambience in which we live. Various factors can numb this capacity, such as occupations which require callousness, or too much exposure to violence or explicit sex, or even just an overload of other people's experience, as might be encountered in a densely populated city. Anger, or intense preoccupation with self, seem to numb many people to empathy. And like any psychological trait, the degree to which empathy is innately present varies with each individual. But latently at least, it is usually there. If our unconscious minds are lagoons of silent hopes and fears, then empathy is the encompassing ocean, the sea in which we swim.

It is a murky and unclear sea. Coming from our unconscious minds, it lacks the clarity and exactitude of conscious thought. Since we are always subject to the whisperings of our unconscious, it is easy to confuse our suppressed desires and fears with authentic understanding of another person. For all its potential power to connect, empathy can be misleading. The sea in which we swim is a dark one.

A Higher Meaning

So, Thomas mused, morality could be derived from Darwinian mechanisms ... at least in its origin. But this might not be a complete picture. Something was missing, something to do with what morality itself seemed to reach toward. Maybe, Thomas thought, morality could only be understood when seen within a larger context.

Take Richard as an example. Richard would certainly deny any need for religion to explain morality, yet it hardly seemed possible to attribute all of Richard's own morals and aspirations to purely materialistic motives. Richard would no doubt like to someday win a Nobel prize, for instance, and that would bring fame and monetary reward. But it had to be about more than money for him. He also wanted to achieve things that transcended his own life. He wanted to expand the limits of human knowledge; he wanted to further vast endeavors—science and broad human understanding—of which he saw himself a part. These goals were not materialistic; they could not be explained as survival mechanisms.

It also seemed to Thomas that these goals were not separate from morality. More than a set of rules, morality was a means to an end. The end might include human flourishing and happiness, but it also encompassed an ambition to advance the species. Morality, in collaboration with a quest for knowledge and understanding, seemed to reach toward some vaguely glimpsed higher level. A more perfect order; a more exalted state for humans. So, Richard's aspirations, in general, were connected to his sense of right and wrong, but they also pointed to a higher meaning. What was this higher meaning, and where had it come from? Maybe a divine being did not have to be posited to explain it, but something transcending materialism, personal gain, or survival, seemed to be required. Could it stem from a non-sentient cosmic principle of some kind? But Thomas saw he had now come full circle: Did a non-sentient cosmic principle create a God? Or did God create the principle? How could either come from a void? A return to the same basic question.

What this was ultimately getting at, Thomas thought, was, Is there a point to it all? Is God the point? Is God required for life to have a point? A point ... that is, meaning in an abstracted, elevated sense. As in the question, Does life have meaning? And what did that question even signify? What, thought Thomas, does "meaning" actually mean? Was *meaning* predicated on an emotional resonance for humans? *Meaning* then would be a felt thing, not a concept. *Meaning* could also denote the completion of some ultimate plan ... but such a plan would need to have that same special sort of emotional power. *Meaning* then, would have to be something that either we humans imbued events with, or that a deity declared. If it came from a deity, we either blindly accepted the god's definition of *meaning*, or decided that His definition intrinsically worked both for Him and for us. *Meaning* seemed to imply a context, however, and the questions arose: what gave that context a meaning, some larger context? How did that larger context achieve significance? And so on ... once again Thomas faced an infinite regression.

At this impasse, Thomas stopped. It was late; he was tired; he had classes in the morning. He would sleep now and think about it again ... some other time.

running, continued ...

Six-year-old Thomas' wild, headlong flight down the hill continues for what seems like minutes. Finally he reaches flat ground, without, he realizes, having run afoul of either a motor vehicle or a macabre creature. He expects to lag from fatigue, and his pace is a little slower without the help of the downward slope, but he doesn't feel any real weariness. He has no concept of adrenaline, but he senses that his fear has in some way boosted his energy. The situation is better now anyway; once off the hill and running along Hatchee Road, he is back among residential buildings, with streetlights and at least the possibility of encountering another human being. He is no longer bounded on either side by dark forests. Thomas swerves away from the center of the street and runs along a sidewalk.

Several blocks pass easily, and Thomas feels increasing relief—he has done it; he has run the dark gauntlet; he will soon be home.

Thomas comes to the quadruplex where he lives. His family residence is, of course, locked and dark. He makes a perfunctory attempt to rouse anyone inside, knocking briefly on doors and windows, calling out quietly, but somehow he knows no one is home. After a brief hesitation, he makes his way a few doors down to the quarters of Sgt. Bradley and his wife. Elgin Bradley is a pleasant, avuncular man; he and his wife are friends of Thomas' parents. Thomas knocks at the door and Elgin takes him in affably; a minute later he's calling Thomas' parents—they're at the base hospital, it turns out.

"I've got Tommy here," Elgin tells them. "He's OK."

It occurs to Thomas, somewhat belatedly, that by now he must have been missed back at the school. He surmises that his parents had been notified of his absence, and people had been looking for him. He sees that, once again, he is in trouble.

But Thomas' brief defection is forgotten in the news Thomas Sr. brings them later that night: Another son, Patrick, has been born to the family. Thomas has a new brother.

* * *

Considering it many years later, Thomas thought that the birth of a child gave a completeness to the evening. In effect, his parents had asserted a tried and true answer to the void: Make a baby. It was a sort of immortality.

*
**

Books of interest

The Reason for God: Belief in an Age of Skepticism
Timothy Keller, 2008

The God Delusion
Richard Dawkins, 2006

The Irrational Atheist: Dissecting the Unholy Trinity of Dawkins, Harris, and Hitchens
Vox Day, 2008

Breaking the Spell: Religion as a Natural Phenomenon
Daniel Dennett, 2006

The Case for God
Karen Armstrong, 2009

God is Not Great: How Religion Poisons Everything
Christopher Hitchens, 2007

Do We Need God to be Good?: An Anthropologist Considers the Evidence
C. R. Hallpike, 2016

Biblical Literacy
Timothy Beale, 2009

The Religions of Man
Huston Smith, 1958

Holy Bible
King James Version

The Meaning of the Glorious Koran
Explanatory Translation, Muhammed Marmaduke Pickthall

Part 2

Sex, Not Sex, and Love

Sex and Not Sex

On the ocean, southeast of Miami ...

*T*he night is mild and clear; Thomas is reclining in a lounge chair, alone in the unlit bow of the cruise ship. The soft, moist darkness is a relief after the weighted heat of the day. From where he's sitting it's impossible to see the fabled phosphorescence of the bow wave; the leading edge of the waterline is far below and behind him. What he *can* see, ahead and to all sides, is an immense sweep of sea and sky. With no intervening terrain, the vista is incredibly vast; the cloud formations, faintly visible under the stars, are huge, complicated, multi-layered. Thomas notices very distant lights along the horizon and realizes they are other ships. Turning his head, he counts three of them, spaced far apart and equidistant against sea and sky. Cruise ships, he thinks, plying the same loop Thomas' boat is on, filled with tourists filled with money. Cruising is a lucrative business.

Thomas doesn't understand why no one else is in the bow of the ship. The serenity, and the grandeur of the vista, should draw at least a few—but he appreciates the solitude. And he's not really that alone. Behind him, in the forward middle section of the ship and just far enough away not to be intrusive, is a recreation area: lights, noise, a crowd of people around a swimming pool.

The light in the recreation area comes mostly from subaquatic lamps in the walls of the pool. The lamps illuminate sideways through the clear water, leaving the crowd partly in shadow, partly in a rippled carnival glow. The noise comes from the crowd, and from a public address system which blasts pop music and the voice-overs of a live DJ. Now the DJ calls out:

"Shake … you-ah … boo-tays!"

His accent, Thomas thinks, is Australian. He turns to look around. The energetic crowd around the pool, young people in swimsuits, long surfer shorts, t-shirts, and slides, obediently shake their booties.

Turning back to the front and relaxing into the chair, Thomas considers the cruise so far:

They left Miami on a Monday afternoon, headed out on a three-day, four-night voyage. They cruise at night and spend the days ashore: Tuesday they're in Nassau; Wednesday Cococay, a small island in the Bahamas, owned and operated by the cruise line and only inhabited when a ship comes in; Thursday it's Key West; and on Friday they're back in Miami. This is Thomas' first cruise; with him are his wife Nancy, his daughter Heather, and her friend Jessica. Heather's fiancé, John, is a workaholic entrepreneur who can't be separated from his latest project. He remains behind in Miami.

Boarding the ship had not been quite the gala affair portrayed in movies. The throng of passengers was festive enough, but any stay-behind well-wishers were separated out at an early stage, and no one went up a gangplank. Instead, they entered a large building on the dock and went through an involved processing that was apparently meant to filter out both terrorists and non-payers. After they had moved through various large rooms and halls for a while, Thomas realized that they were no longer in the building, but had at some point boarded the ship.

This foreshadowed an unexpected aspect of the entire cruise: the sense of still being inside a grounded building, even at sea. Modern cruise ships are enormous. Thomas had found it disconcerting to learn that a modern vessel can have as much as five times the gross tonnage of the ill-fated *Titanic* of a century ago. The great size of this ship means that passengers seldom feel the roll and surge of the waves, even cruising along in mid-ocean. The only movement experienced at all is the initial slow acceleration when they leave a harbor. This is good, of course, as no one gets sea-sick, but it dampens Thomas' sense of being on the bounding main. Though maybe it would be different in rough weather.

Once under way, the overall mood is light and celebratory. No one seems worried they might hit an iceberg (in the eastern Caribbean?), and, as mentioned, no one seems to get sick. And even though being on a ship at sea might be a novel experience for most of them, the passengers in general seem more interested in each other and the on-board diversions than in the ship itself, or the wide ocean.

Maybe this is understandable. This being a brief cruise at a bargain rate near the end of the season, the passengers are mostly people who may not be well off, but are willing to spend what money they have on a short-lived but entertaining diversion such as a cruise. In other words, young people, and young people traditionally apply a lot of energy to seeking each other out.

There is a small cadre of senior citizens aboard. When Thomas or his co-travelers speak with them, they find that they are retired and basically live aboard this ship, or another, year round. They don't even bother to go ashore at the various ports—they've seen them all before. By choosing their cruises knowledgeably they get lower rates, and probably other discounts, such as for being seniors, or for being frequent fliers (frequent cruisers). The bargain fares they pay give them all the on-board perks: a place to sleep, someone to make their beds and clean their rooms, live entertainment, and virtually limitless food—the cruise lines are generous to a fault at the buffets and dinner tables. All in all, the seniors tell them, it is cheaper, or almost cheaper, than living ashore, and a lot more fun. Life is one big cruise.

Thomas notices that the seniors' main interest seems to be the trivia tournaments held in the on-board bars. The seniors are a dominant force at trivia. They've heard most of the answers before, and they've come to grasp the underlying logic of whoever formulated the multiple choice questions. Thomas' daughter Heather, a serious trivia buff herself who will eventually go on to compete on the *Jeopardy!* TV show (crowning glory for trivia-lovers), is able to give them some serious competition.

Aside from the trivia-playing seniors, Thomas' wife, and Thomas himself, it is a young person's voyage. Young people, who want to meet attractive other young people, have fun ... and shake their booties.

Reclining in the bow, Thomas recalls an incident that had occurred earlier in the day:

He had been sitting in another chair, lounging again, in one of the spacious indoor common areas. Sunshine poured in through numerous large windows; music, not overly loud, was piped in through the ship-wide PA. Thomas was idly considering the passengers walking by when a young couple, a gal and a guy in their twenties, caught his attention.

He noticed them because, while the man was merely walking, the woman, demurely built and dressed, medium height, short dark hair, was sort of dancing as she walked, incorporating the rhythm of the overhead music into her gait. This was done more or less gracefully, and was low-key and mild. As Thomas got a better look at her, he decided that she had a lovely face. She also had a look that suggested she wasn't usually a dance-walker, not an extroverted person. There was an underlying sense that she was engaged in an endeavor. Striving to be casual and uninhibited.

As they walked nearer, however, her dancing became more overt. Thomas realized that she had seen him watching her, and the more emphatic movement was a response. He felt a little chagrined—it's rude to stare—but he also pondered her reaction. She could have been flirting with him, though he didn't think so (maybe when he was younger). Perhaps she was being subtly defiant: *Look all you want, you're not going to make me feel self-conscious. I* am *having a good time!* But something else occurred to him:

A beautiful woman must sometimes feel a need to be looked at. Both the woman and her observer may take some pleasure in it. Beyond that, of what use to the woman or to the world is her arresting face if no one sees it? And there is a philosophical question: If no one is looking at her, is she still beautiful? This is analogous to the unheard tree that falls in the forest. Being striking in appearance is a collaborative act, briefly connecting the striking individual and the person looking at her. So, dancing in a more pronounced manner is a way of getting people to look at you. Her reaction could have been a combination of defiance and mild provocation: *Eat your heart out, fellow.*

Problems occur in this type of scenario when one of the collaborators, generally the male observer, makes more of it than it is. Thomas didn't want to be taken like that, so he reluctantly looked away.

Thinking on it now as he reclines in the bow of the ship, Thomas reflects on the female-male dynamic in general, and he recalls a couple of previous conversations he'd had that seemed to bear on the subject:

A few months before, Thomas was exchanging emails with a friend named Mark. In the course of their discussion, Mark mentioned the latest scandal around a famous movie actress. According to tabloid reports, her husband had been caught cheating on her. The conventional question was, why would anyone be unfaithful to a woman who appeared so completely beautiful and desirable?

Mark had an answer, which he called "Mark's Law." Thomas was reluctant to grant this official status, since he and many others had already had a similar thought. However, Mark may be the first to make a formal statement of it. Here is *Mark's Law:*

Show me a beautiful woman, and I'll show you a guy who's tired of making love to her.

(His actual wording was slightly more pungent.)

This in turn leads Thomas to remember a story that had recently been told in the hospital where he works. This vignette may sound a bit incorrect, but, like Mark's Law, it is revealing.

A young resident MD in the Emergency Department is being chastised by the older doctor who is mentoring him; the mentoring doctor is not pleased with the resident's handling of a woman who had come in for treatment. The senior MD begins by pointing out that the woman was homely, and pressures his trainee to agree: "Come on, admit it! She's ugly!" The younger doctor is reluctant at first, but eventually is coerced into conceding that she was homely. The older doctor states that, further, the patient was fat. Again the young MD is hesitant, but again is forced into a concession: Well, yes, she was fat. The older doctor sums it up: "She's ugly and she's fat, and that's why you didn't order the pregnancy test. Listen—for every woman who's fat and ugly, there's a guy who likes fat and ugly. Always order the pregnancy test!"

(The good doctor's actual words were quite a bit more pungent. And if the pregnancy test issue needs to be explained, various treatments performed in hospitals, medications, x-rays and so on, can have dire effects on a fetus, so the protocol is that a pregnancy test is always done if a woman is anywhere near child-bearing age, or has any doubt as to her child-bearing status.)

Mark's Law and the senior doctor/resident story seem to point in opposite directions. On the one hand, men seem willing to have sex with anyone. On the other, they grow weary of even the most desirable women. What's wrong with them? But maybe there is no real conflict here, maybe we're just looking at different points along the same continuum. A need for sex, once fulfilled, can evolve into a need for variety in sex. If this need is satisfied, we may seek more diversity yet; if it is thwarted, we'll fall back on whatever we can have. A restless need is the unifying theme.

Not every man follows this pattern, of course, and there is certainly more to sexual attraction than sheer physical appearance. Still, the attitudes suggested by these two recountings are sufficiently common to make the indictment ring true. And further perusal of the scandal sheets, not to mention common experience, indicates that women's sexual behavior isn't so different. Ultimately, the problem can't be narrowed down to one gender or the other. It is the interaction between the two that we have to live with.

Of course, our attempts to understand the common ground of our sexuality are limited by our information. How accurate a picture do we ever really have of someone else's sex life? It's difficult to say for sure. Friends may talk about sex among themselves, but there is often a hidden wariness. It's never clear what is being held back. And when people do seem to speak freely, they may disconcertingly show the opposite tendency: Events are exaggerated from a desire to impress, to appear worldly and experienced, or even to titillate the listener. It seems that virtually all sexual confession is disguised boasting. (Especially with women. Men don't bother to disguise it.) This latter impulse, to overstate our sexuality, may also be partly an attempt to compensate for repression. And there is no certainty that we're more honest when we answer questions from a scientific (sexological) researcher. Still, while facts are often fudged and certainty is hard to come by, most of us at least think we have an idea of what human sexual nature is like. And we're likely to think that, as Mark's and the doctor's perceptions suggest, sex has unresolved issues.

* * *

Many pop psychologists, media sages, and libertines tell us the problem isn't sex; it's our reactive attitudes. They say that our repressive sexual conventions thwart our basic instinctual needs, and this is the source of neurosis. If we would just let go—"go for it"—we would be healthy and happy. Experience indicates that this is simplistic, however, that unbridled carnality doesn't solve all problems.

For one, people still seem to crave exclusivity. Couples still get married—several were wed during the cruise—even though in this day and age there is less external incentive to do so. A lot of these marriages don't last, of course, and high divorce rates are presented as evidence of our natural promiscuity. Divorce rates may in fact be high, especially when compared to the early twentieth century and before, but divorce numbers are actually going down in the US, with rates in the twenty-first century lower so far than their peak in the 1980s.

Besides, what is the real significance of a divorce rate? If we compare the current numbers to, say, the much lower numbers of the 1870s, we have a tendency to censure ourselves: Couples now are less committed, we think, more frivolous. But is it reasonable to assume that the rates of one time period are what they should be, while those of another are not? Maybe they were a bunch of miserable, repressed people in the 1870s, enduring lives they never enjoyed. Higher divorce rates since then probably reflect liberalized divorce laws, coupled with women's greater economic independence—

historically the majority of divorce proceedings are initiated by the wife. The drop in birth rate may also be a cause, since childless marriages have always been more likely to end in divorce. And the greater social acceptability of unmarried couples living together is probably another factor. None of these trends seem evil or negative in and of themselves. The current divorce rate probably just represents an adjustment that more accurately reflects uncoerced human nature.

Whatever may be the overall picture with fluctuating divorce statistics, however, it seems clear that people still want to get married, or at least cohabit exclusively. Many of us still want to bind ourselves to each other, even if that binding is the outgrowth of a transient, even irrational emotion.

So, sexual exclusivity is not dead and probably never will be; faithfulness to one sexual partner is still an ideal in the minds of many. On the other hand, our sexual natures seem to crave variety. It may be that almost all of us experience wayward feelings at one time or another, whether or not we act on them. If we can be sexually aroused by one person, it stands to reason that we can also be sexually aroused by another, whatever we may tell our lovers. But why can't we just ignore this wayward impulse? Especially in view of the trouble it causes.

I think the reason has to do with our sense of excitement. As children, many things thrill us: birthdays, theme parks, camping trips, Christmas, and so on. These things seem magical, seem to take us into almost an altered state of reality. As we grow older, the thrill fades from most of these. Not so with sex, however; sex can remain magical well past the point when we've become jaded with other ephemeral enchantments. But in order to retain this magic, or to keep reigniting it, at least some of us seem to require novelty: new partners.

So, if a significant other is unfaithful, there may be no point in the cuckolded party wondering what he or she did wrong. Probably nothing. Probably the straying partner was just trying to find that old magic.

Well, then ... maybe instead of giving up waywardness, we should give up exclusivity. Why not seek sexual diversity, and let our partners do the same? This seems to actually work for some people (maybe), but not so well for others. It conflicts with the monogamous tendency just discussed, the desire to be faithful to someone, and it tends to make relationships too vulnerable. It makes us insecure. If, as seems the case, we identify with a lover we feel very close to, the intrusion of an outside sexual partner can damage or destroy that sense of identification.

Maybe this uneasy dialectic between the wish for faithfulness and a hunger for variety can be seen as a struggle between love and sex. Or maybe this is just misty-eyed romanticism, and we should be looking for an evolutionary explanation.

Scientifically, this conflict is usually explained approximately as follows: On one side, a need to be sure that our children really are *our* children (something that men at least can doubt), combined with the fact that human children require prolonged parenting (requiring a long-term commitment from both parents), gives an evolutionary impetus toward monogamy. On the other, if we spread our genes as far and wide as possible (via promiscuity), we maximize our chances of having descendants. (This works more for men, whose maximum possible number of offspring is not limited by lengthy gestation periods.) Promiscuity means that men, at least, might have more offspring to pass along their genes; monogamy means that, with fathers present to protect and provide for their children, there is a better chance that our children will survive long enough to pass along anything.

This can't be the whole story, though. Sexual guilt, or something like guilt, persists even in individuals who aren't committed to anyone and who don't have children to worry about. If we only care about transmission of our genes, how do we explain true asceticism? St. Paul the Apostle, for example, reluctantly accepted a state of marriage for his followers, but advocated celibacy as the better choice. (It was his personal choice.) If Paul was alone in this attitude, if it didn't connect with others, that part of his teachings would have long since fallen by the wayside. He wasn't—isn't—alone. A negative reaction to sex always seems to lurk just beneath the surface of our desire. This can't be just a matter of making certain of our children's lineage, or of being in (secular) love. It's as though there is something in sex itself that is essentially problematic for humans. Why?

Popular theories as to why sex seems riddled with issues:

We are still steeped in religious guilt.

The religious model of sexuality, at least in western tradition, is of a spiritual soul in mortal struggle with an animal body. The body—the flesh—is harried with carnal desires, which we must rise above to gain the kingdom of heaven. In the conventional western religious paradigm, this is a war between our spirituality and our sex, and in this war spirit is the hero and sex is the villain. Our sexuality is not seen as broken or stifled; sexuality is assumed to be all too able to take care of itself. The problem occurs when our souls allow themselves to be persuaded by our desires.

This picture raises several obvious questions: If sex is sin, why are we made in such a way that sex / sin is the means by which we continue our species? If sex is sinful, why do we find it so delightful? Does God enjoy tormenting us? We apparently must conclude that there is no sex in heaven. (And if our bodies are animal, why do religious fundamentalists have such a problem with the idea that we evolved from animals? ... but this last question takes us beyond the scope of the discussion.)

These are not newly devised objections, but they're worth recapitulating, as they suggest how the traditional religious view of sexual morality clashes with modern sensibility. It is probably reasonable to say that most of us now are not influenced too much by a severe sort of Pauline doctrine. But the most troublesome aspect of the religious guilt explanation is that it leaves the basic question hanging: Why do sex and religion need to be opposed in the first place?

We are influenced by a "Puritan Ethic."

Everyone knows that among the early immigrants to the North American colonies was a strict religious group known as the Puritans. Their mindset included a stern work ethic and a negative view of sex. The second of these is the issue here. The contention is that the Puritans' attitude toward sex has pervaded American culture in general, and still affects us today.

The sexual conflict associated with Puritanism may seem at first to be the same as the one stemming from religion. After all, the Puritans were identified by their religious beliefs, and presumably their disavowal of sex stemmed from the religious idea of carnal bodies at war with spiritual souls. The current notion of the Puritan Ethic, however, implies that what began as a religious-based rejection of sex has migrated beyond theology into the mass consciousness. It now infects people who not only don't share specific Puritan religious beliefs, but who may be only nominally religious, if at all.

For this to have happened, for the Puritan mindset to have spread beyond the realm of religion and infused secular society, we would have to be highly susceptible to an attitude supposedly at odds with our nature. In other words, how could the Puritan Ethic hold such sway over us unless it speaks to an inclination we already have? And if we already have an innate potential for this tendency, why do we need to invoke the Puritans to explain it?

A more likely explanation is that a puritanical response to life is an instinctual option, present to a degree in most of us. Like all biological and psychological traits, it will manifest more forcibly in some individuals than in others. The most reasonable explanation for the Puritans themselves is that they were a group of like-minded people who found each other, as like-minded people tend to do. Once they had coalesced into a group, they reinforced each other's beliefs, as groups tend to do. And then they had children, who were at the mercy of their parents' mindset.

Numerically, the Puritans peaked 400 years ago, and there never were that many of them in America. It is believed that the Puritans who fled to the new world went on to produce a great many offspring, somewhat undercutting their supposed rejection of sex. Despite this, the New England Puritans seem to have been among the most radical in their beliefs, including their belief in the need to reject sexuality. Their stridency means they could have exerted a strong influence among their neighbors, but probably also means they provoked strong opposition. Beyond this, later waves of immigrants have brought alternative viewpoints to North America, which should have had some countering effect. All in all, it is not clear how the Puritans could have exerted the enormous influence we attribute to them. Nonetheless, we still whine about how the Puritans mucked up our sex lives. We are conceding way too much power to this eccentric little group. Such an extraordinary impact, persisting over centuries and affecting huge numbers of people, is not plausible. It's time to give the Puritans a rest.

Society oppresses our natural tendency toward sex and freedom.

In this formulation the conflict is between the individual and society. No instinctual force or religious belief retards our erotic drive; the social structure itself prevents us from being noble savages in the realm of lust. In this view, sex is the good guy, and society the villain.

The first question that comes to mind in response to this idea is, where did this evil society come from? Was it foisted on us by the devil, or by Martians? No; society is a human artifact, and logically it should reflect our nature.

On the other hand, society is not a static entity; it evolves over time and therefore can't be taken at any particular point to perfectly mirror us. Perhaps society started out as a very rough caricature of us, and is gradually evolving toward a more perfect reflection. Or perhaps we change society and it changes us, a sort of mutual, intertwined spiral of development.

Still, and granting that society is a work in progress and there may be periods of adjustment, society is ultimately our creation and should never be completely at odds with who we are. A more likely idea is that society is the way it is because we are the way we are, and even at an incomplete stage of social development (there may never be a complete one) any restrictive, even apparently stunting quality of society must stem from a component of our collective consciousness.

A simple notion of society as oppressor, with no recognition of its relation to us, seems to be an evasion on our part. As with the idea of a Puritan Ethic, we must look to ourselves if we wish to understand what is really happening.

Our erotic impulse is opposed by a death instinct.

Freud does what I have been suggesting in the previous sections: He places the force that opposes our sexuality squarely in our own basic nature. He tells us that we have an instinctive, biological drive toward death, and this continuously struggles with our sex drive. This is a bothersome, even anti-intuitive, concept; Freud arrived at it with difficulty and was never happy about it. In fact, before adopting death as the great nemesis of love, he considered a couple of other candidates.

Initially Freud believed the instinct that opposed our sexuality was something he called the Reality Principle. Here the conflict was between sex, (or E*ros*, by which Freud meant life force, sex in a very broad sense) and self-preservation. Simply put, we want sex, but we also want to avoid being killed, so we rein it in ... sometimes we have to be realistic and defer gratification, even if it causes us frustration. Freud became dissatisfied with this idea, however. He saw that the need to survive is not necessarily in conflict with the need for sex. Such a conflict could occur as a pragmatic issue, in a specific situation, but it does not have deep, instinctual roots. He didn't think it was a *basic* duality. He abandoned the model of Eros versus reality principle.

Freud's second concept was that Eros was opposed by the impulse toward aggression. Our inclination toward sex, which he now allowed to include both the inclination toward survival and cooperation and the desire to create and thrive, was opposed by our need to fight, to make war, to conquer. This duality is suggested by the familiar sixties-era slogan: Make love, not war. But this concept also ultimately failed to work for Freud.

He saw that Eros and aggression convert back and forth too easily. We've all seen how readily love can turn into hate. Also, they can fuse, as in sadism. (It appears that Freud considered aggression synonymous with hate.)

Beyond Freud's reasons for rejection, it could be added that antagonism between sex and aggression sits poorly with direct experience. Even the most gentle and solicitous lover needs a certain amount of aggression in order to get close to anyone. Most of us intuitively understand sex as having an aggressive component.

So Freud came finally to his third idea, a conflict between the sex instinct and a death instinct. (Freud called the death instinct *todestrieb*, "death drive," not the commonly mentioned *Thanatos*.) Here Freud raises the disturbing idea that we want to die, that we are innately compelled toward our own destruction. In this view, Eros is identified with life in general, and the opposing force is the human version of a broad natural tendency, present in all life and maybe in the world in general, toward non-being. Our unconscious mind now becomes the battleground for the war between life and death, the most basic of all struggles. This duality between Eros and death was Freud's final version of the conflict.

How exactly would this death drive function? Why would we have such a thing in the first place?

Freud believed that all animals, and maybe all plants as well, seek rest, a stress-free state, an end to striving. Death is clearly the ultimate form of such a state. Though he didn't originate the term, Freud also called this tendency the "nirvana principle", after the Buddhist concept of nirvana as a condition of serenity associated with freedom from desire. (This state has also been likened to homeostasis, though Freud seems to have had in mind something more inert than mere equilibrium. Equilibrium can be dynamic, a quality of an active system.)

The idea of a universal tendency toward disorder and non-functionality will probably make sense to anyone who has noticed how everything seems to want to break down, to come undone, to work against us. Such a tendency may certainly look plausible to those of us who have had to repair machinery, maintain manmade structures, or even tend gardens against time and weather. Many have commented on what seems a perverse tendency of inanimate objects to seek the most destructive path. But how would this essentially metaphysical trend work within our psyches? Not to mention the psyches of beasts. This gets too mystical, and we could also ask how such an impulse is evolutionary. How does it serve our need to survive?

An instinct to refrain?

What seems more reasonable than a death instinct would be an instinct toward restraint, a sort of psychological balancing mechanism. This idea can be illustrated by considering how our muscles work:

When you activate a muscle to perform a movement, for example contracting your biceps to fold your arm, not only does your biceps contract, but the opposing muscle, the triceps, also activates. This counter contraction by the triceps is weaker than the biceps contraction and so does not prevent movement, but it slows and smooths it. This use of a muscle is called eccentric contraction. Of course, when the object is to straighten a bent arm, the triceps would prevail, and the biceps would perform the weaker, eccentric contraction. In a pair of complementary muscles such as biceps and triceps, either muscle can prevail, depending on what motion is needed.

What Freud calls a death drive may be no more than a retarding, or balancing instinct, performing a function for the mind similar to what the eccentric contraction of a muscle does for the body. An impulse to refrain from erotic activity, if only briefly, might have evolved naturally within us, in response to evolutionary forces.

From a survival standpoint, such a balancing factor could have many advantages. For instance, imagine a stone-age tribe suffering persistent drought or famine, or forced into a long, brutal, migration. In this context, making babies, the biological function of sex, would be a bad idea. Better to wait; the impulse to refrain would need to prevail. Eros may be the life force, but sometimes life is better served by temporarily suppressing sex.

Beyond this, sex is potentially such an intense experience that we risk being devoured by it, abandoning all other concerns, losing ourselves. A moderating factor is required. An impulse to refrain could also prevent overuse from dimming our erotic lightning.

In place of a death instinct, then, maybe we could speak of a restraint instinct. Recalling the earlier discussion of Puritans, those religious souls could be seen as individuals who either had a higher than normal amount of restraint instinct, or had suffered experiences that had imprinted them with a need to hold back, or both. This impulse to refrain would occur to some degree in most of us, though, and probably is as necessary in its own way as our positive drives and impulses.

Our challenge, if our sexuality is in fact problematic, would be to recognize and use the restraint instinct in an appropriate manner. We need to understand when to say no, and when to let go and follow our joy. Clearly things have changed since the hunter-gatherer period, and maybe our erotic and restraint instincts have become a little confused. Understanding ourselves better might resolve this. While Eros is undoubtedly the stronger impulse, and while it is a lot more fun than restraint, we have to learn to ride both these horses.

* * *

A complete alternative to Freud's death drive is not being provided here, nor does it seem that a death instinct can be completely replaced by a restraint instinct alone. Restraint explains neither repetition-compulsion nor sado-masochism, both of which Freud associated with his death instinct. This is easier to sort out if we can give up Freud's insistence that there has to be a duality, that there can be only two basic, contending forces. Why not several different instincts, each with its role to play, each shading into dominance when the situation requires it?

(It isn't clear why Freud was so insistent on dualism. Was this a relic of his early religious training, a scientifically rationalized reflection of the duality of good and evil? Or of God and the devil? Or even of the Christian idea of heaven and hell? But it may be presumptuous to analyze the father of analysts.)

Letting go of the idea of just two instincts, and thinking in terms of several, means that no single instinct has to fulfill so many roles. It becomes easier to reconcile divergent traits and build a coherent picture. Too many instincts, of course, would result in another sort of incoherence.

At this point, it probably helps to be reminded that all these descriptions of psychological tendencies are arbitrary. The brain is a dark brew of hormones, soft structures, and electrical impulses. There isn't a clear-cut death or sex drive in there, running like some deep ocean current, any more than there is a three-level house with superego in the attic, ego on the ground floor, and id in the basement (Freud's hierarchical way of organizing personality). All of these descriptions are like poetic metaphors or scientific theories: attempts to get at something, to capture in words a thing that is not made of words and will never exactly correspond to words. The trick is to find the descriptions, the words, that are most useful. At the broad, overview level we're operating on here, it may not matter whether we attribute a given web of behaviorisms to a single, multi-faceted instinct, to separate instincts, or even to an intermediately related cluster. It can be left to others to figure out repetition-compulsion and sado-masochism. Here we can settle for humbly suggesting a restraint instinct in place of an essential impulse toward being dead.

* * *

An afterthought: Would we really be happier if we were more like the animals, which appear to have a straightforward, non-neurotic approach to sex? Maybe not. Maybe sex is a struggle because, deep down, that's what we want it to be. Maybe sex is an area where the complications add to the zest, and maybe nothing really feels good if it's counterpart doesn't hurt. Pain is the price paid for pleasure. It may also be that the whole complex superstructure our species has built up around sex has added vast richness to our lives. No animal has such variety in how it can think about and experience sex. It isn't all good, of course. Frustration can be painful, instinctual joy might be occasionally shaded by our over-intellectualization of desire, aberrant individuals can become violent, and at times we even become tawdry or silly (as with pornography) ... but it still may be that in our complex elaboration of sex we've gained more than we've lost.

And, without problematic sex, maybe we would never have hit upon the notion of romantic love.

*
**

... and Love

*I*n considering romantic love, we can be guided by another pair of metaphors: the speech of Aristophanes in Plato's *Symposium*, and Anton Chekhov's short story, *The Kiss.*

Aristophanes

Plato records a drinking party, a "symposium," where a group of ancient Greek friends, all male, engage in a discussion of Eros. Each attendee is expected to give a speech on the subject, and various views are presented over the course of the evening. The comic playwright Aristophanes advances a somewhat bizarre hypothesis:

Originally, Aristophanes says, most humans were joined together in pairs, composite beings essentially wheel-shaped, with eight limbs—four arms and four legs—and two faces on a single broad, round neck. Sometimes these paired beings consisted of one female half and one male half, sometimes of two male halves, and sometimes of two female halves. These humans were very robust, physically powerful and able to cover distance quickly by rolling along the ground. In their fierceness they assaulted the gods themselves in their citadel on Mt. Olympus. The gods were not amused, and Zeus decided to punish these primitive humans by splitting them in two. Thus were created humans in the style we are familiar with: linear-shaped, four-limbed, narrow of neck, only one face. In this new form, they—we—were not only much weaker physically, but also psychologically undermined. We have been haunted ever since, says Aristophanes, by the loss of our twin.

Ever since, we have been incomplete. Ever since, each of us has been trying to find his or her other half.

Putting aside the anatomical grotesquerie, this is a romantic, almost touching idea. It speaks to that part of ourselves which thinks that, somewhere out there, we have a perfect match, a mate for life, an individual with whom we can become the person we were truly meant to be. Depending upon which kind of paired being we originally were—female/male (androgyne), male/male, or female/female—we became hetero- or homosexual. Sexual preference has no effect on intensity of need, of course, and only in the arms of our missing other selves will our fears be calmed, our doubts quelled. Thus our most basic ambition in life is to become whole again by meeting that right person.

This view can be disparaged as a sort of clinging insufficiency, but a positive take is also possible. If each individual commits to the other, as kind of an externalized version of her- or himself, this can be an unselfish, supportive sort of love. Or at least the selfishness is turned outward. And of course it is meaningless to ask which is the first, the self, and which is the other. Each is both.

Chekhov

Anton Chekhov, a Russian writer and physician in the late Tsarist period, published a short story in 1887 titled *The Kiss*. Probably Chekhov's most famous story, *The Kiss* describes an event and its aftermath in the life of Ryabovitch, a young officer in the Russian military.

Ryabovitch is shy, awkward, physically unappealing, and completely lacking in confidence, especially at social occasions or with women. When his Cossack brigade is invited to a party at the mansion of General von Rabbek, etiquette requires that Ryabovitch attend, but he lacks any enthusiasm for the event.

At the party, things go as dismally as Ryabovitch had expected, though he has become somewhat inured to his misery. Wandering by himself in an unoccupied part of the general's mansion, trying to be inconspicuous in his aloneness, he finds himself in a darkened room. Abruptly a young woman rushes out of the shadows; Ryabovitch is embraced and passionately kissed. The woman realizes her mistake—Ryabovitch is not the lover she was expecting—and she shrieks faintly and whirls away, fleeing back into the darkness.

Ryabovitch understands that the woman mistook him for someone else, but nonetheless his mind is abuzz. Surely, he thinks, the kiss is a sign of something more to come: fate has made him a promise. He returns to the party, absurdly happy, and wonders who the woman was. (He never got a good look at her.)

Dinner is served and at the table Ryabovitch considers all of the young female guests. Which one kissed him? He picks first one woman, impressed by her graceful shoulders and arms, her clever face, but then discovers she has an artificial laugh and a nose that makes her look old; it can't be her. He tries another lady. She has a charming brow and drinks daintily, but then he decides her face is flat; she also is discarded. He goes on like this with all the young women present, until eventually he has found some endearing trait and some flaw with each of them. Undeterred, he combines the best characteristics of each, the shoulders and arms of one, the brow of another, the eyes of a third, into an idealized composite, and casts this imaginary person as his unknown lover-to-be.

Ryabovitch goes home after the party still ebullient, and the feeling lingers on in the days following. Eventually however, reality imposes itself, and his mood sours. He realizes fate's promise will not be kept, and becomes, if anything, even more unhappy than before. Finally another party is scheduled at the general's house and Ryabovitch receives an invitation. He experiences a brief surge of hope, then quickly, bitterly crushes the feeling. He will not be hurt by this next occasion; he will not attend. He tosses the invitation away.

A possible interpretation of this story is that it is an extreme, telescoped metaphor of relationships based on romantic love. We fall in love with people who are essentially strangers, based upon a quick impression: looks and a hint of mannerism. Since we don't really know these potential consorts, it is easy to assign them the attributes we wish they had, the attributes we would find ideal in a lover. Only later, perhaps after a couple of years of marriage, do we really begin to understand who we've paired ourselves with. Poor Ryabovitch never even achieves the consummation and transient happiness of the newly wed, but the overall trajectory is the same: an encounter with a person we are able to find attractive, under random circumstances that seem portentous, then a period of self-deception, followed eventually by harsh knowledge, disappointment, and disillusionment. Of course, our lover or spouse is having the same realizations about us.

* * *

Looking at these two metaphors, we are again faced with a duality: Aristophanes' love as completion, the ultimate partnership, versus Chekhov's love as self-deception and wishful thinking. Which of these messages should we take to heart? Chekhov's dark vision inarguably has some truth to it; for one, it explains our divorce rate. But the view from Aristophanes has a certain persuasiveness as well (leaving out the human wheel part).

Maybe it would help to make our language more specific. We could distinguish *love* from *being in love*.

Love can connect any two individuals, and can be nonsexual. A parent loves her child. Children love their parents (sometimes). Siblings can love each other, aunts and uncles love nephews and nieces, even friends may love each other. And husband and wife can love.

Being *in love*, on the other hand, means focusing on what you think you can derive from your lover: sexual pleasure, ego inflation, a giddy sense of excitement that is always transient. Where loving can be other-directed, being in love is always essentially selfish. If any proof is needed, look at how quickly this feeling can fade, how easily it turns to resentment and even hate.

Of course, people who are actually *in* love, as defined here, say they *love* each other. In setting up this dichotomy, Thomas realizes he is guilty of a sin common to writers: using everyday words in a specialized way. However, even though *loving* and *in love* are often used interchangeably, the difference in meaning suggested here is already present, at least in latent form, in mass consciousness. These definitions are not invented from scratch, and it's useful to have a way to differentiate two not-so-similar states of mind.

This does not mean that being *in love* is a completely bad thing. The irrational excitement can be wildly enjoyable, if you don't take it too seriously, and don't become addicted to it. Perhaps going through this phase is required for maturation, a normal part of growing up. Have you lived fully if you've never been in love? If we want a long term relationship, though, we probably need to focus on loving, rather than on being in love.

* * *

Thomas and his little group arrive back in Miami without any untoward incidents—no seasickness, no perfect storm, no deep-rising kraken. He is still a little surprised that it happened; he'd always semi-consciously supposed cruising was only for a certain economic class, beyond his range. If the ship didn't sink, he expected at least to be bankrupt. However, they are OK on all fronts. Plus, they seem to have been shipping out on the love boat: While docking they learn from the ship's recreation director that the captain has presided over the wedding vows of four couples during their brief cruise. No data was provided on the number of hook-ups, casual flings, and torrid affairs.

⁎

Part 3

The Art of Living Forever (in this world)

In the Telemetry Unit of a mid-sized hospital ...

'm ready for the big show," Mr. Smith is saying to the nurse as Thomas enters his hospital room. Sitting propped up in bed, Mr. Smith seems clear-headed and at ease. Nothing in his manner suggests that he has any qualms about what the doctors have told him: that he will die very soon. His impressive equanimity is supported by his remark—the "big show" he refers to is whatever will come after death. Thomas doesn't know what religion Mr. Smith professes, if any, so he doesn't know what form his big show will take. Whatever he expects, though, he sounds sincere, optimistic, interested. Thomas is also curious about a possible afterlife, but he's wondering if he will be so at ease when his time comes.

* * *

Finishing his brief conversation with Mr. Smith's nurse, Thomas returns to his seat at the monitor station. The hour is late, and lighting in the telemetry unit has been adjusted accordingly. The hallways and patient rooms are dark. In the center of the unit, a few strategically placed lights cast dim pools of radiance over the tables where the nurses are doing their paperwork. Conversation is minimal and soft spoken. The only other sounds are the fluctuating murmurs of medical equipment, and the occasional soft slap of a nurse's shoes as she enters or leaves a patient's room.

Thomas sits facing a group of CRT terminals: telemetry monitoring devices. There are three terminals, and each terminal's screen is divided into eight rectangular sectors, twenty-four in all, one for each patient on the unit. Each rectangle displays a pale greenish line, which slinks across its sector in six-second intervals. This moving line segment is a visual representation of the electromagnetic pattern cast by a patient's heartbeat. The image will conform to certain general patterns, but each individual's is different, like handwriting. By measuring and timing this squirming line, by recognizing its relation to archetypal forms, and by considering the accompanying numeric data, much can be inferred about the condition of a patient's heart. State law requires health care facilities to have a staff member watching monitors of this type every hour of the day, every day of the year, on any floor designated as a telemetry unit. As the Telemetry Technician currently on duty, this watchfulness is Thomas' primary task.

One of the most important features of the monitors is that they sound an alarm whenever a change occurs in a patient's heart tracing. If the Telemetry Technician decides that the change could be immediately life-threatening, he notifies the patient's nurse and a "code blue" can be called: Overhead alarms sound throughout the hospital and doctors, nurses, and other staff rush into the room and attempt to save the patient's life.

It has already been decided that this will not happen in Mr. Smith's case. He is classified as DNR: Do not resuscitate. His cardiac tracing still displays on the monitor, but all of his alarms have been turned off. For Mr. Smith, medical science has reached the limits of its power; his doctors have acknowledged the inevitable. He will be allowed to die.

* * *

Of the eighteen years Thomas worked in a hospital, the first eight were spent in Telemetry, the last ten in Critical Care.

Critical Care accepted all sorts of patients since severity of ailment, rather than type, was the criterion for admission. The hospital Thomas worked in was a designated regional trauma center, however, so a great many of the admissions were trauma patients. These were most often victims of motor vehicle accidents (MVAs), but they also received people who had fallen from roofs, bicycles, horses and tractors, pedestrians who had been hit by cars (a kind of MVA), victims of gang violence, near suicides, and individuals who had suffered a variety of bizarre and unforeseeable mishaps, almost surreal compoundings of coincidence and error, as though fate indulged some dark humor.

The unfairness of it all was obvious with these trauma patients. No one needs to point out the existential injustice when a seventeen-year-old is brain dead because she rolled her car, or a twenty-two-year-old will spend the rest of his life paralyzed from a diving accident.

The situation on the Telemetry Unit was different. Patients here usually had heart disease, or something closely related. This meant that most of them were older, close to the natural end of their lives: the situation we all eventually face. It should have been a little easier, then, for staff to distance themselves from them, that slight distancing healthcare workers need so they can do an effective job. A dying eighty-year-old won't affect most people the way a dying eighteen-year-old will.

Still, when Thomas considered these elderly patients, he saw a special sort of poignancy in their situation, not lessened by the fact that what was happening to them was not an aberration. Sitting at the monitor, watching their flickering, uncertain vital signs, he was seeing everyone's future.

Thomas thought about it during his years in Telemetry, and eventually came up with the following scenario:

You are, we'll assume, a normal person. You spend most of your time working at some job or other, you have a greater or lesser degree of financial success; you get married, you have children or you don't, maybe the first marriage doesn't work out, so you get divorced and eventually marry someone else, you try to do a good job of raising your kids, maybe you make a few mistakes, maybe you cheat on your spouse, maybe you're tempted but you don't give in. All your big decisions seem reasonable when you make them, though not always in retrospect, and over all you try to do the right thing. Eventually you retire, maybe with some regrets, but maybe with some accomplishments as well. And most of your life has passed.

Then you end up *here*. Lying in a hospital bed. Your bodily functions are attended to by various strangers. Your skin color is pale and sickly, you smell strange, your internal systems are so impaired that you're half conscious and fighting for breath. Your face is contorted into that expression the nurses call "the O-sign"—your gasping, open mouth forms the circle of the "O". Sometimes your tongue lolls out, like a serif on the "O", and then you're making the "Q-sign." In the end, it doesn't seem to matter what kind of life you led, whether you were a good person or bad ... you end up in this same bed.

What's the point? Why does it end like this? Is this what we deserve after a lifetime of effort, of doing the best we can?

Why must we die?

Taking the question philosophically rather than medically, Thomas provided some possible replies, and some rebuttals.

We die because ...

The world grows weary of us and wants something new.

The world is too hasty; I still have interesting possibilities. Besides, if the world is bored it can turn its attention elsewhere. It doesn't have to kill me. I'm not bored with the world.

It's God's way. Don't question it.

Why is it God's way? I *am* questioning it. This answer doesn't actually address the question, just places it at one remove.

You had your chance. Now get out of the way and let others have theirs.

I don't begrudge others their chances, but mine seemed a bit brief. Why can't all of our chances be ongoing?

Stop complaining and take things as they are. Acceptance is the path of wisdom.

All progress comes from a refusal to accept what we don't like. Passivity isn't wisdom.

Who promised you life would be fair? And anyway maybe this is *fair, depending on your perspective. What you call fair is really just what you personally want.*

All right. This might be a valid point. When it comes to life overall, nobody promised us anything ... though it does seem a few things were vaguely implied. Still, why wouldn't we think in terms of what we want? What we want is generally the scheme by which we structure our lives. This doesn't even have to be selfish; maybe we want good things for our children. Anyway, the human impetus to want seems to be a basic part of us, what we're handed at birth. Why should we disavow it? Our wants guide us.

Nonetheless, when all is said and done, death is still there, gazing back at us. No amount of point and counterpoint dismisses its blank-eyed grin.

Anyone who thinks about it at all will see that our attitude toward life is informed by our awareness of death. That life is fleeting is a realization that must affect how we behave, whether or not we consciously realize it. So the first question is, in light of our inevitable demise, how should we conduct our lives?

How we've responded historically to the prospect of death

The practice of philosophy has sometimes been defined as preparation for death. From ancient times forward, philosophers have come up with a wide variety of recommendations as to exactly how we should prepare.

One answer is to live in the moment, immerse yourself completely in the here and now. This seems to be what Zen suggests, as a step along the path to enlightenment. This is also what many of us seem to actually do, without any formalized philosophy to it. We dwell on the everyday issues that we all contend with, nurse our wants, suffer our injustices, embrace our loved ones, scowl at our adversaries, and try to make the best of it. We focus on what we *can* do, rather than worrying too much about a bigger picture.

"Living in the moment" can be taken in different ways, however. Historically, one way people have lived in the moment is by focusing on the pursuit of pleasure. In the absence of other forces, pleasure seems to be what our mind/body unit naturally gravitates toward. We're instinctively geared to seek pleasure, aren't we? Why fight it?

But on further reflection, things get more complicated. If pleasure continues, does it continue to be pleasure? Does it still satisfy us? And are we even sure of what we mean by pleasure? The word conveys different things to different people. In ancient times, rival philosophers came up with conflicting definitions. For example, one style of pleasure was sought by Epicureans, another by Hedonists.

Epicurean pleasure-seeking

The word *epicure,* as used currently, suggests a sybaritic indulgence in luxury and sensuality, but this isn't what the original Epicureans had in mind. Epicurus, who taught his philosophy in the fourth century B.C.E., defined pleasure as the absence of pain, as modesty, as the giving up of sensual desires. He thought the good life would be attained when we renounced ambition and striving, when we became quiet and tranquil. His idea of an enjoyable night out would be a simple dinner with friends, and quiet conversation. Doesn't sound all that bad.

Hedonistic pleasure-seeking

Hedonism, on the other hand, implies a more active, intense sort of enjoyment. While the Epicurean nibbles at an austere meal and takes part in congenial discussion, the hedonist—

- eats rich food with gusto;

- snowboards, snorkels, para-glides;

- plunges into the cool sea on a sweltering day;

- is powerfully moved by emotive music;

- leans his motorcycle through the hilly curves, cruises past the redwoods, and opens it up full throttle on the coast highway;

- has sex, frequently and variously.

Unlike the serene Epicurean, the hedonist engages in activities that require a close focus, an immersion in the immediate, with perhaps an accompanying disinterest in wondering what it's all about.

Though both of these philosophies define themselves as pleasure-seeking, they have emphatic differences. True Epicureans sidestep through the world, avoiding controversy or struggle, while hedonism is more risky. Still, they have enough in common that we can criticize them on the same basic grounds.

Hedonism and Epicureanism appear to satisfy some people, and most of us act in these modes occasionally. By themselves, though, they are not enough. We need to place our indulgences within a framework of meaning. For many of us, our pleasures become unsatisfying, or leave us with a certain uneasiness, if we don't feel we've earned them. This need for pleasure to be part of a transaction with duty or accomplishment may be an evolved trait, something that has furthered our survival … but for whatever reason, most of us seem to need a balance.

If we continue to pursue sensual or aesthetic enjoyment without this balance, a sense of futility may overtake us.

Stoicism

At the other extreme is stoicism, a discipline that teaches calm acceptance of any outrageous sling or arrow fortune may throw at us. If we were to look at the concept of *stoic* in the popular mind, we'd probably find an image of a stony-faced warrior being tortured without flinching.

A leading exponent of stoicism was Marcus Aurelius, emperor of Rome in the second century C.E. Reading his *Meditations,* we are struck by his saint-like tolerance and impassivity, his almost perverse will to abstain from anything enjoyable. These are two sides of the same coin. If we escape life's injuries through a disregard for pain and grief, we escape its joys through an equal indifference to pleasure and affection.

For the true stoic, this loss of engagement is not a disadvantage. His or her goal is to maintain equilibrium; being uncheered by positive events is as important as being undisturbed by negative ones.

Stoicism might sound a little like Epicureanism, in that both are ways to nullify life's ills. But while the Epicurean wants to retreat into a private, pleasant world where bad events don't intrude, the stoic accepts bad events, but seeks to avoid having bad *feelings* about them.

There are days when Thomas finds stoicism very appealing, but all in all he thinks it takes away too much. Giving up the good with the bad seems a dubious trade-off. It's ironic that this philosophy, historically popular with warriors, seems a form of cowardice ... the stoic doesn't want to risk having feelings.

Altruism: fulfilling yourself through service to others

One standard of conventional wisdom is that we find meaning in our lives by living for others. Thomas has heard this in some form since he was very young, and has generally bought into it. Even as a child, though, one question bothered him: If he lives for others, who do they live for? Do they live for some third party, who in turn lives for someone else, and so on, going around in a daisy chain until it finally comes back to Thomas? It would seem to be more efficient if everyone just lived for themselves. Living for each other sounds friendlier, but it would be more straightforward if we each took care of our own situations. After all, who knows what you want and need better than you do?

On the other hand, some people aren't able to take care of themselves. Extending a helping hand to them feels like the right thing to do. Also, a world in which each person only worries about himself or herself sounds like a cold place. Empathy not only moves us toward sympathy and the desire to help others if they need it, it also leads to a sense of connection ... our world becomes larger. If we ignore these emotions, we may feel cut off and isolated, even subtly claustrophobic. If an individual's universe really only consists of one person, it is a small place indeed.

On the rhetorical third hand, selfishness is natural. Your body, with its senses, is your only direct window on the world. Body and mind, in combination, form the totality of your sense of self and your ability to experience life. If you don't survive, you will have no experience to contemplate. If you don't expand your being, you will have little to enjoy. It is logical to protect and preserve yourself before all others.

Life gets complicated, though. Sometimes other individuals become so important to us, we identify with them so closely, that we'd rather forfeit our own existence, our own window on the universe, than see them hurt or removed from the world. Also, altruism seems to return subtle, practical benefits, even when that wasn't our motive for behaving altruistically. Most of us feel intuitively that the presence of altruism in the world creates an environment which is better for us all.

So, how should we act? An individual who has no personal needs or desires, who lives only to please others, seems to lack some basic aspect of common humanity. An individual who lives completely for herself, on the other hand, seems shallow and lacking in resonance. The best course would seem to be a blending of selfishness and altruism. Seek what you want, but help others when they truly need it, and avoid doing harm.

Does any of this help us deal with death?

To start with, anything that causes us to feel we've led meaningful lives may make death easier to face. Beyond that, when we help others we tend to feel more connection with our fellow humans, and ultimately feel we are part of a larger process—we are contributing to a higher effort. If we identify, even semiconsciously, with a larger group, we achieve an indirect sort of immortality. This larger group could be the family, would once have been the tribe, and may ultimately be the human species. In this last instance, as long as there are people on Earth, some part of us lives on. This thought can be comforting, even as we wish for a more personal survival.

* * *

What is striking about these different philosophies is that they seem to embody, in an amplified and formalized way, various innate human tendencies. We can imagine some philosopher, moved by his experiences and personal bent, focusing on one trait of human character—kindness, or the desire for pleasure, or the need to avoid pain, or the impulse toward comradeship, or the wish to rise above circumstance— and taking it to an extreme. Since this is inevitably done at the expense of other traits, the result is an incomplete person. Their imbalances makes such people easy to criticize.

But this doesn't mean these "isms" can't work. While they might seem constricting, inconsistent with broader human nature, they have sufficed for many. You can try them out yourself if you like. Maybe you already have. You may find, on the one hand, that hedonism and Epicureanism fail to prepare most of us for death, while on the other, stoicism prepares us for death well enough, but may devitalize life. That is, it doesn't prepare us to live life completely, to savor the full depth and richness of experience. Altruism gives us a positive feeling about ourselves, but the sense of immortality we could potentially derive from it, a feeling of connection and identity with a larger entity, will be too abstract for some people.

Are there other options?

Exhausting our possibilities

Nietzsche was master of the aphorism, the brief, pithy line that seems to offer a concise quantum of wisdom. He said, for example,

"God is dead." (A contention now become infamous.)

"What doesn't kill us makes us stronger." (Echoed in certain movies, and even in pop music.)

"Man is a rope stretched between the animal and the superhuman." (You get the feeling that Nietzsche really wanted to say, "stretched between the animal and the divine," but that wouldn't have stood too well with his "God is dead" assertion.)

"Convictions are far more dangerous enemies of truth than lies." (A favorite of Thomas'.)

For our purposes here, Nietzsche's most relevant quote is,

"All that is ripe wants to die."

This sounds sort of credible. For produce, the next step after *ripe* is *rotten*, and presumably no one wants that. But what does "ripe" mean for humans? It seems to suggest that we have reached our full potential, fulfilled every aspect of ourselves, done everything we were meant to do. Completion. Live your life as fully as you can, Nietzsche seems to be saying; explore every possibility. If you've done this, you'll be ready for death when the time comes, and you'll accept it without a qualm.

But ... would we really be ready to die, no matter how fulfilled we were? If we achieve personal perfection, why not keep living, why not enjoy our perfect selves as long as we can? Thomas suspects that Nietzsche thinks that since death is the next logical step past perfection, we would naturally move on to it, as part of an intuitive trajectory. (In this Nietzsche may have been foreshadowing Freud's "Todestriebe," the death drive, the instinct that impels us toward oblivion.) This need to die as our final natural impulse probably has to be experienced to be fully understood.

Still, even from the outside Nietzsche's idea has some appeal. Completion implies satisfaction and fulfillment, and the acceptance of death by an individual who has done everything, answered all doubts, and contains within himself or herself the entirety of experience. There is something stoic in it: *You can't hurt me; I've done everything there is to do and I have no regrets. You can't take anything from me. Kill me if you like.* There is at least a hint of altruism: *I have lived fully because I've helped others. I have experienced empathy; I have touched the souls of my fellow humans.* And of course it is hedonistic: *Having tasted all that life has to offer, I am surfeit. I have satisfied every desire.*

In what Thomas takes to be a similar vein, William Blake said,

"The road of excess leads to the palace of wisdom." (This sounds like you already knew where you're headed en route: toward the sad but satiated wisdom of the ex-profligate. But maybe this is a case where getting there is half the fun.)

Nietzsche's sentiment about ripeness and Blake's about excess seem to point to a common theme: Broad and diverse experience lead us to wisdom and completeness; wisdom and completeness make us ready to accept an ending. Nietzsche was explicit about going on to death as the final phase, while Blake was not, but Thomas thinks they were chasing the same thought. Blake omitted Nietzsche's stoic overtones, and maybe even Nietzsche's touch of stoicism needs to be distinguished from the classic form. Nietzsche doesn't seem to require that we give up emotion. In fact, if we eschewed emotion, we could never experience life completely, never achieve "ripeness."

However, this plan has a problem: Is it realistic in this age to suppose that we can exhaust all of our possibilities? Such an encompassing might have been realistic in prehistoric times, when we were hunter-gatherers and didn't have so many choices. To explore all of life's possibilities now, though, is not an option.

But maybe Nietzsche just meant for us to try a reasonable sample of everything. For instance, we could get the idea of what it's like to work for a living, without trying every possible profession. Or, we could try marriage, but keep our number of spouses (or ex-spouses) down to a reasonable number. Or we could live in more than one place, more than one type of climate. But even this becomes problematic when we consider the vast numbers of job categories, potential spouses, and locales, and how each divergent one of these might lead to a radically different life experience.

Completeness, full ripeness, may not be a real possibility. It may still be worth shooting for, not because we can attain it, but because the attempt could be exhilarating.

* * *

Another concept seems to present something of a scheme for how to live. This isn't a philosophy or a system really, and it may or may not be describable as a discipline. This is more just an idea, floating sometimes consciously, sometimes subconsciously, in our collective mind. Though it isn't exclusively associated with any one philosophy or religious belief, it fits well with most, and enhances those that embrace it. Thomas has no idea how old it is; it seems current but is probably very ancient. Once again, it has been articulated by pop musicians (Joni Mitchell, Marvin Gaye). This idea is summarized in four words:

Life is for learning.

The knowledge learned would obviously not be of a type that can be fully understood by the conscious mind. It would not, for example, be subject to memorization, or akin to the abstract mechanisms of math, or law, or symbolic logic.

Instead, it would be something that is felt at least as much as it is understood intellectually, knowledge that imprints on the unconscious, on the soul if you like, a knowledge that transforms our emotions and our character. Knowledge that can only be acquired through direct experience.

But when exactly will we use it? If it's to be in this life, the learning will only be of use if it comes at a young enough age. A profound insight achieved a minute before we die is of little value.

(Of course, maybe our knowledge won't be used in this life; maybe it will come in handy in the next. The possibility of a supernatural afterlife is ancient and momentous. And controversial.)

But there is another point to consider: Is knowledge always worth it?

In Norse myth, Odin, "the All-Father" of the gods, is offered a drink from the pool of wisdom by the giant Mimir. In exchange, all that Mimir asks is that the god give up one of his eyes. Odin scoops out an eye and hands it over, apparently without hesitation. (But gods never hesitate.) On another occasion, Odin seeks further knowledge by impaling himself with a spear on the world tree Yggdrasil and hanging there for nine days. This kills him, though he subsequently resurrects. Apparently wisdom is worth any price.

Those of us who are less than gods may not be so sure of this. Maybe there are times when ignorance really is bliss. Suppose we suddenly lose a person we love, say in a car accident. What lesson could justify such a thing? Those of us who have experienced this sort of loss know that much can be learned from it, but it never feels even remotely worth the cost. Unlike Odin, though, we don't seem to always have a choice. Not about what we learn, not about what price we pay for learning it.

That the goal of life is knowledge, or wisdom, is a satisfying and intuitively credible idea. By itself, however, it is not complete. If life is anything other than random chance, it is likely that learning plays a very significant role, but that learning has to be part of something else. Learning has meaning when we see what it is for.

* * *

There are other approaches. In addition to the obvious—religious faith—a person may devote himself to a life of aestheticism, finding a spiritual timelessness in beauty. Also, it is possible to develop variations on the philosophies already described. None of this seems completely satisfactory, however. This inability to find a final answer may be the dynamic that drives us. If we could settle on one overriding philosophy of life, we might subside into a static mindset, become bored, lose interest. Dissatisfaction, in various forms, is the evolutionary force that has carried us this far. If there is no single answer, each of us must individually grapple with the issue of how to live life and address death. For each person born into the world, the question is again new and relevant.

And there is another problem: If our lives in this world were eternal, would they be bearable?

Living forever

The only alternative to making peace with death is that we attempt to live forever—a far-fetched course. Still, it is an option that our descendants, at least, may someday face. In order to think about how immortality might work, to consider how we might overcome ultimate ennui and a resulting psychological need to die, Thomas considers the following thought experiment:

Let us suppose that in the very distant future human beings are able to reach a state of perfect knowledge and technological mastery. Through advances in medical science, we gradually change our bodies until they are aesthetically perfect and invulnerable to injury, sickness, or death. We become beautiful and immortal. Our technology in such other areas as physics, engineering, electronics, and agriculture is equally advanced, allowing us to have all of our basic needs satisfied, as well as to acquire any material thing we want, without any labor on our part. Automated machinery, probably underground and out of sight, takes care of everything. Challenges are posed only for entertainment or personal satisfaction, and accepted only at our discretion. We never really have to do anything.

The All

This entire perfect world is governed, to the extent that it requires governing, by a human-computer hybrid known as The All. Through countless computer interfaces, we can connect our individual selves with The All. This does not threaten our independence: The machine intelligence is subordinate to us, there merely to be drawn upon. All decisions are ultimately human, though never made by any one human. And participation in The All, like everything else, is voluntary. We can enter into fusion or withdraw whenever we wish, and most of us don't bother most of the time. So absolute is our control of the world that few decisions need to be made anyway. By this means we control the course of life, and are accountable only to ourselves.

This state of affairs takes aeons to achieve, and we are justly proud of it, and for a time we live in peace and contentment. After a while, however, we feel a vague uneasiness. Our lives begin to seem shallow, without purpose. Since no real commitment is ever required, challenges tend to lack meaning. They can always be taken up at another time. We have forever.

And it is worse yet with relationships. Lack of commitment is even more insidious here. Our most intense passions, our most fervent loyalties, fade into insignificance in the long afternoon of eternity. It is horrible to admit, even to ourselves, but ... those individuals we once cherished just don't matter to us as much as they used to. Sometimes, in fact, they don't matter at all. They have always been around, they will always be around, they hold no mystery. They bore us. And it isn't just that others are made insignificant by their immortality. We even become insignificant to ourselves. After thousands of years, how much mystery and surprise do you hold? How much more is there for you to learn about yourself?

So what began as a minor discontent progresses to something that drains our will to live, and eventually threatens our existence. Survival requires more than the physical means to retain awareness; it requires that we find life sufficiently worthwhile to keep on living it.

One solution to this ennui is to join The All completely. It is possible to strip away our conscious identities and merge totally with the human-machine hybrid. Our memories and experiences, our decision-making ability, will still be available as a resource to the vast mentality of the All, but we will no longer have individual selves. This path is chosen by some, but most of us aren't yet

120

ready to let go so completely. There must be some way, we think, to make life fresh and new again, without giving up the seeming perfection we have achieved.

Or at least not give it up permanently. But maybe we can temporarily let it go. Maybe we can arrange to know pain and fear and transience once again, if only for a little while ... a little while lasting seventy or eighty years. Long enough to get the taste of mortality, but only an eye blink in the infinite corridor of time.

So we create The Game.

Reality and The Game

The Game is a virtual reality construct that can generate experiences for us that feel absolutely authentic, even though they are in fact simulated. Instead of nerve impulses from our bodies, images and sensations are input directly into our brains by The Game machine. These simulations have such verisimilitude that we can't differentiate them from actual physical experience. Once we are in The Game, we have no way of telling that we have left normal reality. The illusion, which is not just visual, but aural, tactile, olfactory, kinetic, and equilibrioceptic, completely engulfs us and is completely convincing. In this virtual reality, we can be made to experience not only diverse sensations, but complicated sequences of events that move forward through time: narratives. Illusory lives.

(Watchers of the *Matrix* movies, or readers of the *Otherland* series of books, will have no trouble grasping this concept, but it hardly originated with the Wachowski siblings or Tad Williams. The idea that we lie sleeping while a counterfeit reality is fed into our brains is not new. Even before science fiction writers took it up, philosophers used it as a metaphor to explore our connection with reality. In the earliest philosophical treatises, written during a less technological era, the false experiences were explained as being foisted on us by a demon, rather than by a machine. The underlying thought, though, that our minds are at the mercy of senses that can be deceived, is the same. While we may associate the concept of unreliable sensory perceptions with a relatively recent philosopher like Descartes, the basic concept can be extended all the way back to Plato and his Allegory of the Cave. It's an idea that has bothered us for a long time.)

Participation in this virtual world is, like everything else, voluntary. We can ignore it if we prefer and spend all of our time in the beautiful, comfortable, pleasurable, perfect real world ... which, from here on, we will refer to as Reality.

But though no one is forced into The Game, just about everyone goes there sooner or later ... because, if it continues long enough, perfection is boring, and nothing is worse than boredom.

The Game could, in theory, be played many different ways. Our lives in virtual reality could be completely scripted, with no agency on our parts. This might be enjoyable at first, like a novel or a movie, but eventually would prove too stifling. Or, events could be allowed to proceed as they may, with us having free will, but with certain broad parameters in place. For instance, if we find ourselves in ancient Egypt, we will always be the Pharaoh, never a manual laborer building the pyramid. Or life may seem wild and random but, unknown to us, there is a guarantee in place that no loved one will perish before we do.

A related possibility is that Game programmers will attempt to give us a sort of balancing effect across multiple lives. In this case, a life of success and enthusiasm might be followed with one of frustration, grief, or tedium, then followed again by a more positive experience, alternating back and forth over time. In each round we would still have apparent free will, but this superficial absence of restraint would be circumscribed by hidden, inexorable tendencies. Each of our lives would have a predominant tone and over a number of lives, these contrasting experiences will enrich us more deeply than any one life could.

Still, all of this eventually feels too scripted, and the experience is de-vitalized. We finally realize that to achieve the sheer, raw impact of life at hazard, we have to accept two conditions:

First, every time you are born into The Game, you arrive in a state of total amnesia. It is essential that you remember nothing about Reality. You don't remember who you really are. You don't remember that you've done this before. Most of all, you don't remember that this is just a game. The whole business only works if you think you have no other option, that this is your only life. That you *must* deal with it.

Second, you must be willing to plunge into anything, no matter how sad, painful, or even horrifying.

So, when things get rough, you can't console yourself that this is only a virtual reality. You don't know that, and that reality will not be softened in any way. When your lover leaves, or your stocks become worthless, or you are sentenced to life in prison, when your leg is chopped off, or a loved one dies, or you contract leprosy, the experience is not moderated. If you find yourself in a life where you are captured by Viking warriors who choose to carve the blood eagle on you, you really feel your ribs being split up your back and your lungs being pulled from your body. If you're in a life where you are at the mercy of medieval magistrates who decide that an appropriate punishment would be to thread the wheel with you, it feels exactly as though your limbs are smashed with mallets until they're bonelessly flexible enough to be threaded through the spokes of a wagon wheel. If you're the prisoner of Aztecs who decide to slake your thirst for gold in the most literal way possible (by pouring molten gold down your throat) .. then all these experiences are unstintingly real. Conversely, your sensual pleasures, from a cool breeze at twilight to the feel of your lover's skin, are as sweet as your pains are terrible.

We don't immediately come to this total acceptance of randomness; we each have to live through myriad lives, myriad rounds of The Game, before we see how it must be. To keep The Game experience intense and meaningful, we have to be absolutely brave, absolutely willing to accept anything we are given. This is because it isn't just what we experience in a single round of The Game that matters, it's also what we think about it, how we assimilate it afterwards, back in Reality. The many rounds of The Game are cumulative in our psyches, and the most difficult rounds may be the most enlightening. This cumulative effect even intrudes into our virtual lives: Though we are born amnesiac into each new round, our deep unconscious memories linger. Thus we would sometimes have attitudes and biases that have no explanation in our current existence. They would have carried over from a previous life. (We come back again to the idea that life is for learning.)

Don't look to the Game to simulate emotions or fortitude, however; you yourself must provide these. If your core self is no longer capable of this, if your emotional response has faded too far, or if you can't face another gut-wrenching life, another round on the "wheel of karma", maybe it's time to stay in Reality for an extended period and re-charge. Or maybe it's time to let personal identity drop away and become one with The All.

* * *

Just for a minute, imagine that you do in fact live in Reality, and you are about to enter your next round of the Game. This is your last moment of awareness of your true situation for many years. You know that what comes next is a completely random spin of the wheel, a blind draw of the cards. What will happen? Where will you find yourself? Who will you be? The moment is fearful and exciting, even terrifying and ecstatic.

You enter the Game. A life ensues. Perhaps this time you aren't a diva or a slave or a cavalier or a courtesan or a World War I flying ace or an actress or an international jewel thief or the leader of a major nation. Perhaps your latest round even goes somewhat like the brief synopsis of a life presented earlier, in the discussion of patients in the Telemetry Unit: just a normal life.

In any case, you get through it, you "make it" (of course).

Now it's all over, you've "died," you're back in Reality, and you remember it all, the true nature of things. You track down your friends from the Game who exited before you, then maybe it's hugs all around, share a laugh, relax at a table in a tasteful lounge, and talk over your latest adventures. Maybe you aren't even mad at the individual who was your worst enemy in the Game; maybe you've learned to forgive any evil that occurs in the virtual world ... maybe what happens in the Game, stays in the Game. Then again, maybe not. Your worst enemy, caught up in the illusion, may have taken some very questionable actions, and your pain felt very real. You can't just let that go.

Or, worse yet ... maybe, in your fear and ignorance, *you* took questionable actions. Maybe it's very difficult now to face a person you wronged in the Game. Or even to face yourself.

Your latest round in the Game, your latest "life," may have been absolutely miserable, unrelieved grief and stress, and yet ... for a moment, a moment lasting decades, you can't deny that life was *felt*. Everything mattered. Individuals mattered, commitments mattered, decisions mattered, actions mattered. And, of course, you learned.

An especially painful round of The Game may cause us to find boring Reality a haven newly appreciated. After a particularly harsh life, we might want to kick back in Reality for several Game lifetimes. But probably not forever.

* * *

This concept of life as the ultimate virtual reality construct, set against a backdrop of eternal ease and comfort, suggests that it is at least theoretically possible to imagine a world where all human needs are met: the need for safety and pleasure and the need for challenge and strife, the need for assurance and the need for unpredictability, the need for closure and finitude—the need to reach an ultimate goal—and the need to be unbounded, to always be moving forward. The need to let go of identity and awareness, and the need to never stop existing.

Still … such a world might sustain our interest for an extremely long time, but would it really satisfy us forever? Possibly, but *forever* is hard to think about. Maybe an extremely long time is all we should hope for.

* * *

No need to ask where we get the narrative material for our various pseudo lives. Obviously we are mining history. Or are we? Consider another possibility: Perhaps the Game world is not something we will develop in the future, but something we have already created in the remote past. In this case the history we know may never have happened in the real world; it may be nothing but Game world artifact, the result of a sustained burst of wild creativity. Or perhaps we set up a basic situation and let events unfold as they might.

In other words, it may be that we were always immortal and all powerful, and this world we are in now is one we invented from scratch to amuse ourselves.

Another consideration: All of this may seem to suggest that, as Leibniz contended, we live in the best of all possible worlds. After all, if we either invented our reality or allowed it to evolve in response to our influence, it must reflect our needs. But maybe this is too simple.

First, we run into the obvious problem that this is far from being the same world for each person in it. Two individuals living not so far from each other in time and space can have radically different life experiences.

Second, the history that we are familiar with may be only one of many. A multitude of different timelines could be run simultaneously by the Game machine, each having a completely different general history. These could lurk in our unconscious memories and would correspond to the alternate realities, or other dimensions, proposed by physicists. Which of these would then be "the best of all possible worlds"?

Third, even if the timeline we've experienced so far is the only one, and even if it were approximately the same for every one (within very broad parameters), that could just mean that we've adapted to the situation we were faced with. It's possible we could adapt to a better world, if we could find it ... and maybe we could find it, if we ran the Game long enough. If we allow our virtual world to evolve without restraint, we might eventually chance upon a life more perfect than any we've imagined. Then we would be free to scrap the Game and manipulate the real world to fit this virtual ideal we'd stumbled upon. The Game would have turned out to be a sort of experiment, a testing ground for possible futures.

* * *

A final concern: All of this might seem to make it too easy. Regardless of what we consciously know (or don't know) during the Game, we are in fact living in a kind of illusion; everything is false. But maybe it isn't. If we respond with true feeling to what happens—and why would we not, since we'll think it's real—then the emotional bonds and conflicts that develop will be authentic. The background may be illusory, but *we* will be real, and our choices and emotional responses will be real. These are what ultimately matter, not how the external circumstances are presented to our minds.

Also: Since we will be at least partly molded by our current life's circumstances, each of us will be a somewhat different individual in every round of the Game. This means that a person who was willing to marry you in one life might never feel that way in any other. Or your closest friend will be a cold stranger, or your brother will look at you with blank indifference, in every subsequent round (and maybe even in Reality). A particular set of identities and the relationships between them may never occur again. Grief and transience will still exist; poignancy will still exist.

* * *

All right, you may be thinking, all sorts of things are possible, but so what? What good does this contrived scenario really do us? Does Thomas think The Game represents the true state of affairs?

No. The goal here is to investigate whether it is possible to even imagine a world that would fulfill all the needs of our complicated human selves … a world we could tolerate for an immense span of time.

However, the virtual reality of the Game could be based on the same digital matrix that present day computers use. The Game world could ultimately reduce to bits: a gigantic number of electronic switches that have only two settings: *no/yes*, or *off/on*, or *zero/one*, however we wish to designate them. Very little data can be conveyed by a single bit, but by using a sufficiently large number of them, a near infinite range of finely nuanced information can be represented.

This complexity built from an aggregate of simple units is reminiscent of our natural world. Galaxies, planets, trees, humans, all of it, are built from unthinkably small pieces such as quarks. According to quantum theory, these physical units at the smallest level can change only in a discrete process, not in a continuously varying—analog—way. In other words, such an infinitesimal unit has one status, then it has another; there is no in-between. It is all one thing, or it is all something else. So, our universe ultimately reduces to quanta that are indivisible, that can only be altered in an all-or-nothing way. Like computer bits. At the most basic level, our world resembles a vast digital computer.

Still, Thomas is not really suggesting we live in the Game. Though he sees no conflict in the internal logic of the idea, there is also nothing to suggest that it's true. You would be justified in dismissing it as a triumph of wishful thinking.

But stay with it a moment longer. The world presented in this thought experiment should seem a little familiar. Doesn't it, in fact, resemble concepts made familiar by the major religions? Because it offers both a sort of reincarnation and the opportunity to merge with a greater mentality (the All), the universe of The Game most closely resembles Hinduism. Perfect Reality, though, is sort of a generalized version of the heaven that many religious belief systems feature. And the whole situation could be configured to correspond to any theistic vision. We can imagine creating various concepts of paradise: a gymnasium where you fight to the death with blunt and edged weapons every day, only to be resurrected in time for dinner (for ancient Vikings yearning for Asgard). Or a brothel that offers youthful virgins (for Islamic terrorists). White clouds and harps for traditional Christians. And so on.

Thomas isn't thinking too much about any version of hell, another popular religious concept, because he doubts that many of us would voluntarily go there. Some guilt-ridden individuals might, however. They could use The Game machine to construct a nightmare world where they could expiate their crimes and ease their consciences … though probably few would make their damnation eternal. What good would unending misery do, anyway? After a few centuries in hell, you probably wouldn't even remember why you were there. The effect would be wasted.

The Game world's similarity to religious concepts is important in another sense. Logically, the eternal ennui that the Game world attempts to deal with would also be an issue in a theistic hereafter.

The basis of a religious afterlife is supernatural, while that of the Game world is technological. A religious afterlife is considered, at least by believers, to be an ultimate context, to need no further explanation. The Game world, conversely, would still require an origin. This is significant in various ways. One is that if the Game world existed in the larger context of a supernatural cosmos, choosing to live forever in the secular world would mean that we forego any chance to reunite with friends or loved ones who died before immortality was achieved. Beyond this, while the Game world and a supernatural afterlife would have profoundly meaningful differences, the two situations could feel very similar from the viewpoint of the mind experiencing them. Observed from the outside, it might even seem that both a religious cosmology and the Game world are triumphs of wishful thinking.

But a belief in a supernatural afterlife, and in religion itself, is something that a vast number of people have accepted and advocated, sometimes fanatically, for millennia. Religions give us a way to tie everything together, to find ultimate fulfillment, to have it all finally make sense. Of course, we must pick the right religion: one that accurately describes reality. To be meaningful, religion has to be more than just believed. It has to be true.

Theism is the looming presence in the room that is not being engaged here. It clearly needs to be engaged, but that's beyond the scope of this discussion. God, religion, and the incomprehensible notion of an uncaused Cause, are discussed in Part 1, *Fear of the Dark.*

* * *

Later that night: Thomas is still watching the telemetry CRTs. Twenty-three of the monitor sectors display heartbeat tracings. One sector is blank, turned off. If it were still on, it would present a flat line. Mr. Smith has gone on to his big show. Or maybe back to Reality.

*
**

Part 4

Ideology and the Real World

A Day on the Green: *Style as Ideology*

Oakland Coliseum, Oakland, California, August 1985

The pattern repeats periodically throughout the day: The voice on the public address system echoes over the vast, noisy crowd, announcing upcoming concerts. The crowd, Thomas notices, responds in one of two ways: If the event being touted features a heavy metal band such as those that are playing here today, applause, cheers, and whistles fill the outdoor arena. If the advertised group has more of a pop sound, for instance *Wham!* (appearing here tomorrow), the response is a chorus of boos, jeers, and, inevitably, a forest of upraised arms with middle fingers extended.

Thomas thinks it must be useful for a musical group to know where they stand with an audience, and the audience here at the Oakland outdoor coliseum makes it really clear. The upcoming groups probably aren't actually present, though, so they can't be getting the message. Maybe the members of the crowd hope their sentiments will be noted by the anonymous person on the PA, or the promoters who put on these concerts (*Bill Graham Presents*, in the case of today's and tomorrow's shows). But the reality, Thomas realizes, is that the guys in the crowd are sending a message to each other: We share tastes, they are saying, we share beliefs; we affirm the machismo of the heavy metalists, and even more we scorn the triviality—the effeminacy—of the pop musicians. We want to identify ourselves with the first group, and separate ourselves from the second. We are *hardcore*.

Based on his own experience, Thomas thinks the fans are often more hardcore than the musicians themselves. Musicians have to live up to the expectations of their fans, of course, but if they want to keep growing artistically, they have to be open to what inspiration the world throws their way. They will be most creative if they listen to a range of music. Both fans and musicians have to define themselves, but the musicians also need to be artists.

Thomas understands that the specific form of self-assertion displayed today involves rejecting cultural mores, and he foresees the older person's (the straight person's) common objection: If these kids are trying so hard to be their own individuals, why do they seem to so closely copy each other in dress and manner?

Thomas thinks it is because even rejecting the norm requires guidelines. Individuality and rebellion require a plan. Who is so brilliantly original that he can create himself out of nothing? We need a map of the new territory; ultimately we can only escape the old norm by creating a new one. Beyond this, all of us seem to be afflicted with an ongoing need to both fit in and stand out. We want to be somehow exceptional, but we also want to be accepted.

* * *

While Thomas enjoys some heavy metal music, he is not here today as a fan. He has brought his twelve-year-old son, Konan. Konan is a serious metal enthusiast. Thomas is here as his driver and, though this is not mentioned, his protector.

Looking back, Thomas saw that his oldest son's musical interests could have been predicted at an early age:

On a day several years before, Thomas was walking with Konan and his daughter, Heather, past a construction zone. The site was partitioned off from the sidewalk with a chain-link fence covered with vertical wooden slats. In places the slats were missing, however, and Thomas and his two children stopped and looked through. They saw hard-hatted men at work, and growling, struggling caterpillar tractors carving deep ditches in the bare ground; they felt the burn of dust and diesel fumes; they heard their throbbing, pounding, godawful *noise.*

Heather, about six, turned away from the fence. She closed her eyes, covered her ears with both hands, and was grimacing as though in pain. She implored Thomas to get them out of there. But four-year-old Konan stood poised on the balls of his feet, a huge grin on his face, staring in delight at the hectic scene. He was bouncing up and down slightly, in time with the pulse of the machines. He didn't want to leave.

At that moment, Konan's musical fate was clear. Heather grew up to like the Beatles and folk music; Konan is here today in Oakland cheering to the uncompromising metal sounds of *Ratt, Metallica, Y&T, Rising Force*, and the headline group, *The Scorpions.* Eventually Konan will become vocalist, lead guitarist, and songwriter for various local rock groups.

* * *

Thomas considers the crowd: Members of the audience come from every demographic, but the mode heavy metal fan today seems to be a seventeen-year-old white male, long-haired (shoulder length) but clean-shaven: a youthful, macho hippy accessorized in metal-studded black leather. The effect is a fusion of late sixties flower child and outlaw biker. Most of them don't ride motorcycles, however, and among themselves they use the term *hippie* as an insult. (Other insults include *stroker*—apparently someone who masturbates—and *gay*. Gay is kind of all-purpose; it doesn't necessarily have anything to do with sexual preference. For example, if someone borrowed something from you and returned it in trashed condition, you could confront him with "Dude! This is so gay!")

Thomas is aware of another divergence from the hippies: The heavy metalists don't preach peace and love. The overpowering guitar riffs—massive bass lines, buzz saw leads—scream aggression, force, violence, the masculine idealization of physical strength and energy.

Thomas doesn't find this sinister. Vehemence is common among young guys, easily explained by youthful exuberance, a short but intense acquaintance with testosterone, and the crowd effect. ("Crowd effect" —"mob effect" sounds too menacing.) In Thomas' experience, the heavy metal hardcore aren't wildly different from sports fans. In fact, sports fans are often more violent.

The metal fans' mode is to assert selfhood by identifying so enthusiastically with their chosen groups, their music and their accompanying clothing and personal manner, that the style itself becomes a sort of ideology. Even when it's inchoate, a style is a reaction to life, and can imply an underlying world view. As do all ideologies.

Thomas decides it would be too simple to interpret the metalists' world view as pure defiance, or even indifference, toward the adult order. As with most rebels, there is an underlying desire to gain acceptance and respect from the reigning group. Whenever someone attempts to claim identity, one of the primary goals is to avoid being ignored and made insignificant by the world at large.

* * *

The late summer day is clear and mild; the music moves everything forward at a tolerable pace. Thomas enjoys at least some of the performances, though when he and Konan stand near the stage (what would be the infield during baseball season), as they do at first, the music is too loud to hear. They are extremely aware of it of course, but not exactly as music, more as a wall of sound. Individual songs are hard to distinguish. Still, Thomas enjoys watching the crowd and trying to understand the tone of the event. Later, they move up into the stands, and songs become more recognizable.

By mid-afternoon, one of the covered access corridors is strewn with retching teenage boys. They have somehow managed to acquire alcohol in the first place, and then somehow managed to smuggle it in. The smell in that corridor is harsh; Thomas avoids that part of the stadium. Away from that one area, however, the crowd doesn't seem drunk or overly rowdy.

Then the voice on the PA announces another upcoming concert: The group Dire Straits will be playing locally within the next few months.

This catches Thomas' ear. Dire Straits, in his opinion, is one of the best rock groups around. Their blues/folk-inflected sound combines sophisticated lyrics and sentiments with some of the most emotive, intensely-felt guitar work Thomas has heard. The PA announcement interests him for another reason, though. Dire Straits definitely does not belong in the pop category with *Wham!*, but they aren't heavy metal either. How will this crowd react? Cheers? Or middle fingers?

Thomas waits. There is kind of a restless quiet. Thomas realizes that neither reaction will be forthcoming: no cheers, no middle fingers. The fans aren't sure how they're supposed to feel about Dire Straits.

On a sudden impulse, Thomas begins clapping loudly. He even adds a few cheers. Partly this reflects his sincere admiration for Dire Straits, but he is also moved by that obscure impulse that makes a person want to speak louder, walk taller, *stand out* when he is anonymous in a large crowd. And Thomas wants to see how the crowd reacts to his enthusiastic appreciation for a group they can't decide about.

Nobody follows Thomas' lead; nobody joins in. Nobody heckles him, either. They look at Thomas, or look away from him, a little uncomfortably: Why this sudden eruption from an old guy? (Thomas is in his thirties.) Is he mocking them? Or what?

Konan gestures at his father uneasily. Konan will grow up to be a very confident and extroverted individual, but right now he is still only twelve years old, and he worries about the older boys' opinions.

"Uh, Dad ...?" He says. "Maybe, you know ... you shouldn't do that?"

Thomas pauses and pretends to consider this. He nods soberly and lowers his hands.

*
**

A Day in the Classroom:
Ideology as Style

Thomas acts as a judge at a high school forensics (debate) tournament, on a Saturday in the Spring of 1988

forensic:

1. The art or study of formal debate; argumentation.

2. The use of science and technology to investigate and establish facts in criminal or civil courts of law.

*T*hirty minutes into the competition, having listened to maybe ten students present their cases, Thomas has narrowed the field down to two primary contenders. One of these is number three, a tall, attractive, well-dressed young woman of somewhat matronly build; she gives the impression of being in her twenties, though Thomas knows these contestants are all still in high school. She has a certain air of sympathy, even kindness. Her approach to the topic seems to be politically liberal.

The other primary contender is number seven, a male of medium height and build, lean face, close-cropped hair, glasses; he is dressed in a nondescript casual way. His most notable feature is the faintly derisive look that seems to be his habitual expression. At times this expression becomes more acute. His approach to the topic being debated is conservative. Hearing his arguments, Thomas suspects that his look of contempt is aimed at an abstract target that might be loosely labeled "bleeding heart liberals."

The two of them seem almost too perfectly stereotypical, incarnations of liberal and conservative clichés.

As a volunteer judge in this competition, Thomas is a silent presence in the aging classroom. He is currently employed as a public relations writer for a company that develops operational systems and computer software for the financial industry. An outside observer might suppose he is here because his profession in some way qualifies him to be a judge. The outside observer would be wrong. Thomas is here because the school teachers, deans, and so forth who hold these events on their days off are desperate to find judges. Anyone who is not an employee of the school system can judge, and the likeliest candidates turn out to be the parents of the contestants. Their children benefit, so their parents provide the free labor.

The only stipulation is that a parent can't judge any event in which his or her own child is competing. So, in the morning parents and students bus together to the school hosting the tournament, then the two groups are immediately separated, and usually don't see each other again until the end of the day. (Later in the season there will be a serious scandal when a student from the school Thomas is associated with wins first place in an event his mother judged: The mother will be guilty of a failure to recuse. She had always been a simplistic and very aggressive cheerleader for her son, so Thomas doesn't find her unethical action all that surprising. Despite the need for judges, she will not be invited back.)

It is considered desirable also to avoid judging events in which students on the same team (that is, from your high school) are taking part. Given the number of events and the scarcity of judges, however, such avoidance isn't always possible.

So, Thomas is present today because his daughter Heather is a highly motivated and serious contender at these tournaments, and Thomas is a dutiful parent. He doesn't mind being here; the whole business is interesting, and he comes out of it with a positive impression of high school students. The main negative (aside from giving up part or all of his weekend) is that he is seldom able to watch his daughter compete.

The topic of the debate Thomas is currently judging has been formulated as follows:

The United States holds a leadership position in NATO, and as part of this role maintains a current military presence of 100,000 troops in Europe. Should the US reduce this number down to 50,000, leaving the European nations to take up more of the burden? Or should we maintain our current military presence?

Thomas thinks the numbers are arbitrary, too even, as though made up for the occasion. Thomas suspects that if the numbers were doubled or halved, the same students would argue the same way: If the current number had been stated as 200,000, the students arguing in favor of a reduction to 50,000 would instead be arguing for a reduction to 100,000. The students arguing for the status quo would find that nothing less than 200,000 would suffice. The numbers are essentially meaningless, markers to formalize the game.

Thomas thinks that if the numbers *had* been meant to be taken seriously, the discussion would require the students to be experts in military logistics: How many soldiers and airmen are actually needed to fulfill the required tasks? Which would require a detailed analysis of just what those tasks were. Wisely, no student takes this approach. The debate becomes a referendum on the US being a policeman for the world, and even on militarism and war in general. Thus, the sympathetic liberal gal, number three, argues to decrease the numbers, while lean, mean number seven takes a hawkish stance: Militarism is a realistic necessity—no reduction in forces.

In the era in which Thomas grew up, especially in the turbulent sixties and the post-Vietnam era, these two students would seem to represent stereotypically liberal and conservative positions. Thomas even recalls a commentator on radio during the Vietnam War advancing his theory that we elect Democrats (liberals, more or less) in times of peace, but when we need someone to fight the bad guys, we turn to the Republicans (more or less conservatives). So, liberals are anti-war, anti-militaristic, and generally kind of soft, while conservatives are pro-war, pro-military, and tough. Really?

Thomas didn't believe it. He wanted to point out to the radio talk show host that we chose Franklin Delano Roosevelt and Harry Truman to lead us into and through World War II, the largest and most devastating war of all time. John F. Kennedy took a few tentative steps toward the Vietnam involvement, and then Lyndon Baines Johnson really took the plunge. All these individuals were, of course, Democrats. (Johnson was succeeded by Richard Nixon, a Republican, but all experts at the time agreed that Lyndon would have been re-elected if he'd run.)

Conservatives are allegedly opposed to big government, but there is hardly a larger, more interventional move that a government can make than to lead us into war. Nor a more costly one, though conservatives say they are opposed to taxes.

Thomas remembers his history classes: In earlier periods of US history, isolationism—the shunning of any involvement with foreign nations—was considered a *conservative* stance. So is war-making actually a liberal, big-government kind of enterprise? Maybe, but at this point in time society seems to be stuck with the stereotype of liberal doves and conservative hawks.

* * *

The subject of American military servicemen in Europe is one that Thomas can relate to personally. In 1960 his father, Thomas Sr., was transferred to a NATO base in West Germany, and a few months later, Thomas and the rest of the family joined him. They lived at Ramstein for a little more than three years, and travelled widely in surrounding countries. It was a great opportunity to see Europe on the cheap. Thomas Sr. was given the German tour of duty because he requested it; a few years later, he would request and be given a three year assignment in Japan. Thomas used to wonder if his dad, a World War II veteran, was on a mission to visit all of our erstwhile enemies. A vacation in Italy, another former adversary, was one of their longer trips while in Europe.

Their tour in Germany was almost cut short. In Fall of 1960, John F. Kennedy was elected President. In the time between the election and Kennedy's assuming of office in 1961, the outgoing president, Dwight Eisenhower, decided to act on the same issue the students are debating in 1988: He decided to drastically reduce American military presence in Europe. This was viewed as a highly unpopular move, but Eisenhower had little to lose. A lame-duck president whose party had lost the election, he meant to use his final days in office to take actions he felt needed to be taken, popular or otherwise. One of the military bases that would have been affected by Eisenhower's decision was Ramstein. Thomas' family would have been sent back to the states after only thirteen months—much earlier than originally planned.

Thomas Sr. was sternly patriotic and a great supporter of Eisenhower, positions he regarded as more or less inseparable, but he was much disturbed by Ike's decision. He and Thomas' mother didn't want to go home after only a year in Germany. They wanted to see the capitals of Europe, stay in hotels in Paris, lounge on the Italian Riviera, buy frivolous but prestigious items at low price, and so on. Eisenhower's move was most unwelcome, and Thomas thought that his father even saw it as a kind of betrayal. It turned out he needn't have worried: Kennedy reversed Eisenhower's edict when he assumed office. Thomas' family got their whole three years in Europe, and a bit more.

Thus it was the liberal Kennedy who maintained military presence in Europe and the old soldier and Republican Eisenhower that wanted to curtail it. Maybe no one should have been too surprised by this. Eisenhower was, after all, the man who first warned us about the military-industrial complex. He was also a man who, according to Henry Kissinger, had become "passionately opposed to war in the way only an experienced military man can be."

What about Kennedy? Thomas' father had always disliked him, as he was a Democrat and a Catholic, both affiliations Thomas Sr. had issues with. In his capacity serving in the Air Force PIO (Public Information Office), Thomas Sr. actually met Kennedy during his visit to Germany in the early 1960s (during which JFK made his famous but ungrammatical "ich bin ein Berliner" speech). Thomas' father warmed to Kennedy somewhat, at least briefly. He grudgingly admitted that JFK had "a certain charisma." This was short-lived, however. Once Kennedy's visit was a thing of the past, Thomas Sr. reverted to his previous biases. For him, the power of stereotypes ultimately trumped any personal interest or personal experience. He never seemed to really get it that, in this case, it was the perceived liberal who emphasized the role of the military, the perceived conservative that wanted to reduce it.

* * *

But Thomas has already decided that the liberal and conservative stances were inconsistent in other ways. Right-wingers see themselves as the defenders of individual liberty against the encroachment of big government, but it actually depends on the issue. If the issue is censorship, the Right seems to favor government intervention—apparently they feel that the government should tell people what to read. The liberals take a dissenting view; they oppose censorship. (Though that subsequently changed. See the section further along on modern political correctness.)

But change the issue to gun control, and the two sides reverse polarity: Liberals favor gun control (government intervention); conservatives oppose it.

* * *

So, Thomas wondered, what are the *real* differences between conservatives and liberals?

Certain constellations of ideas are at issue: personal responsibility versus governmental protectiveness; elitism versus inclusiveness; merit versus luck; the sanctity of private property versus the humanitarian admonition to help the down-trodden. All of these seem to resolve down to two opposed views of human nature. We can highlight these different views by considering poverty and wealth: Why are some people poor, and others rich?

Since Thomas is interested in the liberal / conservative distinction as it would be seen by the average person, rather than by academics, he decides to eschew an abstract philosophical approach and think about people he knows. He considers two representative individuals: Janey and Marie. Using government income guidelines, both Janey and Marie are below poverty level. They are both technically poor, though their lives are very different. We'll take Janey first.

Janey is in her early thirties. She is presently unemployed, though she has held jobs in the past. Never for very long, though. She finds it difficult to get out of bed after a night of booze and partying, so she frequently decided to skip work "just for that day." When she did go in, she was often late as well as hung-over. While she actually showed promise in a few of her jobs—most notably telemarketing, as she was always a good talker—she had a hard time with company policies, supervisors, and that sort of thing. In fact, she was known to sometimes be angrily defiant, and profane in her language, when bosses tried to gain her compliance. The underlying problem seemed to be her general scorn for gainful employment. Why face the drudgery of a job? Other people have things—cars, houses, meals—why didn't she have them too? After all, she's been around these middle class people who own things, she walks the same earth, speaks the same language; why don't these desirable possessions accrue to her, as they do to everyone else? (Sort of by osmosis, perhaps.) Why can't people who *do* have things just share? It was useless to point out to her that other people have things because they work for them.

Away from jobs, Janey has a predilection for booze, street drugs, and promiscuous sex. Though the promiscuity often seems aimed more at finding a place to crash for the night than at sensual pleasure. While Janey has been married more than once, she isn't now, and her children are being raised by relatives. She says she dearly loves her kids, and wants to be there for them, but somehow that never inspires Janey to do anything—like stay at a job—that might enable her to take back custody and provide her children a stable home. Beyond this, Janey lies habitually, and is an occasional petty thief. Currently she is dodging drunk-driving, drug possession, and failure-to-appear warrants; she vanishes quickly when a police officer enters the scene. If she becomes angry at her current boyfriend—and there always is one—she feels no qualms about physically attacking him. With fists, flung objects, or even her teeth.

When Janey looks at her overall situation, which is not often, she considers herself a victim.

On the other hand, there is Marie.

Marie is no longer young. Though she married when she was eighteen and had four children, she has been spouseless for years. She might prefer to be with someone, but she realizes that her abusive husband's abrupt departure and continuing absence is overall a good thing. She is not exactly hostile toward men, but she doesn't have any naive expectations about them either. She raised her children entirely without help.

Marie has worked all of her life. While not lacking intelligence, she had little education and her jobs tend to be unskilled and low-paying. Often she has had to work at two or even three jobs at a time to feed her children and make ends meet. Now middle-aged, she is stuck with raising three grandchildren. Most of her children turned out all right, but one daughter became a drug abuser incapable of raising her own children, so Marie took over the task for her. Marie loves children, and is fiercely loyal to family.

Marie knows her life is not easy, of course, but she doesn't think of herself as a victim. She never had the idea that life would be a picnic (though she thought it might be better than it has been), and she doesn't bother with self-pity. She does occasionally spend a few of her hard-earned dollars on the lottery, but at her present age, she doesn't really expect her life to turn around. Basically, Marie lowers her head, hunches her shoulders, and keeps trudging on. She takes life with a certain fatalistic calm. She does what she has to do.

It should be noted also that Marie is a member of what is called *the working poor*. The very label, and the reality it represents, undermine the idea that all poor people are shiftless leeches.

So what does Thomas draw from the examples of Janey and Marie?

Janey, he thinks, is where she is because of how she behaves. One interpretation of her would be that she has a mental impairment that prevents her from connecting past, present, and future. Janey doesn't seem to understand how what she did last month put her in the situation she's in now, or how her present actions will put her in a bad place next month. It is almost as though experience comes at her in a random, meaningless pattern, which she reacts to in whatever way promises some immediate if trivial gain. Life is an ever-changing present; the past is vague; the future doesn't really exist.

She views herself as the victim, but Thomas thinks otherwise. Thomas believes she has made a habit of short-sighted, self-indulgent decisions, the consequences of which usually catch up with her sooner or later. Paraphrasing Cassius in Shakespeare's *Julius Caesar*, Thomas might say, "The fault is not in Janey's stars, but in herself." Or as Heraclitus more succinctly put it, "Character is fate." However she may attempt to blame everyone but herself, Janey is usually the author of her own misfortune.

Marie illustrates the opposite point. While she doesn't consider herself a victim, she does seem to suffer because of random misfortunes that are, in fact, beyond her control. The negative aspects of her fate are not the result of her character, and the fault does indeed seem to be in her stars (her luck). Looking at her, Thomas might say, along with Phil Ochs, "There but for fortune go you and I."

The simplistic conservative thinks that Janey represents all poor people, and he wants very much *not* to help her. After all, helping people like that won't do them any good; they must make up their minds to change themselves. Until they do, pouring charity into them changes nothing; you just feed their pathology. And why should a hard-working citizen have to subsidize people whose actions are beyond his control? It isn't fair.

The more thoughtful conservative understands that Marie also exists, but he thinks she can best be helped by an indirect method: raising the general level of prosperity. Also, his attitude toward Janey is so vehement that it eclipses Marie's plight. He feels sorry for Marie but Janey irritates him so much—he wants so much not to be taken advantage of by her—that he dismisses Marie. After all, Marie might still get ahead if she keeps trying. Even if she doesn't, a lot of people have it tough. Life's like that. Nobody promised you a rose garden.

Conversely, the simplistic liberal sees all poor people as Marie: a woman who clearly deserves our kindness. The more perceptive liberal realizes that Janey is out there too, but he feels that helping Marie is the more important issue ... so he shrugs off Janey. If lending Marie a hand means aiding and abetting a few Janeys along the way, so be it.

* * *

It's clear that Janey is the poster child for the conservative view of the poor, as Marie is for the liberal, but which view is accurate? Will the real poor person please stand up?

The obvious response is that both Janey and Marie exist. Of course they both exist, Thomas thinks, but which is representative? How many are Janey? (Not 47% of the entire population, we hope.) How many are Marie? Thomas has no way of knowing, especially since the criteria for differentiating them would be at least partly subjective, and the range between the two would contain a vast number of in-between points and borderline cases. Whatever the actual numbers, though, and even if there is an even balance, the conservative will focus on Janey, while the liberal will focus on Marie.

* * *

Thomas reflects that, when considering individuals at the other end of the income scale, the wealthy, conservatives and liberals have a similar divergence of opinion.

Conservatives admire the ultra-rich businessman. They see his success as evidence of his boldness and imagination, his organized approach to life, his willingness to take risks. He got to where he is through intelligence, self-discipline, and perseverance. He and those like him drive the economic growth that made this country great. We reward them with crippling taxes and a morass of regulatory hobbles.

Liberals, on the other hand, see the rich businessman as someone who resents the government and whines about taxes, even while trying to take every advantage of the government that he can. Liberals think the wealthy entrepreneur ignores the fact that his success is partially made possible by the legal context and physical infrastructure that the government provides. This top of the food chain businessman externalizes his expenses onto the rest of us every chance he gets—for example, pressuring the government to build roads, at taxpayers' expense, that will serve his factories. At the same time he milks the tax-payers through bloated government contracts that his lobbyists make sure get routed to his company. And so on. And what about that golden parachute waiting for him at the end, the bailout that he seems to get no matter how he performs?

Liberals believe that for the rich, as for the poor, luck is a major factor. However hard-driving the top-level executive or entrepreneur may be, almost certainly luck played some part in his success. Many people are intelligent and hard-working, after all, but only a few achieve the highest levels of wealth and power. The difference must be luck.

* * *

For Thomas, these differences between liberal and conservative viewpoints raise some very basic questions: How much control do we really have over our lives? How accountable are we for our successes and failures? Suppose individuals fail to thrive because, to put it bluntly, they aren't very smart. Should this be considered their fault? Are they responsible for their IQs? Are they less deserving because their genetics put them at a disadvantage?

Which ultimately leads us to wonder about the whole concept of free will.

* * *

While conservatives fear that the alleged self-correcting mechanisms of capitalism will be sabotaged by welfare recipients, and others wanting a hand-out—the hidden hand of capitalism subverted from below—liberals suspect capitalism is more likely to be thrown off course by the rich, with their lobbyists and the financial power which enables them to get laws passed that favor their interests over those of the public: capitalism subverted from above.

Thomas has read *Wealth of Nations*, Adam Smith's treatise on capitalism. (Smith was not the inventor of capitalism, no one person was, but he was certainly one of its earliest and greatest explicators.) Though Smith was an ardent believer in the capitalistic system, he warned repeatedly that people with like interests, generally the rich and powerful, will band together to get laws and policies enacted that favor them, that give them an unfair advantage. Perhaps this could be seen as subversion from the side, if the royalty and aristocracy of Smith's time are considered *the above.*. Smith never mentions subversion from below, but the welfare state wasn't much of an issue in his day.

Conservatives

At best, the conservative vision of life is heroic. The conservative is willing to be accountable, to take risks, to put himself on the line.

At worst, he is self-absorbed and arrogant. He is willing to use the perceived inferiority of others as a rationale to dismiss them, or to treat them in an abusive or even brutal manner. And his self-explanations often sound an annoyingly self-congratulatory note.

The conservative's ideal person is the self-reliant individualist.

Liberals

The liberal view, conversely, stresses cooperation and kindness over individual heroism. The liberal believes that civilization only exists because we work together, because we don't compete like beasts in a jungle. Competition may have a place for liberals, but only in the highly controlled arena of regulated capitalism, or in sports.

At best, the liberal is cooperative, flexible, and inclusive. He wants to be certain that all members of society have a place at the table.

At worst, he refuses to recognize the role of the individual in advancing the general cause of society, and he can be patronizing and paternalistic. He may overstate the necessity of government intervention in social issues, and understate the resilience of the individual. His policies may even hold back people of ability. He is also annoying when he tries to glaze over reality with political correctness: jargon, euphemisms, and sentimentalized stereotypes.

The liberal's ideal person is the beneficent sharer.

* * *

Thomas realizes that these are generalizations, and the actual people he meets, whichever political side they claim, usually have some inconsistent combination of these attitudes. Since the major political parties are not themselves paragons of consistency (as already discussed), this is reasonable. Beyond any of this,

Thomas finds certain basic aspects of the Right-Left polarity worth pondering:

When you observe two opposing points of view, both of which are widely held (perhaps held by approximately the same number of people, allowing for fluctuation), you have to conclude that either half of all people are idiots, or that the ideas of both sides have some merit. Neither is completely correct and neither is completely wrong. Of course, deciding that half of the people are idiots, whichever half you're not a member of, is exactly what dogmatic members of the Left and Right do.

When faced with this situation, a private individual and voter may find it expedient to at least tentatively choose one side over the other. This is usually the most effective strategy, staying with the ideology or party that *generally*, if not exactly and always, goes in the direction you think should be taken. Thomas thought it best to do this, however, with a certain detachment, a realization that your chosen side probably isn't perfect either. And maybe the other side occasionally has something worthwhile to say.

To a degree, all political affiliations are a compromise. Political followers of whatever stripe buy into a package deal, at least if they toe the party line. Certain ideas cluster together, regardless of their actual philosophical consistency. Ultimately, we proclaim our politics, at least partially, as a way to assert our identity. Thomas concludes that we are not so different from the heavy metal rockers he saw in the Oakland Coliseum. Our politics reflect our taste and style at least as much as our rationality.

Thomas thought this was a logical necessity. The world bombards us with myriad facts, and it is impossible to assimilate them all into a coherent picture. We must ignore some, dismissing them as irrelevant, reinterpret others to force sense into them, and fixate on a few. Depending on which subset of facts we choose to pay attention to, it's possible to support, with apparent logic, very different ideologies. Our personal style guides us in this fact selection process, and that style is itself then reinforced and elaborated by the rationalizing logic we applied to our data. Full circle.

And, as stated, we are not always consistent.

* * *

On the other hand, Thomas thinks, what's so hot about consistency? Perhaps this hobgoblin needn't always be guiding us in the first place. There is a reason why Democrats are only more-or-less liberals, and Republicans only more-or-less conservatives. The reason is pragmatics. The various political systems and ideologies are means to an end, after all, not ends in themselves. If we can achieve justice and prosperity, the greatest good for the greatest number, by compromising our ideologies a bit, why not do it?

Capitalism versus Communism

It occurred to Thomas to extend this idea to economic theories. In this arena, the two great adversaries in our era have been capitalism and communism.

Thomas first encountered communism in a meaningful way (other than as an all-purpose label for anyone who disagreed with you) when he was in college. What he actually read about as a student was Marxism, rather than communism per se. The difference between the two is described variously: Marxism is more the philosophy or ideology, communism more the system or implementation based on the ideology. Or, Marxism is a specific type of communism, communism the more general idea. (Though Marxism was overwhelmingly the predominant type of communism in the twentieth century).

Marx, it seemed to Thomas when he read him, had very astute criticisms of capitalism, but there were a couple of problems.

First, the capitalism Marx seemed to be critiquing was the uncontrolled, robber baron, monopoly'ed, kicback'ed, "public be damned" style that was rampant in the nineteenth, and early part of the twentieth, century. Thomas doesn't think Marx's objections are as valid when applied to the regulated capitalism of the present day. Even if we did grant Marx's critiques, maybe it is unnecessary to supersede capitalism entirely; maybe it would be enough to merely regulate it a bit.

The second problem with Marxist thought was the obvious fact that, because Marx could find flaws in capitalism, doesn't mean his system is better.

Marxism makes predictions about human behavior and the direction of history that at least some of his proponents have labeled as "scientific." Thomas, however, thinks the belief that history is moving toward some pre-determined goal, a classless, stateless, egalitarian utopia of worldwide socialism, with the government withering way, seems more mystical than empirical. (Of course, Thomas reflects, it could be argued that our confidence in capitalism's self-correcting "hidden hand" is also more faith than science.) In any case, Marx's theory, elegant though it sometimes is, does not really appear to be based on anything most people would call either science or empiricism. It is based on a personal impression of history, and an abstract logic carried forward from a set of insights that Marx had about that history. In other words, it developed much like the classic but non-scientific philosophies of old.

At present, communism is in world-wide disarray. There are a few minor holdouts, but overall capitalism appears to have won. Thomas doesn't find this surprising, considering the origin of each system. Despite the populist spin proponents try to give it, Marxism never seems to evolve spontaneously; it never seems to be a verdict of history pronounced by the proletariat. Instead, it is usually implemented by violent zealots, professional revolutionaries, who are able to foist it on down-trodden people desperate for any kind of change. And contrary to Marxist predictions, this seems to happen more in feudal than capitalist societies. In fact, the theory of Marxism was developed by a small group of intellectuals, you might even say in an ivory tower. Capitalism, on the other hand, evolved over a significant period of time through the day-to-day interactions of a vast number of people. Which process is more likely to result in a system that reflects human nature? Communism's wishful-thinking predictions of human motivation have never been born out; capitalism seems overall the more realistic approach.

So, capitalism has won and we should adhere to a capitalist model in all aspects of life? Thomas thought that it might not be quite that easy. Beyond doubt capitalism is the more powerful engine of productivity, but productivity is not our only concern. Certain services, such as fire and police, seem better suited to state control. Having these services provided privately is neither logistically practical nor economically viable, but we still must get them some way. They are required for the survival of our society.

Other areas where the state seems to best serve as agent include the military—we don't want to rely on mercenaries—and taxation. (It may seem obvious that it is the state that gathers taxes, but in eighteenth century France, at least, sufficiently well-off individuals could purchase the right to collect taxes. The king still got his money, but the tax franchisee kept a cut for himself. These "tax farmers" had little motivation to be kind or just; like most businessmen they were oriented toward the bottom line. Not surprisingly, some of them ended up on the guillotine when the Revolution came. But the idea must have seemed logical enough beforehand.)

So, Thomas decided, we should grant government a few areas of control. How about healthcare? Does healthcare seem to fit the engine of productivity model, or is it more a function that should be regulated so that it serves the interests of the society at large? The concerns of both individual and society are at issue with healthcare, as we wish to avoid the spread of epidemics and plagues, just as we wish to avoid the spread of fire, of one house burning unchecked and taking out an entire city.

Another consideration: Is the healthcare patient-consumer really in a position to make informed choices? Does she have any real control over what happens to her once she enters the healthcare system? Does she really have enough knowledge to "comparison shop"? Once the papers are signed and she is admitted to the hospital, she is almost totally subject to the decisions of others: doctors, insurance companies, hospital administrators and their policies, even third-party billing services. (The government is emphatically not the only source of red-taped bureaucracy.) If she feels sufficiently abused, she can walk out "AMA" (against medical advice), but if she does the insurance company won't pay her bill. The one decision the patient is allowed to make (sometimes) is whether she wants to have heroic measures taken or be allowed to die, should the penultimate moment come. Little else is left to her, at least little else that she understands well enough to make life-and-death choices about. The capitalist paradigm is based on consumer choice. Patient choice is conspicuously constrained or absent in the health care world.

In other words, does the hidden hand of capitalism prevail here? Is capitalism the appropriate paradigm?

The issue is further complicated by doctors, many of whom resent governmental involvement in medical practice. This antipathy is largely assumed to be rooted in a fear that their income will diminish; even some doctors seem to think this. Thomas wasn't so sure this was really their issue. Under any system, medical training will require a great deal of education and a lot of years before it begins to pay you back. How likely is anyone to go into this if they don't expect to be generously reimbursed? It's likely that doctors will always be paid well, though exactly to what degree may vary. European doctors, practicing in the context of socialized medical care, don't seem to be financially deprived. Also, if MDs don't have to worry about buying equipment, paying office staff, renting or buying office space, and so forth, maybe they would actually come out better financially, not to mention being able to focus more on the medical aspect of their practice.

Thomas thought the doctors' real concern was that they wanted to be independent businesspersons, not civil servants.

Still, healthcare seems more comparable to police or fire services than to retail merchandizing. There are probably ways to balance the interests of various factions: provide healthcare for everyone, still give MDs at least some of the free agency they want, and so on. However we finally do it, and the trend worldwide seems toward more government involvement, the decision will be much easier if we aren't bound by ideological purity. We need to use whichever process best serves us, regardless of abstract philosophy.

* * *

Thomas finally ends up giving first place to number seven, the hawkish male. Thomas finds his arguments are well-presented, thorough, and logical. To number three Thomas awards second place. She also did a good job, but he thinks number seven edged her. But later Thomas wonders: In his zeal to be objective, did he try too hard to avoid being swayed by his personal responses to the two of them? He certainly found the gal more appealing, more sympathetic. Thomas smiles wryly to himself. Overcompensating, perhaps, he thinks. *A typical bleeding heart liberal.*

*
**

Thomas' political odyssey ...

any years later, Thomas has occasion to wonder about his own ideological biases. As a young child, he remembers being overwhelmingly influenced by Thomas Sr.'s conservative opinions. He recalls being beaten up as a five-year-old by an older boy for saying he hated FDR and Truman. He was, of course, merely repeating his father's words; Thomas had no actual animosity toward men that were abstractions to him. And the older boy probably wasn't a diehard Democrat. He just seemed to think it was blasphemous to hate American presidents.

As he got older, Thomas' opinions grew more mixed. He continued to share his father's enthusiasm (in general) for Eisenhower, but developed a favorable opinion of John F. Kennedy. In 1964, as a teenager too young to vote, Thomas was drawn to Ayn Rand's views and mildly supported Goldwater, mostly because Thomas' Marin County classmates universally despised him. By the time he reached voting age, however, Thomas considered himself anti-racism, pro-environment, a strong supporter of free speech, and a person who believed in assessing others based on their individual merits, rather than on what group (race, gender, ethnic) they involuntarily belonged to. And he therefore considered himself a liberal.

Race

It seemed to Thomas that anyone of good will and a sanguine mindset would not be a racist. We humans are all in it together; we should be watching out for others, not finding excuses to denigrate them. Thomas theorized that while overt physical traits may vary among races, good and evil were universals that didn't play favorites by group. As a military brat and afterward, he had traveled to various parts of the world. It seemed to him that, while superficialities varied, the deep structure of human nature was the same everywhere. Similarities greatly overshadowed differences.

Also, who did the widely used racial label "black" actually refer to? Anyone who had a darker skin tone than the average Norwegian? Or persons or descendants of persons from a specific area of Africa? Different populations around the world had dark skin, but these populations often seemed to have little to do with each other. They did not appear to be all one people.

After having these thoughts, Thomas read a book on black athleticism that made the following assertion: Based on DNA studies, black people from different areas of Africa, particularly from the west coast and from Eastern Africa, genetically differed from each other, at least athletically and probably in general, more than either group differed from white people. That is, west coast Africans were more similar to Caucasians than they were to East Africans, and East Africans were more similar to whites than to West Africans. It further stated that Africans were genetically the most diverse group on Earth. This makes sense if humans originated in Africa: Having been around longer, Africans would have had more time to diversify.

To Thomas, this meant that if you used skin pigmentation as the sole marker for genetic identity, you would be seriously misled. His policy of looking at people as individuals, rather than assessing them by what group they belonged to, seemed further confirmed.

Political correctness

Thomas maintained his self-perception as a liberal for decades, though bothered by what at first seemed the minor excesses of political correctness. Later the PC effect began to disturb him more, especially the opposition to free speech and what's called reverse racism (though in fact it was just racism), to the extent that gradually he withdrew from taking sides politically. He decided he was done with tribalism in any form, that he would from now on judge situations and policies on their own merits, as he did individuals, rather than by where they fell on the ideological spectrum.

What was Thomas' issue with political correctness? Wasn't it the bastion of anti-racism and anti-sexism, the advocate of fair play for everyone? Wasn't the avoidance of possibly insulting remarks and behaviors desirable? Well ...

Incorrect?

The acrimonious response of the politically correct to anything even slightly ambiguous sometimes seemed unbalanced, and more divisive than reconciling. No benefit of the doubt was ever given. It was as though PC individuals sought any opportunity to be offended and resentful. Being self-righteous or sanctimonious, trying to force your way onto some supposed moral high ground with concepts such as cultural appropriation or micro-aggression, hardly seemed productive. Or valid: with sufficiently convoluted arguments, virtually anything could be interpreted in a way that permitted the vilification of an opposing viewpoint.

Beyond that, should even genuine insults be silenced? Clearly, racist violence, and prejudice in housing, employment, and so on, should not be tolerated. But should the government attempt to micro-manage rudeness? At what point did such an attempt usurp basic political freedoms, such as that of speech? And was it better to suppress an odious view, or allow it to be heard, and then refute it with reason?

It occurred to Thomas that the suppression of ugly views such as Nazism meant that Nazism's advocates seldom heard forceful arguments refuting their beliefs. They were merely told they were bad, without much explanation. They were left free to reinforce their beliefs among themselves, and to consider themselves heroic outsiders, superior to those with the lemming-like mindset of the politically correct. By allowing fascistic arguments to be heard, the counter arguments could also be heard. Even if few fascists were persuaded to change sides (though a few probably would be), the majority of people could understand the arguments, and understand why Nazism is an evil thing. Not just be told by the politically correct to shut up and take it on faith.

If a just and egalitarian society was the objective, why was it politically correct to attack certain groups, such as whites and males? Wasn't having an allowed target, a scapegoat group, the essence of the problem in the first place?

Thomas doubted that political correctness would cause white males to suffer much, at least in the short term, but that wasn't the point. Prejudice, regardless of direction, diverts us away from what we claim is our goal. Thomas thought that one of the worst aspects of it was that denigrating any group, whatever its history, would ultimately be injurious not just to that group, but to the minorities that had already suffered. One effect would be pushback. But more significantly, an unjust frame of mind was being propagated. This is detrimental for everyone.

If equality is the objective, the playing field must be absolutely level. Nobody will truly believe in a just state unless they can see that its principles apply to everyone. An egalitarian mindset must be engendered across the board; it must be internalized. By its nature, equality does not exist unless it exists for all.

***

Lost in Yosemite:
View from a Mind's Eye

Yosemite National Park: Spring, 1980

Thomas had left the lodge when it closed at 2:00 AM. It doesn't reopen until six in the morning; he knows that's a long way off. He also knows that he is in Yosemite National Park in California. Beyond that, Thomas doesn't know too much. He has walked far enough from the lodge that there is no sight or sound of it; there is, in fact, no manmade light or object visible anywhere. Also, due to the high fog, no moon and no stars. The misty sky is faintly luminous, but not enough for him to make out much of the surrounding landscape.

Thomas is hiking along the edge of a narrow, paved road that leads from the lodge up into the climbing areas. He stays in contact with the road by walking with one foot on asphalt and the other on the moist dirt shoulder (there is no curb). By this means he knows he is moving in the direction the road leads, rather than wandering back and forth across it. Back and forth meandering could eventually turn him around, send him back the way he came, or even place him in danger of being hit by a vehicle—if there were any. There aren't. An occasional slow-moving car would actually be a blessing. Thomas would probably see it or hear it far enough way to avoid being hit, and its headlights would give him a chance to orient himself. They would also give him a break from what seems to be solitary confinement in a very large sensory deprivation arena.

The air is cool but Thomas is dressed for it, and he is not particularly hungry or thirsty. Except for being lost, he is OK. He keeps wondering how this is supposed to work, how you're supposed to find your way around here at night. Down in the valley are crowds of people, with their electric lanterns and campfires and noise. Here it's just nature and Thomas. An aesthetic concept in the abstract, but now the beauties of nature are invisible, and Thomas is lost.

Somewhere up in the higher reach of these mountains is the camp of the junior college mountaineering class that Thomas is with. They've been climbing all day; Thomas will climb with them again tomorrow, if he can find his way back. For now, Thomas is carefully keeping his mind relaxed, not letting this spook him. What can happen? Spring is arriving in the mountains, though it's still chill after dark. Thomas is fit, young; not likely to freeze to death overnight. In the dawn he'll certainly find his camp, if he doesn't stumble across it sooner. If he stays in contact with this paved road, nothing too bad should happen. Still, the situation makes him a little uneasy.

Then he sees the campfire, far away in the woods beyond the opposite side of the road. He knows his class had built a large bonfire, but the distance and the intervening underbrush make it look small. He also knows there is some way to get to that campfire via a trail that leads from the road, but his impulse is to forget about trying to find the trail in the darkness and set out directly across country. Now that he has sight of the campfire, he doesn't want to do anything that would cause him to lose it again. Common sense might suggest that he stay on the road and try to find the trail, rather than go stumbling across rough ground that he can barely see. But being an impatient person who has survived so far by occasionally ignoring common sense (maybe more than occasionally), Thomas starts walking straight across an almost invisible, uneven landscape toward the distant fire.

At least he is trying to walk straight across. He has to keep swerving at the last instant to avoid head-high branches, and he is half-tripping over roots, dead logs, fallen timber. The ground abruptly dips, and he half runs, half stumbles, down into a gully, barely managing to stay on his feet. Pine needles tear at his face and he turns his head just in time to protect his eyes. Still, the fire is getting closer. He'll be there soon.

Thomas staggers through rises, stumbles into more gullies, and he has definitely learned the value of proceeding slowly. As he gets closer, he sees what appears to be a very oddly shaped tree, or maybe a pair of trees, not too far from the bonfire: Two side by side tree trunks ascend into an oddly shaped conjunction of branches and pine needles. The tree—if it isn't two trees—rises about forty feet above the ground, towering over the fire, which casts a muted light over its lower trunk. But Thomas becomes increasingly puzzled as he nears the tree. It looks less and less like a tree ... and more and more like a huge human figure.

The tree-figure turns it head, looks at Thomas, nods in a polite but guarded way.

"Howdy," it says.

Thomas experiences a brief interval, a second or so, of inexpressible strangeness. Then everything shifts into perspective. The fire is not the head-high bonfire he was expecting. It is only a small blaze, its flames reaching a foot or two above the ground. The talking tree, is of course, a man. The man is wearing a plaid flannel coat and jeans and is moderately tall, but not Paul Bunyan. His entire campsite is much closer than Thomas thought it was. In fact, Thomas realizes that he is standing on the edge of it.

Thomas says something to the effect that he guesses this isn't the camp he is looking for.

"Most likely not," the man says.

Thomas apologizes for barging into his camp. The man nods and asks Thomas if he is with the large group camped a little way north. Figuring this has to be his class, Thomas says that he is. The man gives Thomas brief directions and a nod toward the path he needs to take. Feeling like an amateur, Thomas thanks him and leaves. Within a short time he finds the right campsite and rejoins his group.

Once Thomas gets over his initial sense of relief, he feels chagrin and bewilderment. Even allowing for the lack of light, the unfamiliar territory, and the sensory deprivation, how was he so deceived that he mistook a six-foot tall man for a forty-foot tall tree? Yes, Thomas thought the campfire was larger and further away. Also, the campsite sat alone in almost total darkness, so there was nothing around it to provide a reference for size or distance. More important yet, the campsite was on higher ground than Thomas was. Without realizing it, he had been in another gully. This caused the campsite to sit high in his field of vision. If the campfire and Thomas had been on the same plane, he would have been looking down on it and it would have obviously not been a large bonfire. Instead, the fire was elevated in his angle of vision to the plane of the invisible horizon. A small-appearing ground-level object that high is far away, if it is level with your head.

So, the surrounding landscape was too dark to give any spatial clues, and the fire was on higher ground. But that leaves out the most important aspect. Thomas was looking for, really wanted to see, that big inviting fire in front of his camp. What deceived him most was his own expectation.

* * *

Though this was his most disconcerting experience with optical misjudgment, Thomas has had others. For example ...

When he was a child his family lived for a while in a house near the top of a hill.

From their front window, Thomas could look out across the valley and the rest of the residential area. On the far hillside, a large house sat facing him. It was in a group of rather closely spaced houses, and there didn't seem to be too much beyond it. The large house was only a short distance beyond the center of the valley. Or so Thomas thought.

If Thomas had never visited the house on the far hillside, he might have kept this same perception of things for the rest of his life, or as long as memory allowed. However, one day Thomas met the boy, about his own age, who lived in that large house. The boy invited Thomas over for a visit. As they approached his house Thomas could see, first of all, that the neighboring houses were much farther apart and more scattered than he had thought, more varied in design, and extending a good distance beyond his new friend's house. Thomas also saw that this house sat farther back from the center of the valley than he had previously thought. Up close, the world around this house seemed to open up; there was much more going on, more depth and variation, than Thomas had realized.

Reaching the house, Thomas turned and looked back. To his consternation, he saw that his own home, now small and distant, looked like part of a low-relief frieze of flat, closely spaced houses. With distance, depth and complexity faded away.

* * *

As visual phenomena, adult Thomas thought this was all fairly obvious, but he saw that it also applies more abstractly.

In the situation in Yosemite, an image or message is misleading because there is no way to know how it fits into a larger picture, and because we superimpose expectations, fears and desires, on what we perceive.

Consider a story in the news media. In and of itself, it might mean almost anything, and maybe something different for each person who reads it. Your political philosophy, for example, can completely change the import of a story. An event may appear random and unimportant if you are neutral toward or favor the politicians involved. If you dislike them, then obviously they are trying to slip some dark design past us: a cover-up is in progress.

Thomas decided that we have a previously constructed image of reality which we use all the time, generally without realizing it, to fill in the gaps that are always present in our information. It allows us to connect all the seemingly unrelated and partial truths into a pattern coherent enough to deal with. As can be seen from the Yosemite example, the impulse to apply closure can be so strong that it asserts itself even when there is little or no information to close with. Our unconscious will provide the entire context from memories, hopes, and anxieties.

And when we have an emotional reaction to the people or ideas involved, our perception is even more likely to be distorted. This lack of perfection in our cognitive systems isn't necessarily disastrous; in many areas of life we only need to get things kind of right, or at least not get them too wrong. It's possible that our lives would be more successful if we could discern the world more precisely, but the only completely necessary accuracy of perception is the minimum required for survival.

In the second situation, the houses on hills and the valley between, adult Thomas found it easy to see an ideological metaphor.

If the center of the valley represents the political midpoint between liberal and conservative, then when we stand on that central line and face north along the valley, the liberal hill is on our left, to the west, and the conservative hill is on our right, to the east. From this centrist stance we can see that the extreme left and right positions, symbolized by the highest points of their respective mountains, seem equally far away in opposite directions. We can also make a reasonable assessment of the distance to and between various positions on either side. However, if we view the ideological valley from the top of the far right hill, the conservative mountain, the center of the valley appears very close to the western hill. Clearly, liberalism and even centrism are mere inches from communism, and our nation's capital is overrun with pinkos. From the most extreme point of the leftist hill, conversely, we see that moderate and extreme conservatives are close to each other, and only a trivial distance away from Nazis. From this perspective, there is no significant variation within the ranks of an opposing ideology.

This effect stems largely from ignorance, the lack of a real understanding of the other side's position, and from being overly familiar with our own territory. We are deceived because we aren't interested in the details of a stance we find unsympathetic. It is easier to let our preconceptions tell us all we think we need to know. In effect, we create a straw man version of our opponents' positions. The straw man in this case is not contrived to fool an audience and win a debate; we use it to unconsciously deceive ourselves ... to create in the adversary an "other" that is easier to contain and defeat in our minds. The ultimate result, as Thomas found in the Yosemite mountains, is that we are misled by our expectations.

Reflecting on all of this, Thomas decides the only way he can break out of the mental trap was to force himself to adopt, at least temporarily, the values and ideas of his political opposite, and then look back at himself from that perspective. This is not easy; it requires a great psychological exertion. Many people consider themselves energetically thoughtful because they spend a good deal of time reflecting on their own entrenched ideology. They endlessly cross the t's and dot the i's of what they think they already know, further refining their ideology without ever questioning it. This only serves to more deeply imprint what is already believed. It is a completely different thing from questioning yourself. Self-corroboration requires very little psychic energy; hauling your thoughts around the same circular track becomes second nature and close to effortless. Trying on the beliefs of people you don't like, on the other hand, is draining and threatening.

What is the survival value of not questioning your beliefs? Group solidarity, Thomas guesses, affinity with your tribe and compliance with their policies, an essential mode in a primitive clan. In the modern world, however, the ability to question received values, to doubt what you think you've always known, might be the more valuable trait. You must look closely and questioningly at your own opinions, as it is difficult to fix or improve something you can't see clearly. Constant re-appraisal becomes essential.

*
**

Books of interest

Diplomacy
         Henry Kissinger, 1994

Taboo: Why Black Africans Dominate Sports and Why We're Afraid to Talk about it
         Jon Entine, 2000

Part 5

Bullies, Victims and Heroes

$\mathcal{F}$rom the patchy, weed-grown vacant lot where they are all standing, Thomas can see their grade school a quarter of a mile away. Directly across the street from them is a row of private houses. These are nearer, but still at a good distance. They should have enough privacy.

About a dozen sixth-grade boys, of which Thomas is one, are gathered in this lot to conduct a fight. Thomas and a boy named Richard are going to be the fighters. The whole business is a little like a duel: arranged in advance, attended by a small group of friends and acquaintances (some of whom might be thought of as seconds), and there is a sort of code in place: Show up at a certain place at a certain time; don't start fighting until both fighters are ready (not always followed); don't kick each other (sometimes—but rarely—ignored); don't tell adults about any of this (scrupulously followed most of the time).

Thomas' prospects are not good: Richard is generally thought to be tougher than him, and Thomas kind of believes that himself, But he has a plan. As with many people, having a plan reduces his anxiety. It doesn't even matter too much how likely the plan is to work. At least there is something he can try to do, rather than just stand there and get hit. And Thomas' plan is even fairly reasonable. On this day, however, events will take a turn no one expects.

* * *

Thomas had met Richard (sometimes called Rich, never Dick) when they were both in fourth grade. This was in a different school; this year the school district has redrawn certain boundaries and now Richard and Thomas are in a new school, with a few of their old friends and a lot of new kids. Richard and Thomas have one mutual friend and the three of them even socialize sometimes. However, their history together isn't favorable.

Thomas first encountered Richard when he was befriended by a boy named Evan. Evan's way of befriending Thomas was unusual: Evan had tripped him from behind. When Thomas jumped up angrily to face him, Evan acted for a moment like he was going to fight, then turned and ran. Thomas chased him. Thomas was considered to be a fast runner among fourth graders, but he was having a hard time catching Evan. Just as he was about to give up, Evan suddenly stopped, threw himself to the sidewalk and begged for mercy. His tone of voice when begging was a strange combination of whining and assertiveness. Thomas discovered later this was his tone in most situations. Thomas didn't know what to make of it, but he accepted Evan's surrender and let him get up peacefully. Evan began talking to Thomas as though they were buddies. He told his story, that he and a friend were being chased by a bunch of bullies led by Richard. Thomas quickly took Evan's side of the conflict, more for the excitement than anything else, and promised to help him with the bullies. Thomas soon met Evan's friend, who seemed quiet and passive, and maybe somewhat slow. The friend didn't appear to add much to their side, but this was their group, the three of them against Richard and his faction.

None of this seems exactly reasonable to Thomas when he looks back on it as an adult, but somehow it made sense at the time. Perhaps Thomas saw himself playing the heroic role in an adventure story.

Thomas mainly helped Evan by warning him when Richard's gang was near, and even momentarily obstructing the gang so Evan and his friend could run, and then running himself. The running seemed justified since Richard's group outnumbered them, and included older boys.

At one point Thomas was cornered by Richard, who told his friends to stand back, as he would take care of this himself. Thomas didn't really know Richard, so he wasn't too worried. Thomas didn't tend to be belligerent, but he didn't restrain his mouth either, and he'd gotten into several fights in grade school. These always took the form of a wrestling match. The struggle continued until one boy got on top of the other, pinned him to the ground, and didn't get off until the boy on his back "gave" (said "I give"). The boy on top was usually Thomas, though not always.

Richard fought differently. He had brothers in high school who had taught him to use his fists. He would give a little jump toward his opponent, gaining momentum, while swinging his arm with all his might. The motion was as though his arm were a rope and his fist a rock swung on the end of it. In their first, brief fight in fourth grade, his fist hit the side of Thomas' head several times with fierce kinetic energy. The strikes could have been easily blocked by a trained fighter, but that wasn't Thomas at the time. His impression at that moment, facing Richard, had been that he was going to get his head knocked off. That fight ended almost immediately when a teacher broke it up. By the time Thomas' dizziness passed, Richard and his friends had left. Thomas had to stand there a while and mentally reconstruct what had happened. This was about two years before today's fight.

The situation between Richard and Evan (and therefore also Thomas) faded away over the course of the school year, but Thomas found that Evan had other problems with tough kids wanting to beat him. He seemed to have some way of attracting adversaries of a certain mindset, and even bringing out that mindset in boys who usually showed no sign of it. Thomas saw Evan draw even normally non-bullying boys into beating on him. Thomas never hit Evan, but came close in moments of extreme frustration, when Evan seemed to be trying to provoke him.

Evan got into other sorts of trouble as well. Climbing through the window into the girls' restroom, making bizarre, often perversely foul statements to adults as well as to other children, constantly defying teachers, running away from them suddenly and inexplicably, and always getting into fights that he seemed to want to lose. As a child Thomas couldn't figure out what was wrong with Evan, and their friendship became very tenuous and occasional. When the school district changed boundaries and they moved to the new school, Evan went to the new school too, but was held back in fifth grade, so Thomas, in sixth grade, had less contact with him.

The fight with Richard

In the gathering dusk, Thomas and Richard square off to fight. Thomas' plan is simple: don't let himself be hit. It sounds like a joke, but one of the maxims of unarmed combat (as Thomas learned years later) is don't box a boxer; don't wrestle a wrestler. That is, don't fight your opponent's fight; make him fight yours. Thomas intends to leap in on Richard before he can swing and wrestle him to the ground. Once on the ground Thomas will try to pin him, something he's reasonably good at, and not let him up until Richard agrees to drop this idea of hitting him. Thomas reminds himself that this fight is not his idea, after all; Richard had offered the challenge.

It had been almost casual; Richard hadn't really expected Thomas to accept. The year before, Richard had made a list of all the other boys in the school (the previous school) that he considered to be tough guys, or at least valid opponents. He had gone to each of them in turn, and tried to goad them into fighting him. Thomas had not even made it onto the list. Nevertheless, Thomas had felt compelled by honor, or some whim, to not back down from today's fight.

The fight starts. Richard draws his arm back, cocking it for the big swing. Thomas jumps on him, grabbing him around his arms and upper body. Richard twists, jerks, tries to spin around, tries to break free. Thomas hangs on with desperate strength, knowing he will get his head pounded if he loses his hold. They go on like this for perhaps as long as a minute, a strange, jerky dance between two pubescent boys. Then Thomas manages to pull the wiry Richard off balance and bear him down to the ground. Thomas thinks, great! It's going my way—

Richard screams wildly, violently tears himself free with hysterical strength, and jumps to his feet, holding his right forearm. He has lost any interest in fighting. He leaps into the air with insane energy, again and again, screaming with each leap: howls of intense, overwhelming pain.

Confused and frightened, Thomas stands and backs away from him. The other boys stare at Richard in perplexity. Thomas is not sure how long this goes on.

They try to calm Richard down, try to figure out what they should do.

Richard's screams are loud enough to be heard by a woman living in one of the houses across the street. She comes over and drives him to a medical office, only a few blocks away in this small town. The rest of them follow on foot. Richard is taken inside the doctor's examination room and the other boys sit uneasily out in the waiting area. They are given to understand that his mother has been called. One of the boys suggests that, when she comes, Thomas should go to her and offer to help, to do whatever he can. Thomas waits nervously, wishing he could just sort of cease to exist for a while.

Richard's mother arrives; Thomas stands and mumbles something to her. She ignores him and goes into the room where Richard is being kept. By now he is no longer screaming. They find out later he has been given a sedative.

It turned out that Richard's right forearm is broken badly, with multiple fractures—"splintered" is the word the doctor uses to describe it. It occurs to Thomas that if his plan had gone as intended, the fight would have been a relatively benign affair. A wrestling match between two sixth-graders is not that lethal. Richard, Thomas tells himself somewhat defensively, was trying to smash Thomas' head, while all Thomas was trying to do was to nullify him. True, Richard's welfare hadn't been a consideration when Thomas formed the plan; he was only trying to avoid being hit. Still, his intentions weren't malicious. This thought doesn't help his state of mind.

Over the next week or so, events unfold: Richard's arm requires expensive reconstructive surgery. There is a rumor that his parents are considering a lawsuit against Thomas' parents. Who are not well off. What would be Thomas' defense in court? That Richard started it? This tended to be the all-purpose excuse in childhood; at this point it sounds weak even to Thomas. But the lawsuit never materializes.

Richard heals well, rebounds quickly. By the Spring semester he and Thomas are vying against each other for top honors in the school in tetherball. Thomas notices that Richard's tetherball-hitting style is similar to his fighting style: he cocks back his right arm and swings his fist like a rock on a rope. He adds a little jump if he has time, to lend power to the move. Richard and Thomas trade off tetherball victories. Somehow Thomas wins more often.

After the fight

In the following year or two, before Thomas leaves California and moves to Germany at age thirteen, he continues to interact with the same group of boys, including Richard, and has little contact with Evan.

Richard

Richard has not been impressed enough by pain to change his tough guy ways. He still takes on anyone, even older boys, and consistently wins. He never wants to fight Thomas again, however. To his face Richard is usually civil enough, but he tells their mutual friends his violent fantasies of coming up behind Thomas and taking him out with a baseball bat. This never happens. But the fact that he would think of it, combined with the lack of any face-to-face confrontation, tells Thomas that the agony of Richard's broken arm did leave an imprint on him. Only in regard to Thomas, however; he fears no one else.

Thomas thinks he understands Richard's treatment of Evan. Bullying others is a most emphatic way of differentiating yourself from them: You are asserting that you are not them. You are not a member of the victim caste. The need to do this can be especially compelling for those who have been victimized by bullies themselves.

Before their fight, Thomas had heard Richard tell stories about his older brothers, about their fights in high school and other trouble they found their way into. At least at times, they must have bullied Richard himself, as older brothers frequently do. Thomas suspects Richard's attitude toward them was a mixture of respect, anger, fear, and a desire to emulate them.

Thomas thinks Richard grew up with the sense that violence always lurked nearby and you had to be ready for it. He didn't wait for it to come to him, however; Richard was proactive to perceived threat. He sought out conflict, usually with people he saw as a challenge. Certainly he didn't lack courage. His dark mumblings about attacking Thomas with a bat were just talk, a way to vent frustrated anger.

Richard had some ennobling characteristics. During the previous year, when he thought that a girl he liked, was "going with," preferred Thomas, Richard came to him, explained the situation, and said he was willing to step aside for the better man (and this in fifth grade!).

Richard never bullied his friends; he usually spared the obviously weak, seeking fights with boys he saw as tough (and therefore a threat). Evan was an exception to this. He was no challenge to Richard, but you hate most in others that trait you can't tolerate in yourself. Evan's demeanor, short-lived assertiveness followed immediately by raucous submission, followed by sniveling insolence, must have been especially incendiary to Richard. Evan clearly represented what Richard did not want to be.

Thomas

Thomas is deeply imprinted by the fight and the broken arm. For years after the confrontation with Richard, he never fights anyone. He goes to schools where bullying is a constant. (Maybe all schools are like that). Through junior high and early high school, Thomas avoids confrontations. In the bully/victim scenario, he always felt like he was forced to come down on one side or other of the equation: Either you were a tough guy or you were preyed upon by tough guys. Trying to walk a middle path, neither provoking a fight or allowing yourself to be intimidated, was difficult, and readily seen by your peers as cowardice. To avoid this perception, and still avoid fights, was a balancing act not easy for most adolescent boys. You had to project a certain confidence, combined with neutrality, and a sense of what was fair. A useful skill for later in life, perhaps.

Thomas tries to walk this middle path a lot after the arm-breaking fight. He is not always successful. "Chickened out," or "chicken sh--t" are phrases he hears applied to himself. He found you can avoid most fights by simply accepting the shove or the insult, hunching your shoulders, and walking away ... but this is also difficult to do. Especially at a time in life when self-esteem tends to be an issue.

In ninth grade, attending an American junior high on an air base in Germany, Thomas encounters a boy named Mike. Mike turns out to be the worst of the bullies. Thomas originally meets him when Mike comes up behind him and punches him. (For no known reason.) Thomas almost turns and hits him back, but he is still held by the incident with Richard. After that Thomas tries to avoid Mike. His attempts are usually successful, but not always. When Mike catches Thomas, he does things like shove him against lockers, write on his neck with a ballpoint pen while Thomas is seated at lunch, bash him with his gym bag, and so on. His goal seems to be humiliation more than injury.

Finally, in the Spring semester of tenth grade, Thomas finds that he is through with it. One day Mike approaches from the rear and applies a football-style block (Mike is on the school team) to Thomas' lower back. Thomas' anger boils over. He abruptly realizes that he no longer cares if he breaks Mike's arm. He actually doesn't care if he breaks his neck. Thomas turns around and leaps into Mike in a berserk fury of flying fists. Mike cowers back, doubling over and covering up. The fight, in a school hallway at lunch, is broken up quickly. Mike never bothers Thomas again, however. As with Richard.

Richard contradicted the cliché that all bullies are cowards. Mike struck a different note. He continually bullied his closest friends, dominating them, even while scurrying away (despite his impressive height and shoulder width) from older boys. He also probably grew up with a sense of eminent violence, and also proactive toward threat, but his response involved posturing more than fighting prowess. His physical features, both face and build, were unusually intimidating. This probably taught him to rely on appearance and bluff. Sometimes the clichés are true.

The fight with Mike breaks Thomas out of his fight-phobic mindset. After that, through the end of high school, he is in one or two more fights of no great consequence. He considers himself to have become "normal" once again about fighting. "Normal" is a relative status, of course. It occurred to Thomas much later that fighting to save face, fighting over insults and attitudes, not in physical self-defense, is probably not rational, however normal it may be in some circles.

Like Richard, Thomas had been motivated by a fear of being oppressed. In Thomas' case, that feeling was combined with a sense of heroism absorbed from comic books, novels and movies. Of course he saw himself as the good guy of the story; it was his duty to defend people like Evan. To some degree this attitude stemmed from a child's romanticized view of life, but it was also based partly on a sense of justice that was offended when he saw someone being bullied. Many years passed before he realized that another part of it might have been that Thomas also felt a need to differentiate himself from victims, to assert that he was not Evan. If he could defend a victim, he proves he is not a victim.

Evan

Evan is hardest to understand. In Thomas' experience, most victims of bullies don't do anything to provoke abuse—at least not anything that a reasonable person, a non-bully, would view as provocation. Evan, however, seemed to want to be bullied. It was as though he had a neurotic need to seek out what he fears most, bring it down on himself, and almost revel in the consequences.

He seemed to be caught in some repetition/frustration cycle, continually compelled to seek pain and humiliation. Thomas saw him act out the same pattern again and again: raucous assertiveness (he had a hoarse, croaky voice, deep for a fifth-grader), followed by abrupt, insolent submission. He would suddenly fall to the ground, almost hugging it, and allow himself to be struck again and again. He would swear angrily while this happened, but he wouldn't fight back. He reminded Thomas of someone who knows that the stove top will burn his hand, but somehow is compelled to touch it. Again and again. Evan was neither small nor weak for his age.

In repeated fifth grade, Evan fell under the sway of a popular male teacher with a large and dominating presence. Mr. S. seemed to understand Evan, to know how to deal with him. At that time, Thomas thinks maybe Evan will be okay.

Much later

Richard

After leaving California at the end of seventh grade, Thomas never sees Richard again. When Thomas returns to California years later, the mutual friend tells him that, at least into first adulthood, Richard has turned out all right. The friend had expected him to get deeper into trouble as he got older, maybe wind up in jail, but none of that had happened. Thomas doesn't know where Richard eventually ended up.

Thomas

Thomas never gets into another uncontrolled fight after high school, but it seems like he was haunted by the possibility. Maybe this is because of his experiences in school, perhaps it is because he had a father who never wanted to spare the backhand and spoil the child. For whatever reason, Thomas also lived with the not quite conscious idea that violence is always lurking close by, and he had to be ready for it. In his twenties, Thomas begins studying Asian martial arts. This led to various strange paths in his life, including taking part in an international full contact martial arts tournament in Taiwan. Eventually it leads to Thomas' acquaintance with Alan, and his involvement with emerald-smuggling in Central America. This is discussed in Part 8, *Chaos Theory in a Tokyo Bar*.

Thomas knew that he was at least partly motivated by the desire to be a hero. In heroic mode, it's even acceptable to lose the fight, to get beat up, because you're still the good guy. Breaking another boy's arm knocked that feeling askew. Thomas was confused, no longer sure he had the moral high ground.

Evan

Thomas never sees Evan again, but in the early seventies, when Evan and Thomas are both about 25, he sees Evan's name in the newspapers. Evan has been murdered, apparently by drug pushers. According to the newspaper, Evan had become a heroin addict, and later a police informant. He was eventually murdered, along with his girlfriend, in a hotel room in a nearby town. They were killed by the forced injection of lethal overdoses of heroin. It seemed that with Mr. S. no longer around to guide him, Evan's life had gone in a dark direction.

At the time, an infamous outlaw motorcycle gang was reputed to be the largest drug-dealing organization in California. Thomas wondered if they were the ones who had killed Evan. It seemed he would be drawn to them: the individual with the need to be a victim magnetically attracted to the famous stereotypical gang of bullies. Maybe the collision was inevitable.

*
**

Part 6

Critical Numbers

Travels with Zeno

Between Phoenix and Tucson, Arizona

Though Interstate Highway 10 runs mostly west and east, from Santa Monica, California to Jacksonville, Florida, for the 116 miles between Phoenix and Tucson it takes a north-south slant. Thomas is cruising along this stretch of road late one night in December, a few days before Christmas. They had left early that morning from Marin County in California, and Thomas has been driving all day and deep into the night. In the back seat his wife Nancy and the two children they have so far are asleep. In the front seat, Thomas is trying not to be asleep.

They are going to visit Thomas' family in Tucson for Christmas. This is not exactly going home, since Thomas never lived in Tucson; his family moved there after he moved out. After a lifetime of never living in any one place too long, Tucson is where Thomas' family finally settled, so it has become the focal point for family reunions. Thomas' wife's parents live in Indiana, substantially further away, and they don't seem to have much interest in Thomas' and Nancy's family anyway. For Christmas, then, it's Tucson.

Thomas is trying in various ways to stay awake. The open desert and the not-so-distant mountains can be inspiring in the sunlight, but at night they're nearly invisible and offer little to think about. Thomas employs a mental exercise: He watches the road signs showing the mileage to Tucson, and tries to calculate arrival times at different speeds. For example, the green sign ahead tells him that Tucson is 80 miles away, and the speedometer says they're going 80 miles per hour (top and cruising speed in their 71 Volkswagen): An easy calculation—they'll be in Tucson in one hour.

Arrival can't happen too soon, but 80 is a little fast. Without Thomas realizing it, the wide, straight, almost traffic-free highway has seduced him into speeding. And his family is on board.

Thomas slows to 70. A while later he sees another sign: Tucson 70 miles. Fine, they've covered ten miles since the last sign; they're making progress. But ... at 70 miles per hour Tucson is still an hour away. Another hour to fight his sagging eyelids. In a sense, they've made no progress at all.

It occurs to Thomas that he might slow to 60 and then encounter a sign indicating Tucson is 60 miles away. There would still be an hour to go. His mind runs away with this. He could slow to 50 when Tucson is 50 miles away, to 40 when Tucson is 40 miles away, to 30 at 30 miles out, and so on. They will always be getting closer in space, but never any closer in time. They will always be drawing nearer to Tucson, but they will always be an hour away. They will never arrive.

This is at least theoretically possible. Actualizing it would get ridiculous. Eventually they would be one inch from Tucson, moving at one inch per hour. A half-inch out, Thomas would slow to half an inch per hour. A quarter of an inch from Tucson, he would slow to a quarter of an inch per hour.

At another time Thomas might have dismissed this as an idle fancy, but he has recently gone back to college, re-entering as a junior at a California state university, and he has just finished his first semester as a Philosophy major. He has studied the ancient Greek philosophers, one of whom was Zeno. The thought brings Thomas fully awake:

He has actualized Zeno's Paradox.

Sort of. All you have to do to actualize Zeno's paradox, it seems, is to always be slowing down.

* * *

The ancient philosopher Zeno of Elea, who lived from approximately 490 BC to 430 BC, actually presented a series of paradoxes, not just one. Looked at closely, though, these paradoxes are quite similar—variations on a theme. This theme can be briefly summarized:

The distance between any two points can be divided into a number of smaller distances, and each of these can be subdivided further into still smaller distances, which can themselves be subdivided into distances smaller yet ... and this process can go on forever, resulting, theoretically, in an infinite number of very small (or perhaps infinitesimal) distances. Since it is impossible to cross something that is infinite—because infinite means "without limit," "never-ending"—Zeno contends that it is therefore impossible to cross the distance between any two points. This logic can be applied to any movement across any distance between two points, no matter how close together or far apart the points are. It doesn't matter whether you are flying across the ocean or reaching down to scratch your ankle, you can't do it. Any sort of motion is impossible. You can never get from point A to point B: You can't tour the city, you can't leave the room, you can't kiss your sweetheart.

The obvious response to this is that Zeno's logic may be clever, but we *can* do all of these things, so what is his purpose? One of Zeno's purposes was to show that the world of motion, time, and change is an illusion, that there is only the indivisible, unchanging reality, "the One." This sounds like Eastern mysticism, but if you study the various ancient Greek philosophers, you'll find they often foreshadowed the tenets of later religion and science: everything from Eastern mysticism, to monotheism, to atoms, to the curved space of relativity.

Zeno's other purpose in creating his paradoxes was to respond to the doctrines of competing philosophical schools. These rival philosophers had created their own paradoxes to discredit the teachings of Parmenides' school, of which Zeno was a leading member. Zeno wanted to counter-attack.

Though most of us would dismiss Zeno's paradoxes on the basis of everyday experience, philosophers want to be able to explain logically why he is wrong. This need has kept Zeno's clever arguments alive for more than two millennia.

* * *

Previously, Thomas had tried to answer Zeno by arguing that, as the number of divisions of a space increased, the amount of time needed to cross each one decreased. So while you could, in theory, divide a distance into an infinite number of spaces, each space would then be infinitely small, and should thus take no time, or an infinitely small amount of time, to cross. (An infinitely small space of time should equate to no time at all.) In math, an infinitesimal is the reciprocal of an infinite number. The problem, therefore, would be self-canceling. Maybe you could even develop an argument claiming we should be able to cross infinite space in zero time, a counter paradox. Of course, that argument, the counter paradox, should also be defeated by the same general sort of logic.

Apparently Thomas' answer was not satisfactory, and he later learned that the great Aristotle had come up with an argument somewhat similar. Aristotle subsequently found fault with his own solution ... still, Aristotle's proposal was more or less accepted for centuries, until mathematicians in the nineteenth century claimed they had come up with a better answer. Latter day mathematicians treated the paradox of motion as a mathematical problem, solvable through application of calculus (or "The Calculus"), which wasn't invented until after the time of either Zeno or Aristotle.

The problem with the calculus solution is that it doesn't translate well into anything empirical, anything a non-mathematician can understand.

But now Thomas had another angle: He could sort of actualize Zeno's paradox by adding the factor of deceleration. Did this open the door to a deeper understanding, and maybe an experiential (non-mathematical) solution?

Well ... no, it turned out. At least Thomas wasn't able to come up with such a solution. Once again, if we want any resolution at all, we have to take the mathematicians' word for it.

*
**

Thresholds

$\mathcal{T}$homas is driving his son Shane home from school. Though Shane is only six years old, the lines of concentration in his forehead make it clear that he is pondering something profound. Thomas speculates that he has heard something new and provocative in his first grade class.

"Uh … Dad?" Shane says after a while.

"Yeah Shane?"

"How many people are there in the whole world?"

"Three-and-a-half billion." Thomas gives the number agreed on at the time by most authorities.

"Dad?"

"Yes?"

"Is that counting yourself?"

No, son. Counting me it's three-and-a-half-billion and one. Thomas doesn't actually say this, and he doesn't try too seriously to explain the insignificance of precision in very large numbers, or the futility of being exact with a number that constantly fluctuates. He knows that this is the type of concept that is difficult to explain to a child before a certain age, and unnecessary to explain only a short while later. The natural growth of his brain will resolve the issue for him; in a few years, or maybe even a few months, he will intuitively understand why the "counting yourself" question is irrelevant.

But Shane's question lingers in Thomas' mind. At what point does a number's increase or decrease matter? Not with the addition of Thomas to the population of the world, of course, nor even the addition of their entire family. How about adding the population of Cotati, the small town in which they live? Still no. The population of the state of California? Well ... still not that much, though it depends on what your purposes are. But California is the most populous state in the US; its numbers seems significant by any reasonable standard. How about the number of people in the United States, does that impinge on the world census? Yes; now it's significant, regardless of why you're counting. But the United States is the third most populous country in the world. It seems the number should start mattering before that.

The issue here is the concept of a *threshold*. A numeric threshold is the point where a change in number becomes meaningful. That is, the point at which a quantitative change becomes a qualitative change.

None of this should be confused, by the way, with *metaphorical quantification*, such as "I'm 90% certain ..." or, "I've told you a million times ..." Or "I'd walk a hundred miles for ..." Or with *spurious quantification*, where numbers are used to imply a clarity and certainty that doesn't exist. (Or to tell an outright lie.) In these uses, the speaker is employing quantitative terms to illuminate something that is actually qualitative. It can be a tool for deception, including self-deception, but it demonstrates how psychologically powerful numbers are for us.

Simple thresholds

Sometimes the threshold is *one*; sometimes the biggest difference is between *nothing* and *something*. For instance, the biggest change in a couple's life may be their first child, the difference between having a child and not having one. Each succeeding child will have less impact. Usually the second child will have significant impact, but will alter its parents' lives less than the first, the third less than the second, the fourth less than the third, and so on. Thomas once met a couple who had recently been written about in the local papers because they had just had their eighteenth child. The father, an out-of-work carpenter, seemed a perky, happy-go-lucky sort, and Thomas got the distinct impression that this most recent baby, the eighteenth, hardly impinged at all on his state of mind, or his existence. He had seventeen already; what was one more? It may have been different for his wife, of course, but Thomas saw that they had worked out a system where the older children took care of the younger ones, and the entirety of the kids formed their own peer group, a small nation of solicitous older brothers and sisters and cared-for younger siblings. Clearly a great group of kids, with the result that, even for the mother, each new birth was on a curve of diminishing significance.

Occasionally we see quiz shows where contestants continue to win money as long as they answer questions correctly, but lose it all with their first wrong response. The positive side of it is they can quit and take the money they have whenever they choose (prior to the next question). Faced with this decision, how would you decide when to risk another question and when to bow out, to take the money and run?

Mathematicians have tried to provide answers to this calculated on the statistical likelihood of answering the next question correctly, by guessing or however, based on some algorithm. (No doubt Marilyn vos Savant could do a masterful job of calculating these factors.) It seems, though, that the issue is not necessarily mathematical. Maybe you should quit when the amount of money you've won will have some significant impact on your life. If you get an answer wrong and lose before that, you haven't lost anything that would change your life, so you shouldn't really care. Any winnings beyond the point of life-altering impact are just gravy, not worth risking the potential life-change you've already won. So, if you're a person of normal income and you've won a million dollars, and you face an even chance of winning a million more or losing it all if you continue—don't continue. The first million will change your life more than the second million would have. Unless, of course, you already have a comfortable income and you're striving toward a specific goal, a goal that you've calculated will cost two million. Starting a business, perhaps. At that point, two million becomes the life-altering number.

Indeterminate thresholds

In a traffic school Thomas once attended, the retired CHP officer teaching the class was asked the quota question. The quota question is, do CHP officers have a certain number of tickets they have to hand out every month, a *quota*, in order to keep their jobs? This is a significant matter for some people, people who get a lot of tickets, since if there is a quota, they can rationalize their infractions by arguing they only got the tickets because the officers were trying to meet quotas. Otherwise, they would not have received tickets for crimes that were minor or non-existent. Meaning they aren't to blame; they aren't bad drivers. They're just victims of the CHP's quota system.

The retired patrolman's answer was, "Well … they don't *call* it a quota. But your basic job as a CHP officer is to give tickets. If you're not doing that, your superiors are going to start asking you questions."

In the interest of fair play for the officers, the point at which superiors start asking questions should be standardized. The superiors should have a number in mind. So that is a quota, isn't it?

But maybe the number is flexible. Maybe circumstances are taken into account. Maybe different supervising officers use different numbers. (To be clear, Thomas knows nothing of the inner workings of the California Highway Patrol; the traffic school officer's comment is his sole source of information.)

It seems that what actually matters is what the patrolling officer *thinks* the quota is. If there is no set number, or at least none that he or she knows of, then the officer may feel more able to use discretion when deciding whether to give a ticket for a marginal offense. Not giving a specific number, then, might mean that in a certain significant sense there isn't a quota. Uncertainty about just what the quota is could affect an officer either way, of course. Not knowing they are above quota, they may decide they better go ahead and give that ticket. Not knowing they are below quota, they may decide not to.

So a CHP officer's quota would be a type of threshold, the type that has an abrupt point of change. Above a certain number of tickets, the officer has met his quota, crossed the threshold. Below that number, he hasn't. Theoretically at least, there is a hinge point, a single number that changes the entire situation. This is a fork in the road, an *either/or*. Whatever ambivalence we may feel about highway patrol officers or quotas, our brains generally understand this sort of bifurcation, brought on by an exact whole number. As drivers, we face a similar threshold, possibly losing our licenses if we get more than a certain number of tickets.

The more difficult type of threshold is one where there does not seem to be an exact number. At some abstract point, a qualitative change begins to occur, but this doesn't seem like an either/or. One quality of the situation, previously dominant, begins to recede, while a quality which had been secondary comes increasingly to prevail. At some maybe intangible point they are exactly equal, then the ascending quality begins to redefine the nature of the situation. Is this imaginary point of equality the threshold? Or is it merely a point within a threshold effect, useless because it can't be precisely specified? This may seem like splitting imaginary hairs: Aren't all thresholds ultimately of the same nature, even if some are harder to define? This can be approached from another angle.

Imagine a circle. A circle is a line that maintains an equal curvature throughout and reconnects with itself at an imaginary point, enclosing an area. This is not the technical definition of a circle. A mathematician would say something like a circle is a plane curve, every point of which is equidistant from a fixed center point. However, we'll use the first definition, since it underlines the quality of equal and continuous curvature.

If you were to divide a circle into smaller and smaller segments, and then observe these segments close up, they would appear more and more straight. This, of course, is why the Earth, our spherical planet, appears to be flat when we experience it on a personal scale. It should be true, however, that no matter how fine you make the divisions, the line segments of a circle retain some curvature, even if too subtle to detect. If the segments could ever be divided until they became completely straight, the totality of them would not necessarily recombine to form a curve. You would have lost your circle.

What this is getting at is that the essential quality of the circle, its curvature, must always be present. There is no threshold where straight line segments start to be curved. The curvature may be imperceptible, but is still there, at the microcosmic and the macrocosmic level.

Shouldn't this apply to everything?

But if we take an object and break it down into subatomic particles, into its most basic entities, where exactly do we find the (metaphorical) curvature? At what point does an innate tendency begin to manifest, and where does it come from in its most basic essence? Why do atoms combine in different ways into different elements?

Again, a different angle:

Laypersons may or may not know much about credit scoring. Thomas worked several years for a company prominent in this industry; the difficulty of explaining to outsiders what they did was a standing joke among employees. Almost two decade into the 21st century, maybe the scoring concept has become more commonplace. Credit scoring will be briefly explained in the next few paragraphs; those already familiar with the idea can skip ahead.

Credit Scoring

At its simplest, credit scoring is a system in which statistical analysis has been used to develop a quick, objective way to decide which would-be borrowers should be granted credit by lenders. These lenders may be banks, credit unions, finance companies, and so on, but we're not talking about loans made by individuals. (You probably won't apply credit scoring algorithms when your friend asks for a loan. Though in some cases maybe you should.)

Presenting this in more detail:

Assume you want a credit card. You apply to some bank, which has you fill out an on-line or hard copy application form. The form asks you various questions, such as *What is your annual income?* The choices presented might be, "under $50,000", "$50,000 to $99,999", "$100,000 to $149,999" and so on. (These application forms sometimes read like multiple choice tests. Please note that the numbers used here are arbitrary; all credit scoring systems are different.) You will probably receive less points for your answer to that question if you select "under $50,000" than if you check off "$50,000 to $99,999." Better yet if you select "$150,000 and over."

When you've finished filling out the form, your application is evaluated: A clerk or a computer program assigns points to each of your answers and adds them all up. If your total is above a certain cut-off point, another threshold, you get the loan or credit card. If your score is below the threshold, you don't.

In the example above, it may seem like the credit score card favors people who are financially better off. We might suppose this is because the scoring system developers assume rich people are more able to repay a debt. This would be a misunderstanding. The score card favors applicants who are similar in their responses to credit receivers who repaid their debts in the past. This might be the more affluent, but the scoring system makes no assumptions. If people who are less well-off have previously been better about repaying—this sometimes happens—the score card will favor them. It is meant to be empirical and purely objective.

Beyond this, however, even if higher income numbers win more points, the scorecard is merely favoring you if you *say* you earn more money. You could be lying about your income; the lender may or may not make any attempt to verify your answers. But ... it's not really that important to the score card how truthful you are. All its algorithms do is compare your answers to those of previous credit seekers. If your answers match up well with previous applicants who turned out to be reliable payers, the system will like you. It is useful to realize that those previous reliable customers could have been lying about their income too. It doesn't matter; they repaid their loans.

(By the way, this is not to advise lying on credit application forms. Or getting traffic tickets.)

The above description of credit scoring is slightly simplified. For example, some answers may result in points being deducted, and different questions may cross relate in complex ways. Still, this is how credit scoring essentially works.

(Or at least it's how it worked when Thomas was employed in the field. He gets the impression that nowadays the scoring algorithms are applied mostly to credit bureau data. All the personal questions, such as do you rent or own your residence? What is your job? How old are you? and so on, have been left behind. Maybe a good thing?)

The Mechanics of Randomness

A crucial point about credit scoring, for our purposes here, is that it doesn't work on individuals. This may sound ridiculous, since it is individuals that it is usually applied to, and Thomas' company truthfully told lenders that they could improve loan portfolio performance by an average of 30%. What is meant, though, is that it is not guaranteed to predict the behavior of any particular person. A scorecard could never tell a bank for certain whether a given credit seeker would actually pay them back. Given a sufficient number of credit applicants, however, again above some threshold, these scoring systems were extremely effective. (*Robust* was the preferred word.) Since group behavior can be predicted even though personal behavior is harder to pin down, it all just meant that the lenders needed to have a certain minimum volume of business for scoring to work for them.

Why does prediction work for groups, but not so well for specific individuals? It seems that every person must possess, at some level, the same traits as the group. If not, the total individual behaviors would not add up to predictable group behavior.

As with the curvature of the line segments of a circle, the essential characteristic should always be present. The psychological has to be implicit in the sociological.

To put it another way, the tendency to repay or not repay your loans actually should be predictable on an individual basis. It appears not to be, because in any given case, random, unaccounted-for factors may override the prediction system's essential accuracy. With a large enough number of applicants, however, these random elements cancel each other out, and the applicants' shared traits will dominate the picture. The scoring system's predictions become meaningful.

Compare this to something accepted as completely random, like flipping a coin. An honest coin will come up heads roughly half the time, and tails half the time, because it has no innate tendency to do one more than the other. Metaphorically, the line segments here, the individual flips, have no curvature. The inability to guarantee the result of a specific coin flip is absolute. Still, if you flip the coin a large number of times, you will have a predictable outcome: about the same number of heads and tails will turn up. This predictability increases as the number of flips increases. Viewed as a general principle, it seems as though probability takes on weight, or inertia, as the number of individual cases goes up.

The point that nagged Thomas is, with both coin-flipping and credit scoring, a sufficient number (of flips or credit applicants) will reveal a predictable pattern. So are coin flipping and credit scoring strictly comparable? No. They are different in a profound way. Coin-flipping merely demonstrates the mechanics of randomness; other than sheer neutrality, no intrinsic quality of coins or coin-flipping is revealed. With credit scoring, on the other hand, the predictable pattern that emerges would seem to be the result of individual traits writ large. Humans are not random and neutral, even if the butterfly effect of their personal behavior is too complicated to extrapolate on an individual basis. Extending the earlier metaphor, individual credit users, unlike coin flips, *do* have curvature.

Self-organization

The idea that behavior can be predicted for groups but not for individuals is reminiscent of what physicists tell us about matter. The movement of an individual atom is not foreseeable. It may go left, right, up, down, or off in any random direction. Get enough atoms together, however, and their motion becomes very predictable: a flung stone will move in a parabola in a gravitational field, a falling object will accelerate at a rate of 32 feet per second every second at the Earth's surface, and so on. Since increasing the number of individual units increases predictability, the tendency is especially marked with matter because of the enormous number of atoms even in small objects.

The fact is that the tendency to self-organize apparently manifests any time a sufficiently large number of individual units comes together in an aggregate.

This principle of self-organization through clustering is true with coarse material reality. The laws of physics and engineering (patterns observed repeatedly and explained by theories) attest to this. On the smallest scale, individual atoms are so random, their behavior so incomprehensible, that we can grasp them only through the counter-intuitive processes of quantum theory. At this tiny level, gravity, a highly organizing force, is weak to the point of being meaningless. But increase size, increase mass, and gravity becomes significant. At the macrocosmic level, gravity is the most powerful force in the universe.

The principle of self-organization is true of human behavior. People thrown together randomly, say on a desert island after a shipwreck, will begin to self-organize. Leaders will emerge, individuals will be assigned roles, etc. If you doubt this, consider that the history of our species on this planet is basically the story of groups of people self-organizing for survival. Don't be misled by *Lord of the Flies*. If Golding's metaphor was accurate, we never would have socially evolved to be where we are today.

Whether this self-organizing principle needs to be explained by something like divine intention, or is just intrinsically logical and requires no further rationale, is another question. Thomas was satisfied to conclude that groups of any type tend to self-organize as the number of their individual components increases, and this tendency is a basic ordering principle of reality. That's probably grandiose enough.

⁎
⁎⁎

Part 7

Living the Dream, Dreaming the Life

Q famous optical illusion presents an image that can be interpreted as either a rabbit or a duck. In its essential form, the image consists of a circle with a dot in the center, and two parallel stretched ovals extending horizontally from one side of the circle, usually in contact with each other. The dot in the center reads as the eye of an animal's head in profile, and the two horizontal elongations are either the ears of a rabbit or the slightly parted beak of a duck. If we see a rabbit, it appears to be facing in one direction; if we see a duck, it faces the opposite way.

This illusion has been rendered many times, in various styles. The reversibility effect generally works best if the depiction is something of a cartoon or an abstraction, not too naturalistic, but some surprisingly detailed images have been successful. Versions exist in which the entire body of the duck/rabbit is shown, rather than just the head, and there are even variations in which the duck's beak and the rabbit's ears are both independently present, so you see sort of a billed rabbit or a long-eared duck. There is at least one children's book based on this illusion.

(Some sources contend that duck/rabbit is not a true illusion, but an "ambiguous" image because it is reversible or "bistable," allowing two different valid interpretations. From a layperson's point of view, the distinction doesn't seem significant. Aren't all optical illusions capable of being taken more than one way?)

Duck/rabbit has been around since the nineteenth century and still hasn't worn out its welcome; recent discussions of it can be found on the Internet. When Thomas first saw the illusion in a book many years before, the accompanying article said that a modern, urbanized human can see the image as either a rabbit or a duck, but not both simultaneously. A primitive person, the article claimed, could see both animals at once, not switching back and forth, but mentally accommodating the paradox. In other words, for a modern, civilized human the duck/rabbit has reversibility, while for a primitive individual the image has simultaneity.

Thomas' first thought on reading this was, how do they know? Can the authors, or whoever's research they're relying on, really tell what is going on in another individual's mind? Especially when the point is so subtle, and there would presumably be a cultural barrier. A modern researcher and a primitive tribesman may not even share the same language ... and Thomas had the underlying suspicion that the idea that the image had simultaneity for a primitive was based on our recurring attraction to the concept of a noble savage, a person who retains perceptual and intuitive qualities we have lost.

Then he realized something that reduced his skepticism.

When Thomas is awake, he is no more able to simultaneously see the rabbit and the duck than any other ostensibly modern human. When he is asleep, however, when he dreams, the restraints of waking life perception no longer apply. Not to say that he has seen this particular image, the rabbit/duck, in his dreams. He has not. But he has experienced many dreams in which he perceived diverse entities as a single, unified image.

Thomas has dreamed that he stood in a room whose perimeter, the line where wall met floor a few feet away, was also the much more distant chalk line marking the edge of a football field, which he stood in the middle of. The corner of the room was also the corner of the end zone—he was at once indoors and outdoors.

In another dream, he was speaking with a woman who was three different women that he knew, their physical selves and their personality traits blending seamlessly. The effect even works for time and place: Thomas is simultaneously old and young, a teenager and a sixty-year-old; he is sitting in a building that is the student center of a college he attended, and is also a meeting room for a company he worked for, and is also the unit on which he worked in a hospital, and at the same time is a lobby in the mental institution where his brother Terry was a patient. (For Terry, Thomas suspects, all experience had the incoherency of a dream.) In some dreams Thomas will even wonder why he is still living at home with his parents in middle age, puzzled because he knows that he moved out as a teenager.

Thomas has had these sorts of dreams again and again. The multiplicity aspect is as common as other, more mundane quirks of his dreams, such as the fact that it is always twilight, or that colors are preternaturally lush. In one dream, he was standing in a room in some sort of institutional building, perhaps the mental hospital where Terry was a patient. Circumstances were unclear, but he had a vague sense that he might have been the inmate (the "client"), rather than his brother. He looked out through the window at a tree silhouetted against a twilit sky. The tree's branches were lushly leaved, but as he watched, the tree shook as in a breeze, and the leaves became stars that fell and lay shining on the ground. They were leaves and stars both.

All in all, Thomas thinks it would be accurate to say that, when dreaming, he rarely perceives anything as a single entity. Almost everything is multiple; streets are rivers, and objects are both far away and near. (The height-within-a-field-of-vision factor discussed in *Ideology and the Real World*—a way to judge distance when other cues are missing—doesn't seem to apply in dreamland.) In fact, upon further consideration, he realized the eternal twilight that his dreams occur in is actually a blending of day and night.

* * *

To link these surreal impressions with the rabbit/duck illusion, Thomas needed to assume two premises:

First, that the simultaneity effect in dreams is true not just for him, but for most people.

Second, that the mental state of dreaming is a reversion to the mindset of a primitive person, perhaps almost to the consciousness of an animal.

On the first point, Thomas has asked various people if they experience simultaneity in dreams. Most readily say they do, sometimes even with comments like, Isn't that the nature of dreams?

One woman said that while she was speaking in a dream to a friend, the friend became someone else— then she realized that the friend had been someone else all along. Thomas wasn't sure whether to count that one as simultaneity or reversibility, but overall his respondents reported simultaneity in a dreaming state. This isn't hard science, of course, but it was sufficient encouragement for Thomas to continue.

What about the second condition? Does dreaming correspond to a pre-civilized mind state? This is harder to establish, and Thomas was willing to admit that the idea was based mainly on intuition. When he watches how animals behave, however, reflexive whole body movements that seem too quick and random for conscious thought, it reminds him of how he himself seemed to behave in a dream. He acts and sometimes speaks with very little conscious volition, almost as though his body is thinking for him. For example, during a phase of his life when he was deeply involved with martial arts, he would sometimes abruptly lash out with his actual, physical arm while asleep, blocking the attack of a dream opponent. Conscious volition was not involved. (This did not go over well with his wife, sleeping next to him.)

So, behavior in dreams has a sort of semi-automatic quality. Conscious, rational thought is rare, if not entirely absent. Emotions are more intense; fear is overwhelming, lust is convulsive, happiness seems total. At the same time, events may also seem distant or detached. There is a kind of fatalism; you know you're not in control, and that seems natural ... in contrast to the focused, self-directing egos we experience while awake. (Sometimes in a dream Thomas' mind will begin to think in an increasingly conscious and purposeful manner. This always signals that he is starting to awaken. At that moment he often makes a brief, useless attempt to stay asleep, to maintain the dream.)

Freud said that modern man is not capable of experiencing the intensity of instinctual pleasure that a primitive feels. We have given away pleasure and intensity for the control, clarity, and stability of rational lives. Again, Thomas was tempted to be skeptical. How does Freud know what primitives feel? How do you quantify pleasure? But again, his skepticism faded. He decided Freud was right, not only because he can interpret this linking of instinctual pleasure and the primitive mind with the dream state, but because it seems intuitively true.

Intuition has been mentioned more than once here; where do intuitive impressions come from? Thomas decides they are echoes from childhood. We weren't born civilized after all, we had to grow into that state. We begin as animals. Our very earliest memories, when we must have had something like the mindset of primitives, seem very much like our dreams.

The process of growing up, then, can be read as a gradual awakening from the dream of childhood to the conscious wakefulness of adulthood. Similarly, our species' millennia-long journey from savagery to civilization could be conceptualized as a progressive awakening of our collective consciousness.

We become rational, clear, consciously directed, but we can't see both the rabbit and the duck.

* * *

A few afterthoughts

First:

Dreams often present narratives, or at least fragments of narratives. A way to think about dreams is to consider them in contrast to formal narrative structures: movies, novels, documentaries, histories, biographies, and so on. None but the most surreal of these conscious narratives approach the randomness and back-handed playfulness of dreams. In fact, our dreams probably become more coherent than they actually are when we attempt to recount them in the morning. Not necessarily because we intentionally organize them, though sometimes this happens, but because our conscious minds are groping to make sense of something that was experienced by a different aspect of our selves.

Part of the nature of formal narratives is their method of presentation. Different forms of presentation affect us in different ways. For example, an effect you get from a movie, even when you're powerfully drawn into it, is that it is always separate from you. The movie is happening on a screen, some distance away physically. The movie and yourself have a subject/object relationship. The price of the sensory fulfillment gotten from a movie, in the form of visual and aural stimulation, is its separateness from the viewer.

Contrast this with written fiction. Compared to movies, novels have almost no direct sensory aspect. (*Almost* none, because the cover, the typeface, the quality of the paper, and the heft of the book may subtly affect the tone of our reading experience.) The cryptic marks on the page, letters and words, have little intrinsic sensory effect. Only when the reader's mind recreates meaning from the author's words does significance emerge. All stories and ideas communicated by writing have to be recreated in the mind of the reader. This means that when you read a novel, for example, it is literally happening inside your head. This gives it an intimacy that other forms of fiction don't achieve. And the story you read is unique to you, because you construct it in your unique mind; it is never exactly the same story the author wrote, nor exactly the same story that anyone else reads.

How does this relate to dreams? It seems that in a dream both the sensory experience of a movie and the intimacy of a novel can be achieved. How exactly this happens is not clear. The dream imposes itself upon you intimately—it is happening inside your head—even as you see and hear apparent external entities.

Sometimes you may even have dreams where you experience the dream narrative both in first and third person. You see yourself in the dream and you also *are* yourself in the dream—the subject/object relationship is erased. This particular bi-stability was most common in Thomas' dreams as a child, and has faded with adulthood. Perhaps unfortunately.

(One aspect of movies is their presentation on screen of an actor, young, vital and attractive, who has long since passed away. The effect is like looking at the light from a distant star that went nova and burned out eons ago. The light is just now reaching us. The juxtaposition of known facts that are contrary to what we are seeing has a haunting effect. And the dual nature of the person we see on the screen, who exists both as a character in a story and as a person in real life, is both intriguing and subtly disturbing, even when the actor is still alive and not much older. In a dream about people we knew that have died—such dreams are apparently common—this poses no paradox to our dreaming selves. Even if we vaguely remember that the individual we are speaking with has died, their presence isn't questioned: They are alive in our minds, and they are alive in our dreams.)

Second afterthought:

An unrelated theory Thomas had about dreams is that the intense, darkly glowing environment and semi-zombie state he experiences while dreaming are a glimmer of the reality in which we exist before life and after death. (This is not meant to advocate religion. It is only a speculation.) Thomas has no empirical support for this idea. It is entirely intuitive, a reaction to the strangeness, sense of wonder, and the felt but unspecified deep meaning that this "place," the dream space, seems to hold.

***

Part 8

Chaos Theory in a Tokyo Bar

Encounter in a Bar

Tokyo, Japan: August, 1967

*T*homas is sitting at a table in the shadowy back room of a bar in Tokyo. With him is an American girl named Luana. Or maybe her name is Lu Ann—her mother calls her that—but she prefers Luana. Thomas is guessing she thinks it's sexier.

Thomas is relatively new here, arrived from California earlier this summer. Luana, on the other hand, has been in-country with her family for the last three years, and is about to return to the states. Her step-father, a US Air Force sergeant assigned to Tachikawa, has reached the end of his tour of duty; Luana and her family fly out tomorrow.

Thomas is aware that this may be the last time he sees Luana, so he is letting time drift by, in no hurry to leave. They have been in the bar a few hours, drinking and talking on random subjects. At their age neither of them could enter a bar in the US ... but drinking age doesn't seem to matter here. Other local Americans have told Thomas that if you can reach up high enough to lay your money on the counter, the bartender will serve you. They've been served: whiskey-and-cokes and sloe gin fizzes, favorites of Luana after three years in-country.

The bar is not crowded. The other denizens, all Japanese, keep to themselves.

* * *

Thomas' father is also in the Air Force and stationed at Tachikawa; Thomas' family lives in Kanto Mura, a military residential enclave in the suburbs of Tokyo. Thomas met Luana because his family and Luana's live on the same court.

Thomas doesn't normally live at home; he's spending the summer with his family now because of a congenial policy of the military: Since he attends college in the states, is the son of a serviceman stationed in a foreign country, and is below a certain age, he can get a free ride from Uncle Sam to visit his family during summer vacation. He flew here "space available": He presented himself at a designated stateside air base with the proper paperwork and waited around for a spare seat on a plane going where he wanted to go. "Space available" is similar to what civilian airlines call "standby," except Thomas didn't have to pay for it. It didn't cost the taxpayers much, either. Thomas had the lowest possible priority; the only seat he could get was one that wasn't going to be used by anyone else. So, having finished his second year of college in California, Thomas is spending the summer in Japan.

He is enjoying his stay in Tokyo, and he's already learned a little. For example:

1) If you ride a train in Japan, the amount of money you give the gate attendant for fare will either be short—in which case he'll gesture for more—or it will be exactly right. No change is ever returned. (Among other excursions, Luana and Thomas made a day trip to Yokohama)

2) The habitual smiling and giggling of the uniformed department store girls is meant in a friendly way. Luana

assures Thomas that he wasn't really being laughed at for his gauche manner.

3) Summer in Tokyo is extremely hot and humid. The minute you step outside, your clothing wilts to your body and becomes semi-transparent. The local Americans run their air conditioners at full power all summer; the Japanese not so much.

4) Thomas has been told that, in stark contrast to the summer heat, the winter snow in Tokyo will be knee deep. Worst of all, apparently, is the Fall monsoon season: Vehicles have to be parked underground or in enclosed areas; in an open parking lot the hurricane-force winds will send cars sliding across the asphalt.

5) Public necking of the type indulged in by American teenagers is frowned upon here. (This is somewhat ironic coming from Luana, who seems to have no qualms about necking with Thomas, wherever they are.)

And of course, Thomas has become familiar with the flexibility about drinking age.

* * *

The room Thomas and Luana are in is separated from the front room of the bar by a wide doorway semi-opaqued by a beaded curtain. Through this curtain now walks a young American in US Army uniform. He is not physically impressive: short, somewhat soft looking, blond crewcut, boyish countenance.

He stops before Thomas' and Luana's table and stares transfixed at Luana.

"Pardon me," he says in what Thomas take to be a rural accent, "but you're the first round-eyed woman I've seen in thirteen months. Can I just *look* at you?"

Luana looks back at him with kind of a wrinkle-nosed frown, then turns to Thomas with an expression that says, Where'd they find *this* guy? One part of her reaction might be the unconsidered racism of the soldier's remarks. Luana disapproves of racism. (Thomas does too.)

"I just got in from Korea," the soldier says. "I haven't talked with a civilian in over a year."

Thomas is not sure how to take him, especially the 'round-eyed woman' remark, but he seems kind of innocent ... without malice. After a moment, Thomas mentally shrugs and invites him to join them. The young soldier sits down at their table and un-self-consciously tells them about himself. He is on R & R (rest and recreation) from an assignment in South Korea, patrolling along the border with the North. A lot of American soldiers are on R & R in Japan at this time, most of them from Vietnam.

"They're shooting at us every day," he says, speaking of Korea. "It's the same as being in a combat zone. The Korean War never ended."

Further conversation reveals that he is a buck private, nineteen years old—of an age with Thomas and Luana—and his father is a Lieutenant-Colonel in the Air Force. He isn't a draftee; he's in the army because he enlisted.

Thomas asks why he joined the Army when his old man is in the Air Force. For a variety of reasons, maybe including which branch his own father is in, Thomas thinks the Air Force is the better deal.

No, the soldier says, it was the Army he wanted. And just recently he has put in for duty in Vietnam. "I want to be where the action is," he tells them.

* * *

While in Japan Thomas has met several military men, mostly in the Army or the Air Force, on R & R from Vietnam. Back in California the same-age males Thomas knew were usually civilians, college guys with student deferments. Thomas had run into a few soldiers in the states, though, and the stories they told were as strange as the ones he heard in Japan. Strange to Thomas, at least, raised in an old military family. Thomas personally had no desire to be in the military, and he wasn't, but he had certain ideas about how soldiers behaved.

For example, Thomas assumed that when a GI receives an order that bothers him, he doesn't react by pointing his loaded rifle at his superior and saying, "Get out of my way before I shoot you, you son of a bitch." One soldier Thomas met in Tokyo told him he had done exactly that. (Thomas guessed that he was a draftee, not a volunteer.) Expecting the soldier would have faced a court-martial if not a firing squad, Thomas asked him how his superiors had responded. The soldier said they took away his stripe—again. He had lost it before; he expected he would gain it back and lose it again. Military family aside, Thomas was glad that demotion was the extent of the soldier's chastisement. Under a somewhat tense and faintly angry manner, he seemed a decent enough fellow. Thomas didn't think he would really have fired on his superior.

A soldier Thomas had encountered in California, an amiable young black man, told him he was on furlough. He was due back with his outfit on a certain date, but had decided he would show up a couple of weeks late. When Thomas looked surprised, he smiled and shook his head. "They won't do nothin'," he said.

Thomas can recount more stories in the same vein. Of course, this is mild compared to what he'd read about in the news, such as the practice of fragging unpopular or distrusted officers. And these were the people who had volunteered for service or been unable to escape the draft. On the other side of the situation was a larger number of young men who had avoided military service entirely: by pursuing higher education (the colleges were so packed during these years it was practically impossible for a student to get into all the required courses), getting married and fathering a child, going underground in the US, or leaving the country. Many went to Canada, some to Mexico, a few to more exotic locations. And some simply never got called.

In short, Tom Brokaw was not about to nominate Thomas' demographic as "the greatest generation."

* * *

World War II and the Vietnam War were about one generation apart. Thomas' father fought in World War II; many of Thomas' cohorts fought in the Vietnam War. What was the difference between Vietnam-war youth and "the greatest generation"? Basic human nature probably hasn't changed much in recorded history; it certainly doesn't change from one generation to the next. Circumstances change however, and maybe Thomas' generation just changed with them. Thomas suspects that, like their fathers, his generation merely reacted in the way that seemed most reasonable at the time. For many of them, Lyndon Johnson's decision to go to war in Vietnam looked like a political expedient, a move that had little or nothing to do with the basic survival of their country. Why die or be maimed for so ephemeral a reason?

Thomas and Luana's new-found friend in the bar is coming from another direction, however. For him, it is probably about patriotism, maybe about proving something ... and he wants to be where the action is.

Thomas recalls reading in an article that in Israel, members of the military come from either the lower, less entitled class, young men who can't find good jobs, or they come from old, traditionally military families. Of course this latter group expects to enter the officer caste.

Thomas figures it probably works roughly the same way in the US. His own family would fit into the traditional military class, while at first he would have guessed the private in the bar would come from the rural working class. This assessment is based on his way of speaking, his general manner, and the tackiness of the "round-eyed woman" remark. The young soldier doesn't project confidence, but he doesn't seem afraid of anything either. His manner seems mild and unpretentious, no attempt at machismo. Thomas thinks it significant that he is the son of an officer. Is he trying to demonstrate something to his father? Thomas guesses he also is doing what seems reasonable to him at the time.

Thomas has a bad feeling when he thinks about the soldier going to Vietnam. Thomas' intuition is that he won't survive. And Thomas doesn't get the impression that the young man has ever really considered America's decision to go to war in Vietnam.

Going to war

How does the general public decide how it feels about entering another war? Thomas wonders. He knows that some will be eager to fight no matter what, and will consider it their patriotic duty to support any conflict. They will view as traitors anyone who suggests that a war right now might not be in the country's best interest. Another group, pacifists, will oppose any war. They think nothing justifies the death, the maiming, the relentless cruelty and destruction. They would confront an aggressive invader with Gandhian non-violence.

These two groups aside, most people will try to be rational in deciding what the nation should do. Some scenarios may make the decision obvious: We are being invaded by a belligerent enemy that has already swallowed other countries and treated hostage civilian populations in a bestial manner—atrocities abound. (World War II-era Germany and Japan come to mind.) In this case, pacifism is not an option; non-violent resistance is very unlikely to work. In India, Gandhi's followers lay on the train tracks to disrupt the British. What would have happened if the German Jews had tried that tactic against the Nazis? The efficacy of such a move is very dubious. Facing enemies such as we confronted in the second world war, we clearly needed to fight.

Conversely, suppose our government proposes to invade an apparently non-aggressive foreign power that we don't exactly trust; we're considering a pre-emptive strike. Here the situation seems as clear as with the ferocious aggressor, but with the opposite conclusion: We should *not* fight.

In between these two extremes, the issue becomes cloudy, and it is difficult to devise a formula that gives military action a precise and consistent entry point. And no decision at all, letting the matter slide, is a de facto decision. So we must decide something, to avoid paralysis. In a game of pool, you have to make that initial shot that cracks the balls apart, even though you have no idea how they will scatter. We feel a need to do the same thing in life. We want to get things moving.

But ... we're talking about a proposition that will almost certainly lead to death, maiming, personal pain and horror (barring immediate full surrender by one side or the other). "Getting things moving" is not a compelling basis for action.

A factor that Thomas thinks muddles the issue is that, as a species we have a need to be more sure of our conclusions than the situation often allows. We find it very difficult to abide inaction, and we admire decisiveness: It's "manly," even when the decisiveness is forced, and may be contrary to an optimal outcome. So we contrive within ourselves a spurious certainty, and act on that. But why is a purely rational course so hard to set?

Chaos Theory

Part of the problem seems to be that, consciously or otherwise, we think we live in a "clockwork universe." In a clockwork, or deterministic, world, we would be able to predict with perfect accuracy the outcome of current events, if we could specify initial conditions precisely and completely. Chaos theory denies this.

Chaos theory says that in any system of significant complexity, a minute change in initial conditions can completely alter the outcome of a process. This is true even when the process is deterministic—subject to known rules of behavior—rather than random. In bare essence, this is because in a complex system the number of variables, and the number of possible interactions between those variables, quickly propagate toward infinity. This is popularly referred to as "the butterfly effect," the illustrative idea being that a butterfly flaps its wings in Brazil, leading to a series of unforeseen climatic interactions, that ultimately result in a tornado in Texas.

And even if we had a supercomputer that could track an astronomical number of divergent vectors, we still couldn't make a reliable prediction any distance into the future: We can never exactly determine initial conditions. Partly this is because of the number of variables, and partly because initial events never are exactly initial; they're always the continuation of an endless chain of previous, intertwined events. How far back do you have to look, to find a true starting point? And even trying to specify conditions at finer than a certain level of precision is not possible. The act of attempted measurement itself alters the conditions being measured (to bring in quantum mechanics). Finally, even if the above problems could be somehow gotten around, time is always passing; circumstances are always changing even as we try to determine them. The world doesn't hold still for our calculations.

A war of any magnitude is a supreme demonstration of chaos theory. Too many complications will always be present for us to be completely confident of the outcome.

The lessons of war

The cliché is that the military is always fighting the last war. They've analyzed it exhaustively, have learned all of its lessons (maybe), and will now apply that knowledge to the next conflict. Where it may not apply.

In a similar manner, Thomas suspects that the public, when faced with the prospect of war, decides whether it is warranted by reacting to the previous war. Unwilling to admit our lack of certainty, but unable to predict the future to any meaningful degree, we fall back on what we think was learned from the last war. Then we develop reasons to support our decision. And eventually we will emphasize some facts, forget others, and subtly alter secondary attitudes to fit our primary premises. We need to "consistify" our thinking.

Consider again World War II: England and its allies initially gave way to Hitler, a decision made poignant by Chamberlain's "peace in our time" statement. Hitler exploited his opportunity and the lesson learned was that we have to face our wars; there's no begging off. If we don't go after the enemy, the enemy will come after us, and we'll then be in a worse position to deal with him.

The lesson from the Vietnam War is different. We were told that if we didn't take a stand in Indochina there would be a domino effect; the enemy would be landing on our shores in a generation. If we had won in Vietnam, war advocates could maintain this theory forever. When anyone argued that we needn't have gone into combat, war supporters could list the dark events that would have befallen us, and the world, if we had not fought.

We lost in Vietnam, however, never mind that the South didn't collapse until after we left. We didn't win. And what effect did this have on our lives? For the 58,000 Americans who died there, and for their families, the effect was huge. But how about for our society in general? If a Vietnam War-era American were to be transported via time machine a decade or so into the future, there would be nothing to tell him how the war had turned out. He could look it up in a history book, of course, but the point is the whole business in Vietnam doesn't seem to have made any real difference in how we live. Our day-to-day lives are untouched. So why did we fight there?

Maybe because we can't really process a situation of such complexity, and we can't see or admit this inability.

If the lesson of the World War II is that wars must be fought, the lesson of Vietnam is that at least some wars *don't* need to be fought.

Which lesson will we apply to future conflicts?

* * *

Thinking about chaos theory, Thomas had momentarily flashed on quantum mechanics. It was only a vagrant thought, but now he wonders if there could be some connection: Chaos theory as a macro version of quantum mechanics, perhaps? He mentally shrugs. He doesn't have the mathematics to seriously assess such an idea, but he finds it interesting as a jumping off point.

In the quantum world, he remembers, an event or a state could simultaneously be both true and not true.

Until you opened the box and looked, it is not just that it is unknown whether Schrodinger's cat was dead or alive, it is that the cat, in a sense, is both. Sometimes this is explained in terms of alternate dimensions. Thomas has usually dismissed that as an attempt to actualize a concept that was more mathematical than tangible. But now he wonders, what if history did in fact follow more than one path? Thomas considers his own life. Suppose he had not obtained a student deferment, or suppose he had even volunteered? He remembered he had almost done that, standing outside the Navy recruiting office for a long time while he pondered his options. Suppose some other version of himself had ended up in the war in Vietnam and had died there? The Thomas now sitting in a bar in Tokyo is maybe not even the most real. A mere ghost of the dead Thomas.

It isn't just combat death, he realizes. There are many ways to die. With a certain morbid fascination, Thomas considers his past, looking for possibly fatal moments, points in time where some alternative version of himself *had* died …

✳✳

Encounter in the Ocean

Northern California coast: Ten years before Thomas'
summer in Tokyo

Thomas remembers an event that occurred about a year after his family had moved from Florida to Marin county, in the San Francisco bay area.

At age ten, Thomas has long been used to the white sandy beaches and clear waters of the Gulf of Mexico. He and his parents and brothers look dubiously at the grassy hills, sandy cliffs and twisted trees of the northern California coast. They aren't indifferent to the gnarled beauty and diversity of plant life in places like the Point Reyes National Seashore, but it doesn't really seem like you'd come here to *swim*. Hike, maybe. Walk along the beach and lose yourself gazing out over the endless vista of the Pacific. But the waters don't invite you in. They're silty, not clear. And they're cold. And the waters off the Northern California coast are reputedly a breeding ground for great white sharks.

Nevertheless, Thomas' father, a strong swimmer, a former Daytona Beach lifeguard, and a beach addict since boyhood, forces the family to come along whenever he feels moved to drive out to the coast. Maybe the waters will get more welcoming if they keep checking them. Today they are on one of their visits to the ocean.

For some reason, Thomas has separated himself from his family by walking over a ridge of dunes and finding his own private bay. From the beach he sees that this small bay, technically a cove, perhaps, connects to a larger bay; beyond that Thomas can see the open ocean. The waves are mild, only a slight chop. The cove is totally empty of people or any human sign except, far out in the water, a buoy.

Thomas had learned to swim in Florida, coerced mercilessly by his father, but he's not a very good swimmer. His style is a clumsy flailing, head and shoulders high out of the water, splashing ferociously with his arms while his legs kick in a random, disconnected manner. Despite his awkwardness Thomas can swim a fairly long distance, presumably due to low body mass, youthful vitality, and the fitness that comes from constantly playing outdoors. His rough style makes him unpopular in swimming pools, but he doesn't much like them anyway. Thomas prefers the vast ocean, where the salty smell, the endless stretch of sea and sky, give him a heightened awareness. It is a feeling made up of both fear and fascination.

Thomas tends to take this feeling as a challenge. He usually sets a goal of swimming a certain distance, either along the shore or to some point out in the ocean, if a stable point can be found. In this case, the buoy offers an obvious target. He has achieved this sort of goal in the past (he hasn't drowned yet) by turning off his mind to any doubt or hesitation. He doesn't allow himself to consider anything except the next stroke of his arm. Thomas compensates for his deficiencies as a swimmer with narrowly focused, blind determination. Afterwards, he always returns to the shore exhausted but elated.

Thomas wades out as far as he can, shivering slightly as his body acclimates to the water. When he reaches the farthest point where he can still stand on the bottom, he steels himself for a moment, then plunges ahead, thrashing energetically. He tries to keep his eyes fixed on the distant buoy through the low waves.

He swims about fifty feet. It's going well; he's not tired yet, no feeling of a chill, then—Thomas hits something. His knee slams into a solid, massive object, a foot or two beneath the surface.

The impact stops Thomas dead in the water. Whatever he has hit is not harsh and rocky, the surface might have very faint give to it, but the overall mass didn't move at all. Thomas wonders if he has hit a sandbar. He tries to peer down through the surface, but it's impenetrable. He treads water for a minute, then turns in a slow circle, feeling for an object: nothing. He takes a breath and ducks under. Visibility is not good, a dozen feet or less, but he can see there is no sandbar, nothing in the water in any direction. He can dimly make out the rippled pattern of the bottom, about ten feet down, far too deep for any contact.

Thomas comes up for air, completely baffled. What did he hit? Where did it go?

A flurry of thoughts rushes through his head, mostly ominous, but he pushes them aside without really acknowledging them. Thomas' self-programming re-asserts itself: swim, don't think, don't reconsider; just keep swimming.

He swims. The buoy draws closer. However, it's becoming more and more difficult to keep from thinking about the large, unseen object he had struck. A piece of driftwood? Would driftwood float below the surface? Where did it go so quickly? The thought he's trying to avoid is becoming inescapable: the large *something* he'd hit was something alive. Surprised perhaps, it had fled. Thomas' leg, jack-knifing forward in a jerky motion never executed by more accomplished swimmers, had struck some large living creature with enough suddenness to startle it into fleeing. Even at age ten, Thomas has heard that sometimes you can drive off a large animal, an animal that could easily dominate you, by surprising it. Striking it amounts to a sort of physical bluff. Maybe that is what had just happened. But will it come back?

Thomas is only about ten feet away from the buoy now. He pauses, treading water again, for some reason afraid to make the final distance. One part of his mind says he's come this far, he may as well go ahead and touch the buoy, perform the victory gesture he was planning. But another part of his mind is picturing a ring of sharks circling a few feet below the buoy. Somehow Thomas' hand on the buoy will be their signal to break formation and surge toward him. This is completely illogical. If they're there, and they're going to attack, they wouldn't care about his symbolic hand on the buoy. But something in ten-year-old Thomas' unconscious links the mild egotism of this gesture of triumph with an ensuing punishment for hubris.

Fear takes over. Thomas turns away from the untouched buoy and heads back toward the distant beach. He knows that he can't out swim any pursuing sea creature, so he counsels himself to go slowly, conserve his strength and not draw attention. He succeeds only partially. Almost against his will his hands flash more and more quickly through the water ahead. The distant beach looks tiny, impossibly far away. Thomas can't see through the sea's reflective surface at all; most of his own body is invisible to him.

Thomas would be unable to see something even inches away from his unprotected legs and nether regions. Anything could be below the opaque, gray-green surface.

Now Thomas is thinking not just of sharks, but of every frightening aquatic beast he's ever seen in a science book: He pictures barracuda, sturgeons (freshwater fish, do they even attack humans?), giant squid, saltwater crocodiles. In his mind he sees dunkleosteus, the size of a bus and 350 million years extinct. He fantasizes the huge, anvil-like head staring wide-eyed at him through the silty water. He swims faster and faster.

Thomas finally reaches the shore. He wades out of the water and lies on the beach, panting harshly. He gazes back for a while at the serene and enigmatic ocean. Now that he's safe, anger combines with fear. *What* ... he asks himself in a moment of atypical youthful profanity ... *What the hell was it?*

Later, Thomas will be angry with himself for not touching the buoy. Later yet, looking back on it several years on and from the perspective of the Tokyo bar, Thomas wonders why he didn't immediately turn back to the beach the moment he collided with the creature. Something was in the water with him, quite possibly something dangerous: Turn back! But then he wonders, why does anyone do anything that threatens their survival? Or, at least, take a risk for no real reason. Yet it seems to Thomas that he has often taken such risks.

Thomas remembers another irrational and possibly fatal moment ...

*
**

Breaching the Perimeter

On the autobahn, in Germany: Five years before Tokyo

During the three years Thomas' father served at Ramstein, Thomas attended schools run by the US military for the dependents of servicemen. (Germany was one of the assignments where families were permitted to accompany US servicemen, unlike, for example, Korea.) Thomas went through eighth and ninth grades at Ramstein Junior High, but Ramstein had no high school, so he and his classmates had to be bussed to Kaiserslautern American High School, at a nearby US Army post, for their sophomore year. The school was referred to by its students as "K-town," a label Thomas never liked since it struck him as some lame attempt to make a name from a foreign culture comfortable and familiar, to "Americanize" something that wasn't American. Kind of like referring to your Hispanic friend Carlos as "Charlie," Thomas thought. He stubbornly stuck to calling the school Kaiserslautern, or KAHS.

A worse problem with KAHS was that living on one military base in a foreign country, while attending school at another, made life awkward for Thomas and his friends when they skipped class. How did they get back to base housing in Ramstein at the end of their skip? They solved the problem straightforwardly. They walked the several kilometers along the autobahn from Kaiserslautern to Ramstein. This was a less than perfect solution, for a couple of reasons:

First, walking on the autobahn in Germany is no more legal than walking on the freeway in the US. On the occasion of one skip, two friends and Thomas were walking along the autobahn toward Ramstein when they heard a vehicle pull up behind them. They turned to see a Mercedes Benz police car with two *polizei*, German policemen, inside. (All the polizei Thomas saw in Germany drove either Mercedes Benzs or Volkswagens.) The polizei asked the American teenagers where their vehicle had broken down. Thomas and company explained that they had no vehicle; they were simply walking home. The officers informed them that it was forbidden, "verboten," to walk on the autobahn. Not knowing what to say, the Americans didn't say anything. The German officers thought it over for a minute, then told them to get in the car. They drove Thomas and his friends to the nearest offramp and let them out, with a quite civil admonition not to walk on the autobahn again.

(A few years later, apparently having learned nothing from the previous experience, Thomas was walking alone at night along Highway 101 in Northern California. A black-and-white carrying two CHP officers pulled over, and the officers asked for his ID. Thomas showed them his military dependent ID, not having a driver's a license yet, and tried to tell them that he had lived in foreign countries a lot, and wasn't familiar with California law. They considered it for a minute, then told him that, well-traveled teenager or not, he was old enough to know better than to walk on the freeway. If they caught him again, they said, they would give him a ticket. Then they drove off. Thomas appreciated that they didn't cite him or take him in, though he got the feeling that their reluctance to do so was mostly because they just didn't want to bother with it. Maybe it was more complicated to give tickets to people with non-driver license IDs.

In any case, Thomas' safety apparently wasn't an issue for them, since no ride was offered. He didn't think he deserved a ride, and he didn't expect one, but the contrast in style between polizei and CHP seemed interesting. Of course, maybe the German officers were tolerant because they figured Thomas and his friends were ignorant Americans.)

Another problem was entering Ramstein Air Base proper once Thomas and his friends had arrived outside its gate. The issue here was that they had to pass the American military policemen at the entrance guard station. They carried the proper ID, but thought the Air Policemen (APs) would question why they were wandering the German freeway during school hours. They were too obviously high school students. Whatever civility the polizei may have extended them, and however highway patrol officers might react in the future, even military dependents like Thomas, who rarely got in trouble, knew they wouldn't get any leeway from the APs.

It wasn't clear what the problem was. A lot of APs were fairly young also, only a few years older than Thomas and his cohorts, and that may have made teenagers particularly irritating or challenging to them. Maybe the problem was that APs and teenaged male dependents were too close to being on the same wavelength. Or, maybe it was simply that a sufficient number of high school kids had given them a sufficient amount of trouble to justify their resentment. Thomas noticed, though, that APs didn't usually have the same attitude toward female high schoolers.

In any case, Thomas and his friends usually got around the "why aren't you guys in school?" problem by arriving so late in the day that class would be out. On one occasion, though, Thomas and about a half dozen other teenagers reached Ramstein in the early afternoon. After a brief discussion, they decided to move off to one side, away from the autobahn and the AP gate, and climb the fence.

Technically, this was unnecessary. If they were willing to walk another hour or so, they could circle around the base and enter from "Ramstein town," the German civil community that the air base took its name from. Ramstein town was separated from military family housing only by a small forest, no fences or gates. The reason the group was facing a fence here was because this was the side of the base where runways, airplanes, hangars, and other base operations infrastructure and military technology were located. So, they could have just kept walking, but they had already walked something like 16 kilometers (~10 miles), and nobody wanted to walk any more. They would go over the fence.

They walked around the perimeter of the base until they were well away from the guard station, but otherwise took no particular trouble to find an inconspicuous place to climb.

The barrier was about eight feet high, made of chain link. Overhanging them were struts extending out diagonally from the top of the fence and laced with strands of barbed wire. It looked easy enough to climb chain link, but they somberly considered this barbed wire obstacle jutting out over their heads. Thomas personally felt fairly confident, considering the whole business an interesting problem in the logistics of climbing: How to get over barbed wire without getting caught on it. Some of his friends were more athletic, some less, but everyone was game, or at least acted like they were. With much raucous commentary, challenges to each other, joking, and other banter, they pulled their way up the fence and precariously leveraged their bodies over the barbed wire. Some needed a boost from below or a pull from above, but eventually they all got over.

It took a while for the seven of them to get onto the ground on the far side. They didn't hurry, and they made no attempt at stealth.

To make the point clear: Thomas and his friends were breaching the perimeter of an American military installation. Thomas thought there was probably a federal law against this. Beyond that, this was at the height of the cold war, around the time of the Cuban Missile Crisis. The area where they were climbing was known to be patrolled by guards carrying submachine guns and accompanied by police dogs. This didn't seem to weigh heavily on the teenagers' minds, for reasons that would later strike Thomas as incomprehensible. Suppose APs had come upon them, shot first, and asked questions later? Thomas thinks, we got away with it, but why weren't we more worried about the risk?

* * *

Thomas sits still for a moment, wondering if he actually had died at some point in the past. Maybe upon death your consciousness automatically leaped free of your dead body, to incarnate into the next surviving version of yourself in another historical pathway, a different dimension. In a series of alternative realities, Thomas lies buried, and his family and friends grieve for him.

While he lives blithely on in his next version, unaware of the sorrow and disruption he leaves behind.

It occurs to Thomas that it needn't always be death. He could have been seriously injured, perhaps permanently maimed or disfigured. Thomas considers the possibility that the creature in the water had been a great white, and it had chomped into him. He hadn't died, but his leg had been mangled, to be necessarily amputated. For an uncanny second, Thomas feels an emptiness in a pant leg ... he convulsively grips his jeans ... his thigh is solidly there.

Thomas relaxes. Then it occurs to him that though he has survived past crises, the future stretches ahead, a skein of possibilities, death perhaps hiding behind any cryptic door. What other catastrophes would he need to unknowingly dodge? In Tokyo he has no way of knowing that his future will include rock-climbing, scuba-diving, reckless motorcycle riding, parachute jumping, fighting in full-contact martial arts tournaments ... and maybe smuggling.

*
**

On the Edge of Traction

West Marin: Tokyo plus three years

𝒯he plan is to drive from Inverness out through the rolling highlands of the West Marin dairy country to Limantour Beach—a beautiful and tranquil setting for a hike and a picnic. Thomas' friends Jack and Lynn are driving in front of him in Jack's battered old VW Fastback; Thomas follows on his motorcycle, a new, 1970 Honda CB750, of which he is inordinately proud.

Jack is in his mellow, flower child phase, so he is driving very sedately (in stark contrast to the way he drove only a few years before). Sedate is probably a good idea anyway, since the road is narrow, potholed, very hilly and curvy. It is a clear, mild day and the sunroof of the Fastback has been rolled open. Through the rear window and a little through the sunroof, Thomas can see both Jack and Lynn. Jack is one of those white guys who, for some reason, can grow an impressive Afro. With his great head of hair and at 6 feet 7 inches tall, he is hard to miss, even in a moving car. Lynn, freckled and with curly red hair, also has sort of an Afro, though not so glorious as Jack's. They look back occasionally, maybe to make sure Thomas is still there, smile and wave. Everyone seems in a good mood.

Thomas becomes aware of the roar of a car engine coming up fast behind him. More faintly he hears voices, and then a continuous honking. He looks over his shoulder; a late-model Ford Mustang, apparently filled with teenaged boys, has caught up with them.

Thomas can't tell how many are in the car, at least four, and they look to be around seventeen. Their faces are eager, a little wild-eyed, aggressive but not actually hostile. As they careen around Thomas and Jack and Lynn, the boys in the car give them what are meant to be scornful looks, though there is a hint of uncertainty in their eyes. Once past, they honk for a while longer as they speed away.

Thomas reflectively retracts the motorcycle's clutch and revs the engine. Without giving it any real thought, he makes a decision. He re-engages the clutch, rolls back the accelerator grip, and veers around Jack's car. The bike and Thomas take off like they've been shot out of a gun.

Thomas doesn't know much about Mustang automobiles; he knows some of them have honorifics, like "high performance" or "Shelby," though he doesn't quite understand what these titles signify. In any case, the car in front of him doesn't seem to have been especially tweaked, since Thomas' CB750 is easily overtaking it.

But the boys in the Mustang hadn't yet seen Thomas pursuing them. Now they do, and they accelerate abruptly. Still, Thomas gains on them. Gaining is one thing, passing another; the narrow, winding two-lane road makes it practically impossible to get around. The boys in the car look very excited, worked up, laughing and shouting. Thomas hangs close, just off their rear bumper.

Between slopes and hilltops they reach a short straight-away. This is Thomas' chance. He pulls to their left and accelerates more. The Mustang driver, however, seriously rejects being passed. As Thomas starts to come around him, the other driver pulls his car over into the center of the road. The sudden move is exceedingly dangerous for Thomas; he barely avoids crashing into them. Maybe Thomas should be infuriated at this reckless disregard for his life, but he's not. He is too into the contest: He wants to win and so does the Mustang driver. Thomas accepts the driver's move as part of the game.

Now the Mustang driver has two wheels in each lane; the center of the car straddles the center stripe. This position and the narrowness of the road would make it impossible for a car to pass him. But Thomas is not in a car. His bike's four transversely mounted cylinders make it wide for a motorcycle, but Thomas thinks he can still squeeze around the Mustang. Thomas moves to the left, over to the narrow edge of the road. There is no shoulder, the pavement trails off unevenly into sand and weed. Thomas is now balancing his bike on the uncertain edge of the road, crashing over separated chunks of pavement, patches of sand, and the high, dry stalks, skeetering on the brink of traction. Faintly, through the mind-obliterating roars of two high-revving engines, the thought comes to Thomas that if the Mustang driver is *really* serious, he might veer over again, pushing Thomas off the road and down the slope. Thomas somehow thinks he won't.

Thomas pulls up alongside of the Mustang. Moved by an insane impulse, he glances away from the road and at his speedometer: 90 miles per hour. Thomas has run the bike faster, up to 120 on the open freeway, but this is no freeway and this time there's another speeding, shaking vehicle six inches off his right elbow. Without understanding how, Thomas has become completely committed—there's no going back. He guns the bike on past the Mustang. Before the road begins to curve again, Thomas is pulling away.

When Thomas is far enough ahead that there's no doubt as to who won their little race, he guides his bike over into a turn-out and slows to a stop. A short while later the Mustang comes by, still moving fast but no longer in racing mode. Thomas wonders what sort of looks he'll get from the teenagers. It turns out they are grinning broadly at him, still in an excited state, and raising their fingers to Thomas, not the middle finger insult, but the two-finger "V". During World War II that gesture meant "victory," in this era it usually means "peace." Whatever it exactly means here, their attitude seems clear enough. Apparently Thomas' recklessness has converted them to admiration. "You're cool!" their expressions say.

Later, Thomas thinks they should have been saying, "You're nuts."

After they're gone, Thomas turns the bike around and goes back to find Jack and Lynn, some miles behind. They laugh when he gets to them, affectionately scornful, tolerantly amused. "We could see the whole thing," Lynn tells him. "As soon as they went by, I *knew* you were going to go after them!" Jack says. Thomas hates being predictable.

Later that night, Thomas lies awake and thinks about it. The sense of victory has declined as a more realistic appreciation of his foolhardiness sets in. He wonders if he can officially note this as the stupidest thing he's ever done. There are many candidates for this distinction, but today's event seems special. And didn't he have any moral responsibility toward the kids in the car? Granted he was only a few years older than they were (guessing their ages), and granted they challenged him (sort of), he still didn't have to respond. What would he be thinking right now if he'd come out all right, but their car had flipped over the cliff and they'd all died?

Other, as yet unforeseen future deaths arrow toward Thomas. He sits stiffly in his chair in the bar, refusing to acknowledge anything more. But he remembers one activity he has always thought about trying. How could he know what he would be moved to attempt in the future, when this warning moment has slipped away? He has long been intrigued by the prospect of a sky dive.

*
**

Falling Past the Odds

Antioch, California: 1986

Thomas is working as a computer programmer for a credit-scoring company when the parachute jump happens. The jump comes about because of Jim, a friend of Thomas' who had been his supervisor for a couple of years previously. Jim had decided to try sky-diving. Since the jump school he'd talked to offers a substantial group discount, Jim has asked several of his co-workers if they'd want to come along. He explains to Thomas later that he understood it was risky, so he hadn't tried to persuade anyone, hadn't tried to "sell it." He says he asked each person once; if they said no, he dropped the issue. A fair number of computer software professionals, male and female and presumably cliché computer nerds, have said yes: Yes, they want to plummet through two-thirds of a mile of empty sky, trusting that a piece of cloth on their back would prevent them from being smashed to a bloody pulp on the ground. Perhaps because the software they dealt with was heavily involved with statistics, one of the analysts who was jumping justified the risk by analyzing the odds against a lethal sudden stop. The odds were vastly in his favor, he told the group. Better than 90%. "And I'm Mr. Ninety Percent," he said, perhaps somewhat hopefully. "I'm never the outlier."

When Jim had asked Thomas if he wanted to go along on the jump, Thomas had had mixed emotions. Sky-diving was an idea that he'd considered off and on for a long time. On one side, he liked heights. He liked being up above the surrounding landscape. He had rock-climbed, and he enjoyed visiting the tops of tall buildings: the Space Needle in Seattle, the Sears Tower in Chicago. On the other side, his fascination with heights was ambivalent, strongly infused with fear. He was acrophobic in a way that included both joy and terror. His reaction to heights was similar to his reaction to the sea, but more intense.

So, a question in the back of Thomas' mind had always been, faced with the actual situation, would he be able to jump out of a plane? Life was offering Thomas the chance to find out. He decides to take it.

On the day of the jump, Thomas and his group show up at the school early and spend the morning in a classroom. The teacher/jump master and his assistants teach them how to guide their descent with the parachutes' steering rods, how to fall sideways to the ground when they land, and how to untangle their chutes in the air. A relatively benign form of entanglement, where the chute still opens but the straps between chute and jumper are twisted around each other, is apparently common. In fact, this will happen to one of the jumpers in Thomas' group (Mr. Ninety Percent, as it turned out—but he survived).

The training goes well enough; everything they teach is straight-forward and easy to master. The main problem is that as the day draws on, they are getting closer and closer to that moment when they will be looking out through the open door of a high-flying plane. The moment when it will be their turn to jump. It's clear that Thomas is not the only one in the group who feels a certain tension about this.

Afternoon arrives; they get into the plane and take off.

In order to maximize the airplane's seating capacity, the owners of the jump school have removed all of the seats, except for those of the pilot and co-pilot. The parachutists sit packed closely together on the metal floor, in the seated equivalent of what would be called "spoon style," if they were lying on their sides. They aren't on their sides, however; they sit upright with their legs splayed out, each facing the back of the jumper in front of them, who sits between their legs. The exceptions, of course, are the last jumper, who has no one behind her, and the first jumper, who has no one in front of him.

The disadvantage of this arrangement is that the first jumper *must* jump. If he doesn't, no one else can either; no one can get around him to the jumping bay. (At least, so they were told in the class. It could have been a psychological ploy to make sure the first jumper jumps.) On this particular day, Thomas is the first jumper.

He didn't achieve first jumper status through any particular aptitude; he is first because he weighs the most. Galileo may have asserted that objects of different weight fall at the same speed, all else being equal, but a heavier jumper cuts through air resistance faster than a lighter one, and is sooner out of the way of those behind him. So heaviest jumps first.

Thomas wonders: If he fails to jump, and thus prevents the rest of them from jumping, how will they look at him at work on Monday? Angry, but too polite and professional to say so? (Most of them anyway.) Or secretly glad that Thomas had prevented them from facing their own moments of truth? *I didn't jump to save your lives,* Thomas imagines himself telling them. *Your chutes weren't going to open. I had a premonition.*

The airplane reaches parachuting altitude. The bay door is opened. The moment has come. Thomas stands in the jumping bay, staring out through the bright spring day at the placid green fields 3,500 feet below. *No way!* he tells himself. *Yes way*, he answers himself.

Thomas jumps. His mind goes blank for an instant, but he remembers to splay his limbs and arch his back as they have been taught, a maneuver that causes the jumper to fall face downward and facilitates the opening of the chute. (The chute is hitched to a static line which is fastened to the plane; this pulls the chute open for them; no need to count or manually pull a ripcord.)

Thomas has a moment of blankness, then comes back to himself to find that he seems to be hanging in the sky. Looking down, he sees only his blue jean-clad legs and athletic shoes between him and the distant Earth. He seems to sit fixed and unmoving in the air; he has the inane thought that he is hanging from an immense tree. He looks up; there is nothing above but the fluted rectangle of the parachute, outlined against the sky. That's all that's holding me up, he realizes. He marvels at how perfectly the whole arrangement works.

Thomas realizes now that two things he was uncertain about have both happened: He did jump, and the parachute did open. Everything from here on should be a snap.

On the other hand, he's not on the ground yet, it looks far away, and he senses very little downward movement. A faint uneasiness will persist until his feet touch the grass, but he feels essentially in the clear.

Thomas remembers a question he had had a few years ago when considering sky-diving: If the parachute didn't open, what would he be thinking the rest of the way down? Intense self-reproach? That would be futile, of course, though maybe difficult to repress. How do you face yourself for dying over a risk there was never a need to take? The instructors have told them how soon they will reach the ground if the chute doesn't deploy. They would have about 30 seconds to regret their decision before slamming into the grass.

But Thomas had flashed through the moment of that possibility without thinking about it.

After a while he becomes aware that a tinny, far-away voice has been shouting in his ear for a while. He realizes this is the voice of the jump master on the ground, speaking to him over the radio pick-up in his helmet. The jump master has been giving Thomas instructions as to how to steer his chute so he will land in the assigned area. He has become increasingly agitated, since Thomas has been ignoring him. "All right!" Thomas shouts back. He begins to obey instructions, pulling on one or the other of the two steering rods as ordered. "No problem!" he yells at the tinny voice. "I'm on it!" Their dialogue goes on like this for a while. Eventually Thomas remembers that the radio link is one way only; the jump master can't hear him.

Silently now, Thomas continues to follow instructions, learning to temper his movements since his adrenalized yanks on the steering rods are turning him too quickly and too far around. After a while he gets it right. Finally he reaches the ground.

Thomas stands looking back up at the bright sky. A distance away across the field, another jump-master, the founder of the school, sees Thomas staring upward and shouts, "It's even better the second time!" Thomas believes him.

But Thomas never jumps again. At first he plans to, but then he is deterred by certain realizations: Jumping was one of those things he had to do it because it scared him. Once the jump was done, though, a second time would be nothing. Maybe not "nothing;" it could have been beautiful, surreal, even ethereal. But still risky, and redundant, because the original motivating doubt was gone. Now Thomas knew he could jump out of a plane.

* * *

After the parachute jump, Thomas and several others in the group drive home together, laughing, happy, triumphant, almost giddy with relief. They aren't in any hurry to get back, wanting to prolong the jubilation brought on by the intense day. After they do separate, Thomas has to run a few errands, so by the time he finally arrives home it is late, well after dark.

The first person to meet him at the door is his youngest son, six-year-old Brendan. Though Thomas' wife knows where he had been, and Thomas hadn't exactly kept the jump a secret from the rest of his family, his impression is that the whole business had passed over Bren's head. Thomas is pretty sure his youngest son had no awareness of it. Thomas is wrong.

"Daddy!" Bren shouts, running out the front door and hugging Thomas around the legs. "Daddy! You lived! You lived!"

Thomas' elation ebbs away, replaced by guilt.

* * *

Why take risks?

A metaphysical uber-Thomas reflects on these episodes, past and future. The common theme in these four situations, he decides, is how we think about unnecessary risk-taking. This would be separate from risks undertaken by firemen going into a burning building, rescue divers, policemen, mountain rescue teams, soldiers in combat, and so on. The risk-taking of those people has purpose and justification. The justification for the risks in Thomas' adventures ranged from trivial to non-existent. Is there some connection between the undercurrent of randomness in our lives and the way we think about taking risks? Lurking below our surface consciousness, is there an unacknowledged fatalism ... a need to break the pool balls apart in random directions, death being everyone's ultimate future anyway? So may as well get things moving.

In the first incident, in the ocean, why didn't Thomas turn back immediately? Why did he continue on (almost) to the buoy?

Thomas decides that he had continued on because, before setting out, he had induced in himself a state of mind, almost a self-hypnosis, that would not allow any deviation or questioning of what he was doing. He put himself in this psychological state because what he was doing seemed sufficiently difficult and daunting that he was afraid that, if he let himself do any mid-course reconsidering, he would back down and fail. It was like putting on mental blinders. The problem was they were on so tight that Thomas couldn't immediately get rid of them, even in the face of something that clearly should have made him rethink what he was doing. In this one case at least, he also had the excuse of being a child.

In the motorcycle-car pursuit incident, Thomas thought his judgement was blurred by familiarity and an incremental escalation of risk. When he had bought the bike, he had counseled himself to ride safely and he had done so ... for a while. Before long, however, he found himself starting to push the limits. Over time, the limits became more and more extreme; success (survival) at each level of danger made that level feel comfortable, and he would more or less unconsciously push his luck to the next level. He became acclimated to confronting hazards that he would have thought insane to face only a few months before. Adding to the syndrome of danger feeling normal was the sense he had that he was in control, that he could always back off at the last instant if the situation got out of hand.

Jumping from the airplane Thomas originally saw as an obvious example of risk-taking brought on by social pressure. Looking back on it, he was not so sure this was true; he thought he would have jumped from the plane even if no one else had been aboard. The decision was similar to the encounter with the beast in the water: he was influenced by a prior decision that he had programmed himself into staying with. Maybe ... but peer group pressure was also an influence.

A few of the first-time jumpers that day didn't seem to feel any acrophobia. One woman said it seemed perfectly safe, just like jumping out into a giant relief map. Jim, the initiator, had dived for his high school swim team, and said that it never bothered him to jump from a height. These were the exceptions, though; most of Thomas' fellow jumpers seemed profoundly anxious. Still, not a single one declined to jump. When the moment came, each one of them stepped out into high nothingness. Thomas guessed that social pressure had at least something to do with that.

The business of breaching the perimeter at Ramstein seemed to have elements of all these factors.

A blinkered mindset: Thomas and his friends had been walking doggedly for miles, their minds were dulled but determined; they were going to get home as soon as they could, no matter what.

Familiarity: They were used to the air base, very familiar and comfortable with that environment. A military installation bristling with armed guards it might have been, but it was also home.

Peer pressure: A group of teenaged boys, trying to impress each other without allowing themselves to be impressed. Bravado was inevitable.

Thomas didn't want to over-simplify any of this. Of course there were other factors, the most obvious being egotism. Egotism doesn't necessarily make you behave suicidally, though. Some other judgement-dimming influence needs to be present.

* * *

Looking at all of it, Thomas comes to believe that the three factors discussed—locked-down mindset, acclimation to danger, and social pressure—are valid influences in the psychology of risk-taking.

Beyond this, there is the need to generate an individualized self. We have a need to both fit in and stand out. Risky experiences help with the standing out, partly by providing memories that verify our exceptional identity (assuming we survive to enjoy the memory). In another way, risk-taking also enables us to fit in. By our daring behavior, we become members of an elite group. This can be a formal group, like a special military unit, or a knight, or a Samurai, or it can be something more vague, a group made up of all the random individuals who dared to do a specific risky action: climb a certain mountain, descend to a certain depth in the ocean, jump from a certain height, exceed a certain speed, face a particular foe.

Thomas thinks these might also be factors in criminal behavior, which is similar to general risk-taking in many ways, but has certain differences.

*
**

A Casino at Night, and the dangers of Solipsism

McGuire AFB, New Jersey: four years before Tokyo

Tijuana: three years before

Panama: nine years after

𝒯wo minor incidents foreshadowed Thomas's role as an international smuggler. Both seemed fairly innocuous. The first occurred when he returned to the states after three years in Germany.

When Thomas was 16, in the summer after his sophomore year in high school, he and his family left Germany, returning to the states for Thomas Sr.'s new assignment at Hamilton Air Force Base, in northern California. (In fact, a return to a previous posting.)

They flew out of Frankfurt on a transpolar route that took them to McGuire AFB in New Jersey. They arrived late at night, and perhaps Thomas' father figured the customs agents would be tired and not too alert. Thomas Sr. had three bottles of European wine that he wanted to get into the country without paying import duty. (He was a fierce patriot, but apparently patriotism didn't rule out a minor bit of tariff evasion.) Thomas was charged with the task of actually conveying these bottles through customs.

Thomas and his family and other new arrivals were in a line before a long, low ramp on which they were supposed to put their bags and anything else they were bringing in. As the line moved forward, they pushed their possessions along this ramp until they reached the point where they would be inspected by the customs agents. The top of the ramp was about on a level with Thomas' knees.

The bottles of wine were positioned three in a row in a tall, narrow cardboard box. Thomas Sr.'s idea was for Thomas to leave the box on the floor, up close against the side of the ramp, and casually nudge it along with his knee. In this position, and due to the padded bottom of the box, its top was slightly higher than the top edge of the ramp. This left it marginally visible from the ramp's far side. Where the customs agents would be. Thomas' opinion, not expressed, was that any agent who was even remotely worth his pay would spot the box in a moment.

Whatever his assessment of this plan, however, Thomas did as he was told ... and got away with it. Astonishingly to Thomas, this simple and obvious scheme worked: his first success as a smuggler.

The second incident occurred during a vacation the family took the following Spring. Starting out from Northern California, they drove the station wagon south, first for a visit to Disneyland, and then on across the border into Mexico. They cruised in a relaxed fashion down the Baja peninsula; the weather was clear and bright, and they were on a highway that allowed them to look from a cliff-top down onto a beach and the blue ocean. They stopped at various points, but eventually reached Ensenada, where they checked into a motel and relaxed in the warm weather and scenery. In Ensenada, Thomas acquired a cheap switchblade knife. At that point in his experience, the switchblade seemed an object impressive and fascinating, fraught with meaning. He repeatedly flipped it open, amusing his brothers, until Thomas became worried that he would wear out the spring. His parents never seemed to notice.

After several days in Ensenada, they drove north again. As they approached the border crossing in Tijuana, they came to a halt at the end of an apparently endless line of stopped vehicles. These seemed to be mostly American tourists, waiting to re-enter the United States.

They sat in the heat for an immeasurable length of time. Part of the delay was the sheer number of cars, part was that some border-crossers apparently had to be scrutinized more closely, and in some cases vehicles were searched. As they waited, Thomas belatedly remembered that switchblades were not legal in California ... what if the border guards searched their car? Unlikely, perhaps, but the longer they waited, the more it weighed on his mind.

Finally Thomas came up with a plan. Binding the knife very tightly with a shoelace so it wouldn't pop open accidentally, he hid it in a pocket of the pants worn by his youngest brother, Rod. (Rod was not quite three; he had been born in Germany.) It seemed unlikely to Thomas that the border guards would search a two-year-old. Rod looked at him in a puzzled way, but didn't become annoyed until Thomas began pulling Rod's hand away each time he tried to ferret out what had been put in his pocket.

In retrospect, Thomas thought this ploy didn't seem very admirable. He could later offer himself no excuse, except perhaps that he was learning from his father. Thomas did keep a close eye on Rod, ready to intervene whenever his little brother's hand moved.

It turned out their car wasn't searched and they crossed the border without incident. Thomas took the knife to school subsequently and showed it off to various friends and acquaintances, presenting it not as a threat, but as an object of interest. Eventually he lost interest, and at some point years later the knife disappeared without Thomas really noticing. Possibly stolen by one of his brothers: Rod, if the world was a just place, and assuming Rod wouldn't hurt himself with it.

Though the operation was not very challenging and executed rather ignobly, the border crossing at Tijuana marked Thomas' second success as a smuggler.

An abortive later career in smuggling

Thomas' third adventure in smuggling is more involved, and comes many years later.

After returning from a kuoshu tournament in Taiwan, Thomas works another year as an instructor for a martial arts school. During this time, the small fame of the three team members who had placed in the tournament is enthusiastically exploited by school management. They want to add to their schools' prestige, of course, but not just for the glory. The prospect of being taught by full-contact fighters who have succeeded in an international tournament is a powerful magnet for students; the school's already robust business is to be further boosted. Since Thomas is one of the three who has placed (the other two work at other schools in the chain), Thomas starts seeing a lot of new students. This is welcome, as the more students he teaches, the more money he makes.

One of the new students assigned to him is Alan.

Alan appears to be in his mid-twenties. He has a long, lean, aristocratic face, high forehead over deep-set eyes, longish dark hair combed straight back, and is lean and fit. He says he is from Boston, and speaks with a strong Bostonian accent.

His clothing style is on the edge of hippy, but more refined and more expensive: leather coats, jeans, and low boots, or designer poet shirts and beachcomber slacks, and sandals. He usually accessorizes with a necklace: a silver chain set with a heavy mosaic of green stones. This has a look suggestive of Mesoamerican or Andean civilizations. The green stones, Alan tells Thomas, are emeralds. The necklace is worth thousands; he lets people assume it is a replica. He says that he has become wealthy in the import business, selling both authentic pre-Columbian antiquities and replicas, and that he owns a half-dozen retail stores in California and South America. He says that he also occasionally arranges purchases of high-end emeralds for private buyers.

* * *

As a martial arts student, Alan is strong and well-balanced, athletic in his own way, but he moves a little tightly; it is difficult for Thomas to get him to allow his movements to flow. Still, the lessons go well enough and soon Alan is hiring Thomas for tasks outside of the school: house sitter when he is away on business (frequently), bodyguard at parties, guard dog trainer-assistant (the dogs seemed to be more of a hobby than a business). He is lavish with money, paying Thomas large amounts for simple work.

Thomas meets a few of the people in Alan's circle: his girlfriend, who is an artist; a male friend who is an accomplished keyboard musician, able to play (Alan says) at a concert pianist level; others who have other talents ... Thomas realizes that he himself also has a role: the Kung Fu expert. He sees that Alan collects people; he wants to be surrounded by non-ordinary individuals, men and women with special talents. The school's promotion of Thomas as a winning international tournament fighter makes him a collectible for Alan.

What, if any, is Alan's talent? This isn't immediately obvious, though he projects the feeling that he has one. And clearly he has charisma, an ability to charm people, though this is occasionally side-tracked by arrogance. After Thomas has known him for a while, he sees that Alan can be especially nasty to tradespeople, real estate agents, and the like. This makes Thomas uncomfortable, though Alan seems to feel it is their function in life to be abused.

Though Alan's account of owning stores and trading in emeralds is his most consistent story, he sometimes provides other explanations of himself. One afternoon at his house, after Alan and Thomas have been working with the guard dogs, he tells Thomas he plays bass in the backup band of a famous blues-rocker. He demonstrates with a brief riff on a bass guitar that he has handy (though Thomas has never seen it in his house previously). Thomas thinks his playing, though energetic and basically in tune, has the mark of someone who has some natural facility but picked up a guitar for the first time the week before. Thomas keeps this assessment to himself, but later, after Alan tells him an implausible story about being an ex-professional surfer, Thomas feels moved to object:

"You know Alan, sometimes I get the feeling that half the stuff you're telling me is bullshit.

Alan gives a crooked smile: "You're right."

*　*　*

When Alan hears that Thomas has decided to leave his job at the martial arts school, he suggests that Thomas work for him on a more formal basis. He says he can see working Thomas up through his organization. Exactly what this means, what Thomas would actually do and so on, is left ambiguous. But as a starting point, Alan asks Thomas to accompany him on a business trip to Panama. He may be carrying valuables, at least cash, and Thomas can be useful as a bodyguard and general assistant.

As always, the pay he offers is generous, but the real attraction is the excitement—the adventure of it. Thomas agrees without hesitation.

The plan is that Alan will fly alone to Miami. He'll take care of some business there, and Thomas will join him a day later. Then they'll fly together to Panama City, Panama, where more business will be taken care of. After that, Thomas will return to the states on his own, while Alan goes on to Columbia. Where, of course, he has more business to take care of. He doesn't exactly say he is involved in smuggling emeralds, but Thomas gets the impression this can be assumed.

Thomas thinks it over, especially the Columbia part. Perhaps naively, he asks if Alan's business has anything to do with drugs.

Alan looks at Thomas for a moment. "I'm rich," he says slowly. "I don't need to involve myself with drugs. You might need to, since you're poor."

Thomas feels put down by this answer, but only mildly—he *is* poor. More importantly, Thomas believes what Alan says about drugs. So, is he involved in smuggling emeralds?

"Changes in the law have made it mostly unnecessary to smuggle emeralds," Alan tells Thomas. And leaves it at that.

What is going on then? Apparently nothing; it looks like Thomas really will be just a bodyguard.

* * *

Thomas finishes his last day working for the martial arts school. The night before Alan is to leave for Miami, he asks Thomas to meet him at his house. As kind of a final check, he asks if Thomas is sure he wants to go through with the trip. "Sometimes," he says, "people change their minds at the last minute about this kind of thing." Thomas assures him he's in. Alan then pays Thomas in advance, in cash, and gives him the info regarding ticket pick-up, flight numbers and times, and the address in Miami.

As he finishes Thomas' briefing, Alan adds a wry comment. "Like *I Spy*," he says, referring to the TV series.

They shake hands; Thomas takes the money and leaves. Driving home, cash in the glove compartment, he feels something like an adrenaline high.

Late the following night, Thomas flies out of SFO (San Francisco International). He arrives the next morning in Atlanta and sits around the airport for the half-hour layover. Then he flies on to Miami, where he takes a cab from the airport to the address Alan has given him. It turns out to be a new, high-rise luxury condo complex in an upscale part of town.

Alan meets Thomas out in front with casual friendliness, perhaps faintly relieved. Had he had further doubts that Thomas would show up? A half hour later Thomas has left his suitcase in Alan's condo and they are down by the pool. They sit around a table and talk, shaded by a large umbrella from the bright sun.

Their business in Central America isn't immediately discussed. For a while Alan talks about the merits of the variously appealing young women in skimpy swimwear that are all around them. He also expresses his opinion of the slim, blond young lifeguard, who watched his domain expressionlessly through dark sunglasses. "He's always posing for the women," Alan tells Thomas. "He couldn't save a drowning kitten. He's a joke."

Eventually they get to the business at hand. There are a couple of suitcases filled with emeralds, Alan suggests rather vaguely. Something in the way he mentions them causes Thomas to ask if they are stolen.

"Over the years, they've changed hands several times …" Alan shrugged, as though to say: At this point, who knows where they started out? Who cares?

"We'll fly to Panama City and check into a hotel tonight," Alan says. "Tomorrow I'll go to the bank and set things up."

"Am I going with you to the bank?"

"No. You can stay in the hotel, or look around Panama City if you like. There's nothing much worth seeing." He reflects briefly. "The next day I'll go on to Columbia, and you'll go back to California."

He talks a bit longer. Though Alan tends to be indirect, he does eventually make it clear what they are doing: The point of the trip is to set up an account in a Panamanian bank, which can subsequently be accessed by Alan's contacts from South America. Once they have taken their payment from the account, they will fulfill their part of the transaction—send emeralds from Columbia, presumably. The system will be on-going. "Panamanian bank accounts are what Swiss bank accounts used to be," Alan says. "Secure and secret." Apparently they are doing something that requires these qualities.

At this point Thomas wonders why Alan is bringing him along; it doesn't sound like he will actually do much. Wanting more excitement and doubtful that he is earning his pay, Thomas suggests that he accompany Alan to Columbia.

"Columbia is a whole different trip," Alan says. "Guards, guns, dogs, very secretive people. It's something I have to deal with alone."

Now Thomas wonders if Alan wants to keep him from knowing who these Columbians are, or keep them from knowing who Thomas is. Or both. And maybe for Thomas' own protection; they will probably be suspicious of anyone new to them, and have an abrupt way with suspected spies and informants. Or will

Thomas meet them eventually, when he is more of a known quantity? Thomas raises these questions.

Alan shakes his head. "You don't understand these men." He thinks it over for a minute. "These people are beautiful," he tells Thomas. "They have honor. They are gentlemen." He pauses again, looking for the best way to explain their style of noblesse oblige. "They treat their women with complete respect, much more than Americans do. And they never involve their women in their business. It's never talked about." Thomas understands that this last remark isn't just a comment about Alan's contacts; he is also stating policy: this whole business is not something Thomas is ever to discuss with his wife.

Alan looks for another example. "One of their carriers once ripped them off—$50,000, something like that. They just shrugged. They didn't do anything to him. He just wasn't part of their business anymore." Alan speaks some more about his associates, presenting a picture of paternalistic, old world-style gentlemen, courtly, dignified in spirit and generous to the peasantry. Indeed, he tells Thomas these men's enterprises support a major portion of the local economy.

They are silent for a while after that, then Alan comes back to the business at hand: For Thomas' part, this first trip will be primarily educational. In the future, Thomas will make these trips and deposit the cash by himself. When this happens, he indicates, Thomas' compensation will rise steeply. It sounds good, so Thomas decides not to press the issue about Columbia. He realizes later that a few questions should have occurred to him, though:

If Thomas is going to be making future deposits, shouldn't he at least *see* the bank, know where it is? Wouldn't it be useful for Thomas to meet the bank people he will eventually be dealing with? And familiarize himself with the deposit protocol? (Presumably the protocol will be exact, since discretion—secrecy—is a major concern.) But for some reason Thomas does not think of this at the time.

In the afternoon they fly out of the Miami airport. A short way into the flight, abruptly fatigued by the whole thing, Thomas falls asleep. When he awakes, they are gliding down through twilight toward a runway on the outskirts of Panama City.

* * *

Passing through customs in the Panama City airport is an odd, non-linear process. Along with the other incoming travelers, they wait on wooden benches in a dark, older room, their various bags and suitcases clumped around them. The room is moderately large and presents, on one side, a row of closed, inside windows, like teller windows in an old-fashioned bank. In addition, and for reasons that aren't clear, several cages filled with squawking chickens sit on the floor nearby.

The bank teller windows are tightly shuttered, but once in a while one of them will be opened from inside and a man or woman, presumably customs staff, will look out at the crowd. When this happens, most of the travelers spring to their feet and rush to the window, speaking energetically in Spanish. The customs person answers in the same energetic manner, and after a brief exchange the shutters are slammed shut and the crowd reluctantly sits back down. This happens several times, usually with a different window and a different agent each time. Thomas' sense is that getting up, trying to compete with the excited crowd, would be purposeless. And he doesn't speak Spanish. But he does look at Alan when the windows first open, since he is being paid to be useful. Alan shakes his head; Thomas stays seated.

Finally all of the windows open more or less at the same time, with customs employees behind each of them. One of these briefly addresses the waiting travelers. Thomas can't understand what he is saying, but the crowd rises again, more calmly this time, and he gathers that customs is now really open.

They are shown a raised circular area, like a dais, where they are to spread out their luggage so it can be inspected. Uniformed customs officials have come out to join them; Thomas notices that their chief is an American, though the rest of the inspectors are Panamanian. This pattern, American manager with local rank and file, is something he would see repeatedly in Panama.

Thomas puts their luggage up on the dais. Alan's suit bag partially folds over on itself when he lays it down, so Thomas lifts it again and spreads it out flat. Alan gives him a quick, opaque look, like a caution. Then the particular inspector dealing with their bags begins lifting and manipulating them in a cursory manner. He is younger than the other inspectors, and he actually seems pleasant, a rare trait for Panamanians dealing with Americans, though that hasn't yet become clear to Thomas. The young inspector makes a move to search the bags further, then stops and smiles, gesturing as though to say, never mind; go ahead. They take their luggage and leave.

As they pass through the exit door into the warm night, Alan looks at Thomas and grins. "That was tough."

* * *

They take a taxi to downtown Panama City. The driver asks en route if they are Canadian. Thomas tells him they are from California. The driver's expression becomes sullen, almost bitter. "Oh," he says, "*Yankees.*" The hostility is unmistakable; his reaction reminds Thomas of how their guide in Taiwan had reacted when he found out that one of their team members was Japanese-American. Reflexive; in his subculture, rudeness is the acceptable norm toward certain categories of people.

They check into a large, older hotel, not exactly fancy but with a certain fading grandeur. The rooms in their suite are at least spacious. More significantly perhaps, Thomas discovered that the employees inside the hotel feel some requirement to be polite, even mildly friendly.

After a room-service dinner, Alan wants to go down to the hotel casino. He thinks he can win at baccarat, using his system ... his system is based on a theory that casino policy compels the dealer to always act a certain way in certain game situations, and that Alan can take advantage of this. Thomas thinks it sounds dubious. If it really worked, wouldn't all players be doing it? And wouldn't this then provoke a change in casino policy? A Las Vegas gambling industry worker once told him that Las Vegas had been built on people who thought they had a system.

But Thomas says nothing, and they take the elevator down into the casino, a large, shadowy, crowded room in the hotel basement. Alan is not immediately able to find a baccarat game, either because the game is already in session, or can't start without a minimum number of players. He notices another sort of game, involving a board and dice.

When Alan inquires about the game, the dealer tells him it is called Bank Bingo. "How do you play?" Alan asks. This turns out to be a fateful question.

"I'll show you," the dealer says. "Put a few bucks on the board." The dealer is a skinny American somewhere in middle age. He has a long, thin, world-worn face, heavily oiled and combed back gray hair, and he wears a shiny, burgundy-colored suit, very well-fitted and pressed. His voice is a rich, deep baritone apparently seasoned by decades of alcohol consumption; its strength seems disproportionate to his thin physique. Thomas can't place him by any regional accent, but something in his manner suggests vacation resorts and a nomadic life style. He has a casually friendly manner, an easy confidence.

Thomas' intuitive reaction to him is, Keep your wallet in your pocket and walk away quickly. Alan, however, isn't getting this. He is willing to learn the game by playing it. This is probably a bad idea with any gambling game, but turns out to be especially bad with "Bank Bingo," which leads the player down a slippery slope.

Bank Bingo has no clear exit point (other than bankruptcy), and it is structured so that the only way to recoup the money a player has already bet is to keep adding cash and playing it all the way through to the end. Points are accrued from the results of dice tosses; when a certain point tally is reached, the player wins. If the player withdraws at any point before that, the dealer keeps his money. To stay in the game, then, you had to keep putting more money down—you never win until you win it all. Then you get your money back plus a vast profit. And the points add up very quickly at first; victory seems only a few more dice throws away. Alan even asks the dealer (ironically, as it turns out), "How do you lose at this game?"

In retrospect, Thomas didn't think Bank Bingo was a game at all, in the sense that there was more than one possible outcome, or that any participant other than the dealer had a chance of winning. It was just a psychologically astute system for separating the player from his money. Since the game is being played in what seems to be a moderately upscale casino, rather than on a street corner in a bad part of town, Alan assumes it has to be legitimate. He even tells Thomas later that casino gambling in Panama is regulated by the government, so the game can't be crooked.

As play progresses, the accrual of points slows, and it becomes absurdly difficult for Alan to earn the last few points separating him from victory. And he has to keep throwing in more cash. Thomas takes him aside for a moment and quietly suggests that maybe Bank Bingo is a bad idea; maybe Alan should get out before throwing good money after bad.

Alan assures him that he has this figured out. The problem, he has surmised, is having enough money to stay in the game until you win. Most people don't, and that was the answer to his 'how do you lose?' question. Alan figures *he* will win, because, unlike most people, he has a lot of money. "They don't know how much money I have," he tells Thomas. He returns to the game.

Thomas is thinking that his money won't help him, because the game isn't honest: how could the points have added up so quickly at first, when Alan was being drawn into the game, but accrue so slowly now?

When the dealer is adding up the dice count after a throw, he speaks in a quick, almost hypnotic, monotone, his long, nimble fingers caressing the dice. (Later, Alan is to say, "It did bother me that he touched the dice when he counted them.") When the count is complete, the dealer announces the results with his usual confident resonance. The speed of his counting makes it very hard to follow, to tell if he is counting honestly. Thomas tries to get him to slow down. The dealer ignores his first few attempts to moderate the pace. When Thomas becomes more insistent, the dealer allows himself to look irritated and recounts the last toss—almost as quickly as before. "See?" he says to Thomas, with a trace of belligerence. Then he goes back to his usual quick-counting routine.

By this time a crowd has gathered, more locals than tourists. The casino manager has appeared and stands nearby. He is a large, sleek, white-haired American in glasses and a suit as well-tailored, but not as flamboyant, as the dealer's. The majority of the crowd seem to consist of dark, slick-haired men, apparently locals, wearing Hawaiian shirts, slacks, pointed-toed shoes, and sunglasses (at night, in a subterranean room). They watch silently. Thomas' sense is that they are some sort of undercover private security. There is one individual in guard uniform, a short, developmentally-delayed looking man with an enormous pistol strapped on his hip.

Alan asks if the game could be moved to a private room. This is done; the uniformed guard, the casino manager, and all the men in Hawaiian shirts move with them. The new room is smaller and quieter, which makes the whole business seem more intense. Now Alan finds that he is running out of cash. No problem; he sends Thomas up to their suite to get more.

Per instruction, Thomas opens the correct piece of luggage. Not surprisingly, it is the same suit bag that he had fooled around with in customs, drawing Alan's warning look. He finds the pair of low-top boots in the bottom of the bag, and finds the thick wad of rolled US currency in one of the boots. How much is there? Difficult to tell: the bills are of a variety of denominations, and the roll is large. A significant amount.

Again following Alan's directions, Thomas takes about a third of the money (a third by volume, not by count), fastens everything back up as he'd found it, and returns with the cash down to the casino.

As Thomas hands the bills to Alan, Alan tells him, under his breath, "They were asking about you ... if you worked for me. I said no, that you were my friend. I told them about the kung fu thing ... that you were more deadly than any gun." He smiles slightly. Thomas looks around and sees that the men in sunglasses, who had been watching the game, now are intently watching Thomas. He looks back at them impassively, though at the moment he isn't actually feeling more deadly than a gun.

The game continues. Alan continues to add money to the board; those last few points remain tantalizingly just beyond reach. The casino manager sidles up to Thomas. He seems nervous, or worried. Sensing that Thomas is distrustful of the dealer, he makes small talk, maybe hoping to win Thomas over, or maybe just distract him.

He speaks in a soft, earnest voice, at one point wondering about Thomas' karate background and asking if he is the owner of a chain of karate schools, a rich entrepreneur in the martial arts world. Thomas assures him this isn't the case, that he is just an instructor. The manager nods, speaks a little longer, and eventually drifts away.

Alan is running out of cash again. Once more Thomas suggests he get out of the game. No; Alan is too deeply into it. Thomas is sent back up to the suite to get more money. Again per instruction, he takes about two-thirds of what is left. Back in the casino, he watches Alan keep putting his money down. Alan's movements seem almost reflexive, and Thomas thinks there is a kind of glazed look in his eyes. At one point he stops the action for a moment to ask if the casino will cover their hotel bill if he goes broke. The dealer makes a dismissive gesture, vague but presumably meaning yes.

The casino manager approaches Thomas again and apologizes for something, apparently for assuming earlier that Thomas might be the wealthy owner of a karate school chain. Thomas isn't sure why this requires an apology. Is it offensive for the manager to make assumptions about Thomas' economic status? *Forgive me for thinking you were rich ...* Thomas waves it off, lets him know he isn't thin-skinned about his lack of wealth.

Finally Alan steps back slightly from the table. He releases a slow breath; his posture becomes more relaxed. "Gentlemen," he tells them after a minute, "I hate to admit it, but you've beaten me."

The dealer tries not to show too much satisfaction. "I had a feeling something big was going to happen tonight," he says. "A big win, or a big loss."

"A profitable night for you, I imagine," Alan says to him.

The dealer shrugs it off. "I get a percentage."

"Maybe we can play again some time. First I'll have to sell some more emeralds."

"We don't ask you where you got your money," the dealer says dismissively. His manner suggests that discussing your source is a breach of etiquette, or even dangerous. Perhaps he thinks Alan may get himself in trouble if he says too much. In his years plying the gambling (or con artist) trade, the dealer must have dealt with other men in the cathartic aftermath of a big loss. He's probably found that it is wise to lower the tone.

The dealer, Thomas thinks, wouldn't want to hear any emotional or confessional ramble. He would also have little interest in reflecting on how the loss would affect the loser's life. Thomas doesn't really think Alan is on the verge of collapse, but the dealer is making sure. His stance toward his victim seems to be: We're two men of the world; we take winning and losing in a detached, professional away. A large amount of money has changed hands, but we're going to act like it's no big deal. The gambler's code.

The casino manager looks visibly relieved that the whole business is over.

Alan and Thomas return to their rooms.

* * *

They sit at the table in the dining room of the suite.

"Thank you for not harassing me," Alan says. "A lot of people I've worked with would have been angry. They would've said, 'If you were going to throw that money away, why didn't you give it to me? I could have bought a house with it.' "

One of Thomas' martial arts students back in California is a realtor; he has told Thomas that, at this time, the average three-bedroom home in Marin County was selling for $66,000. This gives Thomas some idea of how much money Alan has lost. It had been impossible to keep track of during the game.

"It's your money," Thomas says. "You get to spend it however you like. Would it really have bought a house?"

"Well … $75,000. It would have paid for the house in San Anselmo" (referring to Alan's current home in the hills above the city).

Alan thinks about it. "But it's not as crazy as it seems. If I had won, I wouldn't have just made money, I'd have a way to explain the money I already have. Explain to the government, to the tax people … "

Gambling as a form of money-laundering has never occurred to Thomas. It makes Alan's behavior in the casino seem more rational … a considered risk, rather than a moment of insanity. But this explanation also sounds like rationalizing after the fact. Thomas doesn't say anything.

The silence stretches on. Finally Alan shakes his head. "I'm a whacko."

After Alan goes to his room, Thomas lies awake for a while on the couch, pondering the whole business. Alan, he thinks, is a guy who acts like he's been around some, but he blundered seriously tonight at the gaming table. It was a mistake, Thomas thinks, that he himself would never have made. Then again, Thomas has never become rich, and Alan has. The reckless attitude that had cost him so dearly this evening might also be what had carried him to wealth in the first place. Maybe it's a trade-off: Someone like Thomas would make fewer mistakes than Alan, but never rise as high. Clearly, Alan's life is the more exciting. Thomas might live longer.

The next morning Thomas is up before Alan. He is at the kitchen table when Alan comes out of his room. He gives Thomas his crooked smile.

"I had the weirdest dream last night," Alan says. "I dreamed I lost $75,000."

* * *

Today Alan has an appointment with the bankers. Thomas tells him he thinks he'll walk around the city, see what there is to be seen. Alan shrugs, again disparages the city and its people, but doesn't seem to really care what Thomas does.

Panama City doesn't have the exotic quality of Japan and Taiwan, nor the steeped-in-old-culture feeling of Europe. It seems like a slightly older version of a US city, maybe 1950s vintage. Thomas eats at a McDonald's that is identical in style and menu to McDonald's restaurants he's visited in the states. The only noticeable difference is the coldness of the staff. Afterwards Thomas goes into a large department store, thinking he'll bring home something for his children. It takes a long time to get noticed; sales ladies continue desultory conversations among themselves, ignoring his repeated attempts to get their attention. He leaves without buying anything. (On the way back to California, Thomas will buy serapes and hats for his kids at an airport shop during a lay-over in Guatemala City.)

Thomas gets the picture regarding how Panamanians feel about Americans. Maybe the hostility is earned. He recalls a newspaper story years before about a dispute between American and Panamanian teenagers in the Canal Zone. The issue was over whether the Panamanian or the US flag would fly over Balboa High, a school in "the zone." The conflict had spiraled out of control when thousands of adults became involved and full-fledged riots ensued; 21 Panamanian citizens and four American soldiers were killed. That fight was probably the tip of an iceberg, the culmination of some ongoing back-and-forth between Panamanians and US citizens living in-country. Or maybe the truculence Thomas meets with just reflects the more general Panamanian dissatisfaction with the US-Panamanian treaty of 1903. The treaty specified control over the canal by the US, and reimbursements for its use to Panama. The terms probably sounded a lot better in 1903 than in the 1970s.

Thomas doesn't like the the local attitude, but he can't really judge it without a fuller understanding of the underlying reasons. What seems striking to him at the moment is the contrast between the hostile attitude of the people here and the hospitable, pro-American attitude of the people he'd met in Taiwan the year before. Of course, Panama isn't worried about being absorbed by mainland China.

Back at the hotel that evening, Thomas sees that Alan's meeting with the bankers has much improved his mood.

"The account's set up. We're ready to go," Alan says.

"No problems?"

"No. The bank manager told me at first that what I wanted to do wasn't legal. I told him the schedule of deposits I had in mind, amounts and so on. He said that would be all right. He asked if I would be making a deposit today …" Alan flashes his wry grin, more of a grimace this time … "I had to say the first deposit would be on the next trip."

This account feels abbreviated to Thomas, as though something had been left out. Didn't the banker need more convincing, didn't he need to be told about some mitigating factor, however spurious, that fixed the 'not legal' part? Thomas tries to picture the conversation:

"What you are proposing is not legal, Señor Alan."

"I'll be depositing shit loads of cash."

"OK then."

Shit loads? Bueno—we're good to go.

Maybe the banker is sufficiently experienced with crooked American businessmen not to bother putting up much of a fight. After a while Thomas mentally shrugs it off.

* * *

Alan has spoken with the general manager of the hotel and the manager has agreed to honor the dealer's casual promise: there will be no charge; their stay at the hotel is *gratis*. Thomas asks Alan if having no cash will make the next part of his trip, to Columbia, more problematic.

"I didn't lose all the money," Alan says. "I held back about ten thousand."

Thomas thinks about it. "You could have deposited that at the bank."

"No ... not after the way I was talking. I'd been throwing big numbers all over the place. These people would've laughed if I tried to give them ten thousand."

Later that evening, Thomas shakes Alan's hand in front of the hotel and watches him get into the cab to go to the airport. Thomas' own flight, back to the states, doesn't leave until the next morning ... he goes back up to the suite and thinks about the whole business.

First question: Where exactly had they been illegal? Half an hour or so before landing in Panama, the flight attendants had given all the passengers forms that inquired about how much money they had on their persons. If an individual was carrying more than five-thousand dollars in cash or a "monetary instrument," he or she was required to declare it. No problem for Thomas; he had little to carry. But what about that wad of bills stuffed into the boot in the suit bag, the money Alan had used to stake his try at Bank Bingo? Very unlikely that Alan had mentioned it on the declaration form. Why hide it in a shoe if you're planning to declare it?

Thomas remembers Alan's earlier comment that changes in the law made it unnecessary to smuggle emeralds. Transactions still probably have to be registered though, a difficulty if the emeralds really were stolen. Moving a large amount of money across a national border would no doubt raise a red flag for customs officials anywhere. So the emeralds didn't exactly have to be smuggled, but the money to pay for them did?

This all seems kind of plausible. As the evening draws on, however, with Alan no longer there to sidetrack Thomas with dubious explanations, the events of the last few days begin to take on a certain unreality. Thomas starts to wonder what he really knows about Alan. After all, Alan has even tacitly admitted that some of his claims (bass player in a major rock band, surfing champion) aren't true.

One of the myths Alan has promoted is that he is a poor boy from the slums of Boston who has lifted himself up by his bootstraps to where he is now. Thomas recalls one martial arts lesson he had given Alan where they had dealt with defense against knife attack. Alan had initially been scornful: "Where I grew up, we ignore knives. They're nothing."

"If you think knives are nothing, you're a fool," Thomas said, momentarily unmindful of diplomacy. "A guy with a knife can kill you in a second."

Would a young male raised in a high-crime area really scorn knives?

A counter hypothesis: Alan is some rich kid playing at being an illicit operator. He has money because he is the heir to an old money family in Boston, not because he'd won it in shadowy ventures. The whole international criminal thing is a pose.

But if the whole business is a charade, for whose benefit is it being acted out? The only person in a position to be taken in by this show is Thomas. If Thomas is going to speculate that he is the target of deception, he has to ask the question that all paranoiacs need to ask. Why me? Why take the trouble? How would I warrant such a scheme? Grand paranoia, after all, is a form of egomania: if you are the target of a vast conspiracy, obviously the world revolves around you. The answer to the question, in Thomas' case, is obvious and mundane: A plot to deceive him makes no sense; he isn't that important.

On the other hand, Alan appears to be insinuating Thomas into his inner circle. Those people, artists, musicians, whatever, might be the target audience of Alan's pose. Thomas would need to be able to corroborate events supporting Alan's presentation. Thomas could be a target of the deception so he could be an accessory to it.

Thomas frowns to himself. Alan is beginning to look like some mythical trickster figure from folklore: the raven of the Pacific northwest Indians, or the coyote of the American southwest, maybe Anansi, the African spider god. Or Loki. Or Hermes.

This is over dramatizing the case, but *trickster* seemed to be the role Alan is playing, at least in Thomas' relatively pedestrian life.

This doesn't help him answer the question he is confronted with: How real is any of this?

A darker possibility occurs to Thomas. What if Alan has slipped something illegal into Thomas' suitcase before he left, with the idea that Thomas will unknowingly carry it through customs back into the states? Since Thomas won't know he is carrying anything, it can be assumed that he will act innocently enough. And if it does go wrong, Alan will be somewhere else. Thomas had packed and closed his one piece of luggage before Alan left; could Alan have gotten into it when Thomas was gone from the living room, showering or whatever? Such a plan would explain something Thomas had wondered about earlier: why Alan hadn't seen any need for Thomas to meet the bankers he'd theoretically be dealing with.

This idea seriously disturbs Thomas, not least because he considers Alan his friend—Thomas *likes* him. Alan is kind of like a casual college buddy, who at the same time is a mysterious man of the world. And he had told the casino manager that Thomas was his friend, or at least he told Thomas that he'd said that. A few weeks before, at a party where he'd used Thomas as a bouncer, Thomas had heard him say the same thing to a group of guests: that Thomas was more friend than employee. Thomas believes him; he can't see Alan duping him.

Still, no harm in going through his suitcase.

But what will Thomas do if he does find something? He can go to the police, but what reaction would that bring on? Unknown, from Alan, how about from the unseen, unknown people behind him? Will Thomas just become "not part of their business anymore"? Or will he meet a more sinister response? This isn't Thomas' world, but he senses that exposing the smugglers to law enforcement

302

is a different level of betrayal than stealing from them. And if Thomas does find contraband in his suitcase, he has no way to contact Alan, to demand that he take this stuff back. And Thomas doesn't know anyone else in his organization.

What makes it much worse, is that it isn't just Thomas that might be at risk. He has a wife and children.

Still, one thing Thomas is certain of is that he isn't going to try to pass something like cocaine through customs. He finally decides that if he finds white powder in his bag ... well, the commode in the suite's bathroom can handle it easily enough. One flush, and it is no longer his problem. And no one can say he "narc-ed" them out.

Of course, how Thomas deals with contraband might depend on just what it is. He keeps thinking of drugs, but what is it really likely to be? The value of marijuana is too low to make the small amount that could be concealed in a suitcase worth the bother. Cocaine sells for more, of course, but even that would need to present in an amount that would be easy for Thomas to spot. The truth is, these thoughts are going through his head, but he really has no clear idea of how much cocaine would be worth how much money. Even with the marijuana, he is just making a common sense guess.

How about one or more emeralds? Thomas has been given to believe that a single emerald of good quality can be worth several thousand dollars, so they seem to fit better, both as a theory and in his suitcase.

Thomas goes through the contents of the bag very carefully, feeling socks for stones, and even turning them inside out. He looks closely at the suitcase's lock mechanism and its hinges, though they seem too small

303

to contain much, especially if they still have to function. He finds nothing, and eventually decides there is nothing to find. His bag search was probably paranoia, but paranoia of a supportable kind. At least now he has satisfied himself that Alan isn't setting Thomas up as an unwitting mule.

The whole episode makes one fact clear: If things aren't as Alan has presented them, Thomas doesn't have the slightest guess as to what is really going on.

* * *

Thomas catches a cab to the airport the next morning (a more pleasant driver, this time) and gets on a plane to Guatemala City.

On the plane he falls into a conversation with a fellow passenger, an older, avuncular-seeming American in a suit. The American tells Thomas he is a businessman whose work takes him to Panama frequently. Thomas asks him about the hostile attitude of the locals. That's mostly in Panama City, the businessman answers. The farther away you get from the capital, the friendlier the locals become.

"By the time you get to the more distant provinces, it's about like being in a city in the states."

Thomas has had varying experiences with the friendliness of city-dwellers in the states, but he lets that go. He has something else on his mind.

"I've heard about emerald mining in Columbia," Thomas says, planning to work the conversation around to emerald robberies. He doesn't have to.

"Some of the world's most valuable emeralds come from Columbia," the older man says. "They got mines in Coscuez, Muzo, a few other places ... but they get a lot of problems with bandits. They close the mines down, then they open 'em again, close 'em again ..." He shrugs dismissively. "They've been robbed so many times, they mostly just leave 'em closed."

This sounds consistent enough with what Alan has told Thomas. Later, back in the states, Thomas looks further into the subject of emerald theft in Columbia. What he reads sounds almost like total chaos: Looting and violence are rampant; emerald consortiums, rival guerrilla groups, death squads, and random outlaws are all fighting it out at gunpoint, with the military trying to establish control. Even drug cartels get into it: one source says that the per-gram value of an uncut emerald might be fifty times the street value of drugs. (Things aren't going to get better soon. Thousands more will die from emerald-related violence in the "Green War," which will start soon after Thomas' visit and continue until 1990.)

A recurrent question for Thomas is whether Alan's business is with emeralds, or actually with drugs. This latest information leans him toward emeralds.

In the states, Columbia is mainly associated with cocaine, but emerald-driven illegality seems to be another of the country's thriving industries. Alan, Thomas now thinks, would view drugs as cliché. He'd want to be where the more glamorous action was: precious stones.

Also, the level of violence around emeralds might explain the Bank Bingo dealer's reaction when Alan mentioned them: *Emeralds ... let's not go there.*

* * *

After a brief layover in Guatemala City (where the businessman got off), Thomas flies on to Los Angeles, where he goes through customs. He is treated suspiciously by the agent, based on his "short stay in a sensitive area", but he gets through without too much hassle. Then another short hop and he arrives in San Francisco. Riding the airporter back to Marin County, the past few days seem even more unreal. Thomas sits in his living room in Novato that evening and almost wonders if he dreamed the whole thing.

* * *

Alan calls Thomas a week after he got back from Columbia. He is his usual self, friendly in sort of a courteous, ironic manner. He talks like he expects Thomas to continue working for him, but not in any way that immediately involves travel. With one exception: he wants Thomas to fly to Los Angeles to mail a letter. The purpose seems to be to get a Los Angeles postmark on the envelope, in the interest of fooling someone about where the letter has originated from. Thomas somehow gets the idea that the person Alan means to deceive is his girlfriend. Alan apparently thinks better of it and the trip never happens. In any case, Thomas doesn't think it had anything to do with their business in Panama.

In fact, from then on the business in Panama is very seldom referred to by Alan, and Thomas isn't bringing it up. Also, no further mention is made of Thomas working for Alan as a courier or "bag man." Thomas doesn't think this is because Alan is no longer in the business. He thinks it is more because Alan has made a negative association, not exactly with Thomas, but with Thomas in connection to Panama, even though he doesn't actually blame Thomas for what happened. It seems to Thomas that Alan let himself get hustled by a carnival barker type in a casino, and felt that he'd thereby lost face—with Thomas, but maybe even more with himself, with Thomas as witness.

* * *

After the letter from Los Angeles idea fades out, Thomas doesn't hear from Alan for a while. This isn't unusual. Every time Thomas took leave of him without anything immediate being planned, Alan would ask him to "keep in touch." It never was possible to do this; phone calls were never answered. Though Thomas sensed Alan probably wouldn't want him to, he once went to Alan's house unannounced. No one was there. In the entire time that Thomas has known him, Alan always initiated contact. This time the wait stretches into a year.

When Alan finally does call again, he directs Thomas to a different address. His previous home, in the hills overlooking San Anselmo, was a recently built redwood house of moderate size and elegant design. The new place is only a few miles further south and further into the mountains, somewhere between San Anselmo and Kentfield and closer to Mt. Tamalpais. It is, however, an entirely different prospect.

The first thing Thomas notices driving up is the absence of nearby structures; the second is the remotely controlled front gate. Once he is admitted, identifying himself over an intercom system, he takes in the extensive grounds, the various unattached garages and outbuildings, and the looming three-story house itself: old but well-maintained, an art deco extravaganza from the thirties. Apparently losing money in Panama hasn't presented Alan with much of a setback.

The German Shepherds are still evident, now held on leashes by muscular young men, obvious bodyguard types. Thomas' first impression is that he has been superseded. Alan's greeting is friendly, however, and as though he had last seen Thomas the week before.

He gives Thomas a tour of the house interior. Everything is unique, special, as Alan explains it. One room's floor is a mosaic composed of some rare type of mineral, flown in from far away and hand-laid by craftsmen. There is a large rear porch/balcony that looks down a forested hillside, stained-glass windows, and statuary: huge wrought iron peacocks, standing suits of armor. Thomas loses count of how many bathrooms there are, but the largest one, upstairs, has a black marble tub you step down into. It is gilt-accented, and large enough for a small, intimate party.

The view from the upstairs rear windows encompasses a large expanse of the bay, as seen from high up the flank of the mountain. Richmond, Oakland, part of San Francisco, the San Rafael-Richmond Bridge and the Bay Bridge are visible; sitting slightly off-center in the bay, small with distance, is Alcatraz Island. To say the panorama is majestic would be ironic understatement. Land in Marin County with a view like this, even if there had been no house at all, would be worth more than Thomas expects to earn in a couple of lifetimes.

Eventually Alan and Thomas settle in a very large room on the second floor, sort of a bedroom/office/library. Alan says he has work for Thomas if he is interested, house-sitting at first, and other activities over time. No dubiosities are mentioned, nothing illegal, or challenging. As usual the pay is generous, the terms easy. Thomas only has to sleep in the house at night, and possibly look in on the place once in a while during the day. Thomas agrees with a nod, an off-hand, *of course I'll take the work* gesture, and that is the end of the employment conversation.

Then Alan talks about how well his life has gone since Thomas has last seen him (in case Thomas can't tell from the new house). A mark of his success, Alan says, is that now other people, attempting to turn deals, pretend to be him. He goes on in this vein for a while, describing various events in his life. One example: He tells Thomas he met a man in Columbia who is a killer for hire.

"I couldn't see it," Alan says. "He was nasty enough, but he didn't seem to have the prowess."

Eventually he asks how Thomas is doing. At this time, the heaviest weight on Thomas' mind is that his brother Stuart has been killed in a car accident. This is too painful to talk about at first. After a while, however, Thomas tells Alan about it. Alan is very kind, very commiserative. They talk a while longer and when Thomas finally leaves, he has the same sense of Alan that he had before: He is basically a decent person, he really wants to be Thomas' friend, and Thomas can trust him in certain unspoken ways ... but Thomas still shouldn't exactly believe everything Alan says.

* * *

When Thomas comes back to watch Alan's house, the bodyguards are absent and the dogs are boarded. Alan is gone about a week; after he returns and pays Thomas, he tells him there is something important he wants to talk about.

Alan has an offer for Thomas: He has a friend that needs a truck, an eighteen-wheeler, driven from Oregon to Chicago. Thomas has worked driving trucks, hasn't he? Yes, Thomas had once worked for a distributor, delivering to retail outlets, but he'd only driven vans, Dodge Tradesman 100s; he doesn't have a class B license. No problem, Alan says, they could get him a license, whatever is needed. The single trip would earn Thomas $200,000.

Thomas asks the obvious question: What will be the truck's cargo?

"Just pot," Alan answers.

Thomas points out that trailer rigs are supposed to stop at weigh stations, and are generally subject to regulation and monitoring above and beyond other vehicles.

"The stuff will probably be in bags marked as fertilizer or animal feed. Something like that," Alan says. "It won't be a problem."

Thomas has never been too interested in drugs, but coming of age in the San Francisco Bay Area in the sixties, he is very familiar with the smell of marijuana. It has a distinct odor, not easily confused with fertilizer, or animal feed, or anything else much. (One of the reasons the hippies were always burning incense was that it cloaked the marijuana smell.) To Thomas, this isn't sounding like a good idea.

"I don't think so, Alan."

"This guy you'd be working for is really a great guy. And the money's good."

Thomas shakes his head. After a moment, Alan shrugs and changes the subject.

The next time Thomas sees Alan, helping him set up a weight-lifting gym in his basement, Alan has a new acquaintance. A youthful, slightly built red-haired man that Alan tells Thomas is a doctor. The young MD is quiet and civil, though distant. Thomas doesn't think much about him at the time.

Later, Thomas asks Alan for a favor. Thomas has discovered that he has a tax liability that he has no way to pay. He needs about $650, a relatively trivial amount, but it is a problem at this point in his life.

Alan has Thomas go upstairs with him to his office/bedroom/library. Alan sits back in his lounge-chair and directs Thomas to a large, antique desk. "Open the top drawer," he says.

The drawer is shallow but wide. It is filled with banded rolls of bills, each sitting on end. There are hundreds of them in the drawer.

"Each roll is a thousand dollars," Alan says. "Take one."

"I only need 650."

"Take a whole roll. It will help you."

Thomas takes a roll and thanks Alan.

"You can pay it back by working for me, or with money, whatever."

Alan reflects for a moment. "You know … you were a fool not to take that truck-driving job I told you about. The guy you would have been working for was me."

Thomas thought, So much for *I'm rich; I don't need to involve myself with drugs.*

Alan goes on to say that the driving job had been handled by the young doctor; Thomas has missed his opportunity.

"He's a doctor and he drives eighteen-wheelers?" Thomas asks. "He's an accomplished guy."

"We didn't do the big rig thing," Alan says. "We hitched a trailer to the back of his car, the kind you'd haul a horse in; the whole thing was a piece of cake. Of course, he couldn't carry as much product, so the pay was less."

Thomas wonders if the man has just graduated from medical school and hasn't established a practice yet. Maybe he has student loan debt. He wonders where Alan finds these people.

"I have another job for you," Alan says. "I need a crew to help me unload a barge on a beach in Oregon. You'll have to really hustle, and we work non-stop through the night until it's done—exhausting labor, but not so much risk. Of course, less risk means less pay … each member of the crew earns 50,000."

Thomas nods noncommittally: He understands what Alan is saying; he isn't agreeing to anything. No need, of course, to ask what the barge will be carrying.

As Thomas is leaving, Alan gives him his half-smile. "This is a good opportunity for you, Thomas. Think about it."

* * *

Thomas doesn't hear from Alan for a month, surprisingly, since his tone had suggested that the barge business was imminent. When Thomas is at his house again, Alan has him come down into the basement gym, as he doesn't want the housekeeper to overhear them. It turns out that his life has changed again.

Alan tells Thomas the Coast Guard intercepted one of his barges off the coast of Oregon, and found it loaded with marijuana. Law enforcement has been able to link it to Alan, and now he is facing a trial.

Thomas visits him periodically over the next few months, usually to house-sit again, and he hears reports of how Alan's situation is evolving:

Alan is found guilty ...

He is sentenced to seven years in prison ...

He is appealing his conviction.

One evening, he tells Thomas that his final appeal is coming up the next day.

"Good luck," Thomas says.

Alan nods.

"After tonight, I may be out of contact for a while," he says.

His statement is accurate. This turns out to be the last time Thomas sees him ...

Thirty-six years pass.

Thomas never knows how Alan's last appeal turned out, or if Alan even appeared in court to find out himself. His last chance to run would have been before the final court appearance, of course, since he would be immediately taken into custody if the conviction was upheld. Thomas thought he was considering flight all along, though he never exactly said so.

Thomas still sometimes wonders where Alan's life went after that night, whether he ultimately landed in jail, or in Columbia, or somewhere else. He wonders where Alan is now. Thomas still owes him a thousand dollars.

* * *

When Thomas later reflects on his experience with Alan, he is haunted by the question raised earlier: How much of the whole business was real? Thomas never saw any mention of Alan's trial in the newspapers, though he did look for it. The trial might have been in another part of the country, of course, considering where the barge was intercepted. It still might have made the local papers, though, since Alan was a resident of Marin County. Or was he? Did he maintain another home somewhere else? Beyond that, most significantly, Thomas never heard any of this from anyone except Alan himself. (With one exception: Alan's friend, the one he likened to a concert pianist, once made a vague remark consistent with Alan's claim that he had been arrested.)

For Thomas' subsequent purposes, analyzing the dynamics of risky behavior, he decides to take Alan at face value. He certainly articulated reckless attitudes. For example:

After returning from one of his early trips, where he allegedly learned to ski, Thomas asked him how that had gone.

"Great," Alan told him. "Skiing's easy if you don't care whether you die."

Another time, after broaching the marijuana barge unloading plan, Alan expressed a philosophy toward smuggling, and maybe risk in general.

"I think the real way to do it is to bring your boat up to a busy wharf in broad daylight. Show them some fake papers and start unloading. Just be relaxed and confident. I think it's the guys who sneak around, unloading at night on deserted beaches, that get caught."

This was ironic, since unloading at night on a deserted beach was exactly what Alan had talked about doing. Maybe the broad daylight scenario was a new plan, based on an evolving philosophy, that he didn't get the chance to try out.

Alan's remarks could be taken as simple bravado. Thomas also got the feeling that even if these attitudes were real, they weren't entrenched yet; Alan was still experimenting with approaches to life. The more he got away with, the more his experiments were validated, the greater his confidence. Were his ideas really feasible? To a point, apparently; by some means or other he had gained wealth. His approach worked, at least until his luck ran out.

If Thomas tried to dissect Alan's attitudes in light of his earlier analysis of his own experiences fence-climbing, sky-diving, and so on, it was clear that some of the elements he'd considered before would apply now. Alan's behavior at the Bank Bingo game, for instance, illustrated the trap of dogged persistence, the obstinate refusal to change course, but it wasn't the whole story.

So: It felt to Thomas as though Alan perceived danger, risk, and reward as markers in some metaphysical game, rather than as external realities. As though Alan thought that if you overcame the barriers in your mind, the world would follow suit. Mindset, then, is everything. Be confident; show no fear; it's all in your head. Guns, cops, rival criminals ... none of it matters. It's all about you.

Thomas thought that another word for this attitude was *solipsism.*

Solipsism is the belief that everything that appears to exist is only in your mind. Whoever you are then, you are the only real person. A solipsist is free to be the ultimate risk-taker. None of it is real, so he can't really be hurt. What he does to other people is equally meaningless, as they are unreal and also can't be hurt. Because reality is all a dream.

At this point Thomas moved beyond Alan specifically and was thinking more of a general idea. Though he thought Alan had some tendency in that direction, Thomas didn't believe Alan was exactly a solipsist. He did connect with other people when he knew them personally. People he didn't know personally, humanity in general, may have been a little abstract to him. Beneath his view, perhaps. In his reflective mode, Alan read like some detached philosopher-criminal: the villain in a Jack Vance novel.

* * *

To the factors Thomas had previously considered that he thought could lead an individual into reckless behavior—egotistical paralysis that won't allow you to deviate from a course once you've taken it; acclimation, when a minor risk increases gradually; social pressure—Thomas could add a fourth: a tendency toward solipsism.

Clearly these same factors could influence an individual toward both legal and illegal risk-taking. What exactly was the element that separated the two? Thomas guessed there was little or no difference between criminal and non-criminal risk-taking in terms of direct cause. The non-criminal risk-taker's need to be liked, accepted, and admired, is significantly greater, however. He sees himself as part of the larger society; he probably wants glory for his dangerous behavior. This was much like Thomas himself: Risk excited him, but he had no wish to harm others. If anything, he had an impulse to protect people. The criminal is different; he has less identification with his fellow humans. This was not an either/or situation, of course. The criminal may have his own peer group, an underlying need for recognition, a desire to be admired for his "achievements." (Often this is how they are caught. Bragging to a cellmate, for instance.) While the extreme sociopath, such as a serial killer, may be willing to be a nation of one, many criminals still need some recognition, if only from their acquaintances in the criminal subculture. While Alan would react with impatience and arrogance to many, he clearly had a need to be liked by his own group.

* * *

Detached Thomas has considered various forms of disaster: death, dismemberment, extensive jail time. But now he realizes the ultimate dismal fate: What if time had branched beforehand, and he had never existed at all? Or had somehow been someone else?

***

An Alternative Self

Various places: *throughout Thomas' life*

Thomas' parents met during the war, at a USO dance in Arkansas. His father was on leave from the Army, and his mother was a USO hostess. Apparently it was love at first sight. Thomas' mother was engaged to someone else at the time, but she seems to have been sort of a southern belle (once a runner-up in the Miss Arkansas pageant) and apparently felt she had the prerogative of reconsidering her options. In any case, she instantly ditched her fiancé, whose name was Bill Wilson, and within a few weeks had eloped with and married Thomas' father.

This led to a certain recurrent scenario during Thomas' childhood. At sporadic moments, usually with little lead-in, Thomas Sr. would regale him:

"You know, if it wasn't for me, you would've been Bill Wilson, Jr.!"

Thomas Sr. always managed to convey that this would have been a fate too dismal to even contemplate. Would it have been? Thomas later wondered. Was his father, sort of an unpredictable, primitive egotist, the gateway to Thomas' best possible life?

Thomas had asked his mother about Bill Wilson.

"Well ..." she thought it over. "He was a nice guy." *Nice guy* is perhaps the kiss of death, when your girlfriend says it about you. Thomas didn't recall his mother ever once using *nice guy* to describe his father, with whom she had an intense relationship. (Intense both positively and negatively—their fights were epic.)

Also, why did Thomas Sr. think the inheritance of identity was matrilineal? If Thomas' parents had never met, why did he assume that his (non)wife's son would still be the same person, no matter who his father was? Isn't it at least possible that Thomas would have been Thomas Sr.'s son by a different woman? And isn't it even more likely that the individual known as Thomas wouldn't exist at all?

His father's pronouncement—"You would've been Bill Wilson, Jr.!"—hints at certain underlying assumptions. First, of course, there is Thomas Sr.'s view of the glory of being his son, and the desirability of being in their particular family (old military and so on). However, if Thomas strips away his father's chauvinism, there seems to be a deeper notion: the need to be exactly who you are, for better or worse. It is too difficult to contemplate being someone else. Better to be the devil you know, than be some strange devil.

Thomas wondered, is there an ultimate *you*, a soul that precedes, and presumably survives, this life? An ultimate *you* that possesses a unique and unalterable identity?

Thomas thought his father might be right about this. Thomas couldn't imagine being anyone else. Even when he saw someone whose life was manifestly better than his own in every way, Thomas could not bring himself to want to be that other person.

Still, you never miss what you've never experienced. If Thomas were someone else, presumably he would have been just as profoundly attached to being that other person.

Who knows? Thomas thought. Maybe being Bill Wilson, Jr. wouldn't have been such a bad deal.

∗∗∗

Epilogue: Exit From a Bar

The young GI, Thomas, and Luana talk for a while longer, then the soldier has somewhere he needs to be. Thomas wishes him luck, they shake hands, and he leaves. Thomas never sees him again. It turns out that Thomas never sees Luana again, either. With her family, she "rotates" back to the USA the next day; Thomas returns to California a few weeks later. She and Thomas had some plan to get together state-side, but it never happens. That any of the three ever met in the first place is of course another butterfly effect, the sort of chance encounter that everyone is subject to every day. And the attitudes of the time, the GI's wish to be in Vietnam, Thomas' seeking of a college deferment, another draft-age individual's decision to flee to Canada, are manifestations of chaos theory working within individual lives: the results of collisions of intrinsic traits, diverse experiences, and the proliferating interactions between the two. The intersection of the personal and the historical worked out differently for each of them, pointing them in unpredictable directions.

* * *

Maybe what he was ultimately getting at, Thomas decided, was, is it possible to live your life rationally? Can you really expect reliable outcomes from your actions? Perhaps ... if you accepted the approximate quality of any large scale results. Steer in what seems the right general direction; expect the unexpected; understand that most aspects of your life will never resolve exactly; accept compromised consequences. Besides, what other choice was there? Chaotic behavior on your own part was usually a quick road to disaster. Be as rational as you could be, and allow fate to decide the rest.

* * *

On his return to the states at the end of summer, Thomas was reminded of his status as a space-available passenger: He was bumped from his scheduled flight to Travis. He waited twelve hours in the lobby below the operations tower in Tokyo, and was finally put on a flight to McChord Air Force Base, near Tacoma, Washington. After arriving at McChord, he spent another day in a lobby waiting for a continuation flight to Travis before operations staff noticed (in response to a question from Thomas) that his paperwork only got him to the west coast. He had already come that far, so now he was on his own. This stressed Thomas briefly, but he soon accepted the situation with equanimity. He could hitchhike down to the bay area if he had to, and anyway it turned out he had enough spare change to pay for a Greyhound bus ride to San Francisco (cheaper in those days). He reminded himself that other men his age were in Vietnam being shot at. Thomas did not allow himself any complaints.

Later that night, cruising in the Greyhound along the Oregon coast, Thomas gazed out the window and tried to see through his own reflection to the dark wooded hills beyond. He thought about his day in the bar, with Luana and the young soldier. Tokyo had become less real, and already he had some inkling that he would never intersect again with anyone he had met there.

Luana, Thomas thought, seemed to have survival instincts; she would probably get through the rest of her life one way or another. He wasn't so sure about the young soldier; his survival in Vietnam seemed more problematic. But then again, he might make it. Chaos theory cuts both ways; a prediction of doom was no more reliable than a prediction of survival.

***

Acknowledgements

This book benefitted greatly from the presence of all the individuals encountered herein. Many thanks for being helpful, obnoxious, loving, hostile, and perplexing. Without you, the events described would not have happened.

Many thanks also to my publisher and gadfly, Mark Charalambous, without whom this book would not have happened.